The Master Chefs of France Recipe Book

The Master Chefs of

France Recipe Book

Recipes from 300 great restaurants of France

Compiled with the cooperation of Carte Blanche®

Edited and with an introduction by

Robert J. Courtine

Food and restaurant critic, *Le Monde*

A publication of The Master Chefs Institute

Sandy Lesberg, *Director*

NEW YORK Everest House PUBLISHERS

Library of Congress Cataloging in Publication Data
Main entry under title:
The master chefs of France recipe book.
    Includes index.
    1. Cookery, French.   I.   Courtine, Robert J.
TX719.M34445   1981   641.5944   81-12466

ISBN: 0-89696-140-0   AACR2

Published simultaneously in Canada
by Beaverbooks, Don Mills, Ontario
Manufactured in the United States of America

Illustrations by Jacques Chazaud
Translation by Patricia Konopka
Graphic Production by Filmar Graphics, Inc., San Diego, California

First Edition

Preface

Robert J. Courtine is the internationally respected food and restaurant critic for the French newspaper Le Monde and for 17 regional newspapers in France. A critic for more than 25 years, he has authored many books, most of which have been translated into other languages. Over the years, he has been intimately involved, on a day-to-day basis, with the world of French cuisine, and he has always shared his observations and opinions with his many readers in a delightful, colourful, and learned manner. Now you, too, can benefit from his years of experience as he takes you on his personal gastronomic tour of France.

In many ways, the book you now hold represents the quintessence of French cuisine as represented by the finest restaurants in France. For the first time, great French chefs — 300 of them — are sharing the secrets of their speciality recipes, and the Master Chefs Institute is delighted to be the instrument of bringing them to the attention of the English speaking world. This English language edition of THE MASTER CHEFS OF FRANCE RECIPE BOOK is an Anglo-American presentation, and we have felt it incumbent upon us to maintain, as closely as possible, the integrity of the recipes as originally published in the French language book. You will note, therefore, that the ingredients are listed in their original French form, and then beside each ingredient is the closest, workable American equivalent. This method, we feel, serves the best interest of the chefs while making this edition completely practical.

The appendices offer a comprehensive recipe index and an alphabetical list of all the restaurants and their locations appearing in this book, as well as a glossary of useful information, including sauce recipes and specialised cooking techniques. Asterisks (*) appearing next to some ingredients, utensils, and techniques within the recipes indicate that they are among those included in the glossary. These have been highlighted because, after 15 years of publishing cookbooks, I have learned that many terms and techniques vary from country to country and that it is advisable to alert the reader to possible unfamiliar applications.

Here, then, is the very real basis for what some have called the finest cuisine in the world. Some recipes are more challenging than others, but all deserve your attention and certainly all are eminently adaptable to your own kitchen. They are wondrous and exciting, and they will allow you to make your own special cooking magic.

Sandy Lesberg, Director
The Master Chefs Institute

Table of Contents

Introduction

The universal appeal of French cuisine has been recognized the world over.

This school of the art of fine cooking made its way through the 18th and 19th centuries, imposing its virtues on the "masters" (as they were called at the time) and, later, the chefs. These ambassadors of this grand cuisine triumphed everywhere. Didn't Talleyrand say, when preparing for the Vienna Congress, "Send me good chefs rather than good diplomats"? Subtle diplomat himself, he wanted to show that what the French could do with their pots and pans might be more effective than cannons and guns.

But with success comes a touch of snobbery. It's the thorn of the rose. These master chefs, paid handsomely to delight imperial, royal, and noble tables, have certainly done much to spread the reputation of French cuisine, or rather, a certain style of French cuisine. It might just as well have been a fashion that would have disappeared when the nobles began to tire of a lack of novelty.

But this did not occur. French cuisine proved to be a source of great culinary riches, which probably explains its enduring international reputation.

Here, we must salute those without whom these master chefs would have been nothing more than mere culinary technicians (albeit talented ones). We must salute the men and women (because at first cooking and preparing meals was woman's work) who, from the produce of the soil, subject to the uncertain tides of climate and history, made of the simple preparation of their food — an art. This is what has given our cuisine its wonderful variety, making it specifically our own, yet characterizing its universal allure.

Gastronomically speaking, France is a happy country "which," said Georges Duhamel, "prepares, at the same time, olive oil and fine butter, wine and beer; harvests chestnuts and oranges, rye and lemons; raises livestock; cares for its game; grinds its wheat; grows all kinds of vegetables (even those of little value); invents cheeses; distills alcohols; sorts out mushrooms; collects honey; goes fishing; makes sugar; honours eggs; and ignores nothing edible, not even frogs or truffles."

It couldn't be said any better, even if nowadays there exists a tendency to eliminate any vegetable, fruit, or the like for its poor market value. A sign of the times!

True, this is happening all over. And it's precisely because France is behind the rest of the world in its "progress" that the reputation of her cuisine persists. For the moment!

Going back to the sources of fine cooking — there lies the hope for the perpetuation of French cuisine in its current status. Paul Bocuse coined the phrase "Cuisine du Marché" (market cuisine). It's an idea as old as when the first homemaker, conscious of spending her budget wisely, became aware of the fact that the most important quality to look for in food is its freshness. This expression has come into vogue today. More than a phrase, it should always be a reality . . . Do all chefs realize this?

There is no "Nouvelle Cuisine." There is no "Grande Cuisine." There are the good and the bad. The good being, by today's necessities, simple cuisine, that which my good friend François Amunatequi defined as one where "the product or products used are not deformed, the dishes neither bloat nor nauseate, and all is easily handled. Simple cuisine, for me," he said, "obviously does not mean poor cuisine but rather intact, sincere, honest, and transparent. A slice of fresh duck liver is a perfect sampling of simple cuisine, but as soon as you decide to mash it and use it to stuff a wood pigeon, it would be like an iconoclast breaking off the legs of a Louis XVI couch to warm his imbecile of a carcass!" May it please heaven and Camus that this may ever be the world's definition of French cuisine.

It is up to the Master Chefs to see to it that it is. It is their honour. But, too, it is to a certain extent the task of all — of all the chefs, of all the homemakers (whom we must not forget), and of all the young people breaking into this joyous, but oh how difficult, exhilarating career!

When the humblest of apprentices sets out to find the secret of an old master, adding a personal touch of intelligence and invention, he not only works for himself but for everyone in the interest of the art of cooking. It is the role of the Institut Culinaire des Chefs de France (the French subsidiary of The Master Chefs Institute) to assemble these discoveries, to collect these secrets, and to preserve these traditions. By publishing this book, THE MASTER CHEFS OF FRANCE RECIPE BOOK, in which many of my friends wanted to appear, the Institute has made an important contribution to our endeavour. One can never do enough to defend one's craft when that craft has become an art!

Robert Courtine

Le Maillet d'Or

rue Robert-Petit, 89300 Joigny
Tel: (86) 62-16-28
Proprietors: The Godard Brothers • Chef: Jean-Claude Godard

Le Maillet d'Or is situated in a modern hotel in Joigny. It was originally founded in an old house by Gaston Godard. Today, the restaurant is managed by Gaston's sons, who are as much in love with cooking as their father was. The decor at Maillet d'Or, which features a friendly patio, is discreetly modern. The menu respects the traditional: the famous Duck à la Gaston and Escargot Fricassee are examples. There are also many interesting creations such as Goose Liver Terrine, Noisettes of Lamb, and Cheese-Filled Corniottes, as well as beautiful wines from Bordeaux. The Burgundy Cocktails are a delightful beverage concoction. The Maillet d'Or is a symbol of those free spirits who fought to save their heritage and their liberty.

Cheese-Filled Corniottes with Burgundy Cocktails

Burgundy wine, Crémant preferred, as needed
2 tbsp lemon syrup (lemon juice)
2 tbsp dry white vermouth
4 slices lemon peels
4 green olives
puff pastry dough,* as needed
4 slices any white cheese, grated
3 eggs
salt, to taste
4 slices Gruyère or Swiss cheese, grated
3 tbsp double cream (whipping cream)

To prepare the cocktails: Fill 4 champagne glasses ¾ full with Crémant Burgundy. Add 1½ tsp lemon syrup and 1½ tsp vermouth to each glass. Place 1 lemon peel and 1 green olive in each glass.

To prepare the corniottes: Roll out the dough evenly and divide into 4 pieces, each 30 cm (12 in) square. Mix the white cheese, eggs, salt, Gruyère cheese, and cream together. Place ¼ of the mixture on each piece of dough. Fold up the 4 corners of each and press together. Bake at 400°F (205°C) for 8 minutes. Serve warm.

Serves: 4

La Renaissance

41, rue A.-Marrel, 42800 Rive-de-Gier
Tel: (77) 75-04-31
Proprietor/Chef: Gilbert Laurent

Since 1920, **La Renaissance** has attracted gourmands to Rive-de-Gier. Gilbert Laurent, a self-taught chef who is passionate about his work, took over the restaurant in 1966.

Gilbert has dedicated himself to the preparation of fine food and is very proud of everything he serves. His menu offers Scrambled Eggs with Duck Liver, Fillet of Lamb, Beef with Cream of Chives, and a wonderful cheese tart. The cheese is from a nearby farm and is fresh and natural.

You will be in for another treat when dining at La Renaissance — the variety of dishes is equalled by the fine selection of wines.

Cheese Tart

1 mound short pastry dough,* 14 cm (5½ in) in diameter
125 g (¼ lb) grated Cantal cheese (or any hard, strong cheese)
125 ml (½ cup) double cream (whipping cream)
2 eggs

Place the dough in a 20 cm (8 in) flan tin (pie pan) and bake the dough in a preheated oven at 400°F (205°C) for 8-9 minutes. Mix the cheese, cream, and eggs together and pour into the crust.

Cook this tart for only 2 minutes longer in the oven, at the same temperature as before. Serve warm.

Wine: Côte du Rhône

Serves: 4

Relais des Gardes

42, avenue du Général-Galliéni, 92190 Meudon-Bellevue
Tel: 534-1179
Proprietors: Pierre and Simone Oudina • Chef: Daniel Bertholom

Pastry Shells Filled with Roquefort Cheese

300 g (7 oz) puff pastry dough*
1 egg, beaten
20 g (¾ oz) butter
100 g (¼ lb) Roquefort cheese
50 ml (3 oz) milk
100 g (¼ lb) grated Gruyère cheese
salt, to taste
1 pinch nutmeg
1 tbsp double cream (whipping cream)

Form the puff pastry dough into 6 - 8 rounds, 4 mm (¼ in) thick and 6 cm (2½ in) in diameter. Lay them on an aluminum cooking sheet and keep slightly humid. Dip each round into beaten egg and fry in butter until golden brown, but not crisp. On half of the rounds, spread pieces of Roquefort cheese, then cover with remaining pastry rounds. Pinch together all sides to close, then bake in the oven at 350°F (175°C) for 35 minutes.

To prepare the sauce: Slowly mix the milk, Gruyère cheese, salt, nutmeg, and cream together.

To serve: Pour the sauce over the pastry shells hot from the oven and serve.

Wine: *A white Bordeaux*   Serves: 3 - 4

The famous **Relais des Gardes** has a prestigious and historical past; it was once a royal domaine. Situated at the edge of the forest, this remote *maison* dates from 1768. It was reconstructed in 1923, and in 1968, Pierre, who was well-acquainted with the *crème de la crème* of restaurants, took over the management. Daniel is the chef; he is a fine gentleman who has spent many years cooking elegant dinners at Le Printemps.

This rustic but elegant restaurant contains a beautiful collection of ancient etchings, a grand fireplace, and an excellent kitchen.

Le Lièvre Amoureux

Saint-Lattier, 38160 Saint-Marcellin
Tel: (76) 36-50-67
Proprietor: Mlle. Caillat • Chef: Robert Gaillard

Ravioles

2 eggs
125 g (¼ lb) butter
250 g (½ lb) flour
salt, to taste
250 ml (1 cup) warm water
50 g (1¾ oz) parsley, chopped and cooked in butter
300 g (10½ oz) grated imported Swiss or Gruyère cheese
125 g (¼ lb) fresh goats cheese
2 eggs
25 g (¾ oz) butter
1 litre (2 pt) salted chicken broth
50 g (1¾ oz) grated Parmesan cheese

To prepare the dough: Knead the first 5 ingredients together until smooth. Let rest 1 hour. Roll out dough very thinly, then cut into ribbons — 3 - 4 cm (1 - 1½ in) wide by 5 - 6 cm (2 - 2½ in) long.

To prepare the stuffing: Mix the parsley, Swiss or Gruyère cheese, goats cheese, eggs, and butter together.

Place the stuffing on ½ the dough strips, then cover the stuffing with the remaining dough to make ravioles. Seal the edges with a fork. Poach the ravioles in salted chicken broth, then drain and serve with grated Parmesan cheese on top. Serve warm.

Here is a small restaurant-hotel of quality — it is located in the lush greenery of Vercors and is run by Mlle. Caillat, assisted by her father, who is the chef.

The menu is rich with specialities — *dauphinoises* that are never to be forgotten, *sauces grilles* with Saint-Joseph wine, Goose Liver in Crust, Ravioles, game and fowl in season, and a vast variety of cheeses, including Saint-Marcellin goats cheese (which has become a rarity) followed by a number of sumptuous desserts. Mlle. Caillat will probably suggest one of her Côtes du Rhône wines to accompany your dinner, for here it is "the right wine in the right place."

Restaurant Greuze

4, rue Albert-Thibaudet, 71700 Tournus
Tel: (85) 51-13-52
Proprietor/Chef: Jean Ducloux

Crayfish Omelette

2 kg (4½ lb) fresh, raw, medium-sized crayfish
4 tbsp oil
½ litre (1 pt) white wine
3 crushed tomatoes
salt and pepper, to taste
1 bouquet garni*
50 g (1¾ oz) butter
250 ml (1 cup) double cream (whipping cream)
12 eggs, scrambled
1 tbsp chopped tarragon

Sauté the crayfish in oil. Wet them with white wine, then add tomatoes, salt, pepper, and the bouquet garni. Cook for 5 minutes, then set crayfish aside to cool. Once cooled, remove the shells from the crayfish. Reduce the cooking liquid to half its original volume, then add a teaspoon of butter and ⅔ of the cream.

Make 4 omelettes using 3 eggs for each and ¼ of the remaining cream. Cook in the remaining butter. On top of each omelette, pour the crayfish sauce. Decorate with chopped tarragon and serve.

Serves: 8

M. Jean Ducloux, a most colourful personage, is also a man of high calibre. He demonstrated his creative imagination when he bought a garage and transformed it into a restaurant which soon became *grand!* The garage was once the home of painter J.B. Greuze. In commemoration of him, Ducloux named his establishment **Restaurant Greuze.** Today, Jean Ducloux continues to blend his work and his passion (cooking and music) within his restaurant. Here he greets his regular customers — well captured by the divine snails, Crayfish Omelette, Gratin of Shrimp, Sole with Broccoli, and an assortment of desserts, both hot and cold, to be enjoyed along with a most sophisticated selection of fine regional wines and champagnes.

La Mère Poulard

50166 Mont-Saint-Michel
Tel: (33) 60-14-01
Proprietors: M. and Mme. Bernard Heyraud

Mother Poulard's Omelette

8 large eggs
320 g (11 oz) semi-salted butter

(To be cooked over an outdoor open fire of burning oak chips.) Beat the eggs until fluffy. In a large pan, place a generous amount of butter and heat it. Add the beaten eggs and bring the omelette to a slight bubble over the burning oak chips, cooking evenly.

When almost cooked, lean the pan toward the scented flame so the fumes from the wood give the omelette flavour and aroma. Do not overcook; the omelette should be moist inside. Serve immediately.

Serves: 4

Mont-Saint-Michel, the "Marvel of the Occident," attracts millions of tourists each year. Erected in the Middle Ages, this awesome castle stands majestically near the blue waters of the English Channel as though frozen in time. Once inside this labyrinth, you will find many shops and restaurants, and even the cemetery where the founders of **La Mère Poulard,** Victor and Annette Poulard, rest. Now this establishment is in the hands of the Heyrauds.

The menu offers fish and other products from the region, such as Fricassee of Angler with Saffron, Turbot with Mustard, Lobster à l'Américaine, Haddock Salad with Two Kinds of Apples, and a very famous omelette, which has been prepared here since 1873.

Le Restaurant du Marché

59, rue de Dantzig, 75015 Paris
Tel: 828-3155 and 532-2688
Proprietor: Michel Massia • Chef: Christiane Massia

Paris is where Christiane Massia started, and it is here where she still reigns over a real local bistro with its bar and slightly provincial style restaurant and fast food boutique. In the evening, all the food-lovers of Paris come here to relax and treat themselves to the wonderful country style delights on her menu that include cracklings, black pudding, skins of duck in an omelette, gizzards and hearts of goose, salads of assorted lentils, cabbage soup, *foie gras* in all its forms, chicken in a pot, stew, or hot-pot, and braised meats. The food is accompanied by exceptional wines and Armagnacs, Arabica coffee sweetened with acacia honey, and herb teas, the list of which is by no means the smallest attraction in this restaurant.

Omelette with Duck Skins

400 g (14 oz) duck skins
100 g (¼ lb) duck or goose fat
8 eggs
pinch of salt
5 g (pinch of) pepper
1 tbsp wine vinegar

Cut the duck skins into fine thin slices. Melt the fat in a frying pan and add the skins. Brown on low heat for 15 minutes until skins become dry and brittle.

Break the eggs into a bowl, add salt and pepper, and whisk for 3 minutes. Remove the hot fat from the frying pan, then pour the egg mixture onto the skins. Increase the heat slightly and let the omelette cook to taste.

Fold the finished omelette onto a warm serving dish, sprinkle with drops of vinegar, and serve.

Wine: *A regional wine*   Serves: 4

Chez Les Anges

54, boulevard de Latour Maubourg, 75007 Paris
Tel: 705-8986
Proprietor/Chef: François Benoist

This restaurant, created and founded by Armand Monassier 20 years ago, was later taken over by the Champagne-born François Benoist. **Chez Les Anges** is chic. It is a venue at lunchtimes for politicians and businessmen who enjoy its terrace, its little recesses, and its salon, which, come evenings, is transformed into a real Parisian restaurant, in the most positive sense of the word.

Thick slices of veal liver compete for your attention along with Tongue "Lucullus" Style, which is garnished with *foie gras*, the delicious Poached Eggs "Les Anges" Style, and many other delights. The selection of cheeses is magnificent (especially the goats cheese), and the desserts are most tasty.

Poached Eggs "Les Anges" Style

50 g (1¾ oz) chopped shallots
150 g (5¼ oz) butter
1 bottle Rully red wine
1 bouquet garni*
250 g (½ lb) lean bacon
250 g (½ lb) onions
10 g (⅓ oz) sugar
250 g (½ lb) mushrooms

juice of ½ lemon
½ litre (1 pt) court bouillon*
1 litre (2 pt) red table wine
12 eggs
½ loaf French bread, sliced
4 garlic cloves
1 tbsp chopped parsley

Sweat* the shallots in ⅙ of the butter, add Rully red wine and bouquet garni, and reduce to ¾. Cut the bacon into pieces and let soak in cold water. Heat the water and remove bacon just before boiling. Peel and scald the onions, then sprinkle sugar over them. Glaze onions under a cover of greaseproof (wax) paper. Cook the mushrooms for 5 minutes in water with lemon juice.

Pour the court bouillon into the reduced shallot and wine preparation and dot with ⅓ of the remaining butter. Season and simmer for ½ hour. Strain through muslin (cheesecloth). Brown the bacon and mushrooms separately, strain, and add to the sauce.

Heat the red table wine and poach the eggs, 2 at a time, in it. Fry the bread slices in garlic and the remaining butter until golden brown. Serve the eggs on the toast on hot plates. Coat with the sauce and sprinkle parlsey on top.

Wine: *Rully red*   Serves: 6

Yan

94, avenue Paul-Doumer, 75116 Paris
Tel: 524-5537
Proprietor/Chef: Yan Jacquot

During an extensive trip through France, Yan Jacquot visited many restaurants (Vivarois, Drouant, and La Bonne Etape, to name a few) and tasted many different foods. Yan then decided to establish himself in Paris and open his own fine restaurant. What he purchased was a mediocre restaurant with a perfect location (exactly in front of the Eiffel Tower) and a large terrace. The cuisine here is now anything but mediocre.

Yan's cooking is everything that could be desired; Haddock with Green Peppers, Scallops with Tomatoes, Scrambled Eggs in Kiwi Shells, Fried Perch with Spinach, Oysters in Truffle-Flavoured Butter, and his cool and refreshing desserts are all here for your pleasure.

Scrambled Eggs in Kiwi Shells

4 kiwi fruits
6 eggs
salt and pepper, to taste
½ tsp butter, melted
2 tbsp double cream (whipping cream)
2 tbsp chopped chives

Cut off the tops of the kiwi fruits. Reserve the tops. Spoon out the insides and reserve. The outsides should look like hollow egg shells. In a grinder, gently grind the kiwi flesh, then put the purée through a strainer to collect all the small black grains. Reserve the grains; discard the pulp.

In a small salad bowl, beat the eggs well and season with salt and pepper. In a pot, blend the melted butter and the eggs. Add cream, chives, and the black grains from the kiwis. Put on the stove over medium heat and scramble.

To serve: Put equal amounts of scrambled egg mixture into each kiwi shell, then put the tops back on and serve.

Suggestion: Serve in egg cups.

Serves: 4

Le Relais des Pyrénées

1, rue du Jourdain, 75020 Paris
Tel: 636-6581
Proprietor/Chef: Jean Marty

It has been a decade since Jean Marty established himself in Paris. He is originally from the Pyrénées and is the second Pyrenean to succeed in this old provincial restaurant. When I say provincial, it is meant as a compliment, for in the provinces, the country air stimulates the appetite. This requires sitting at a truly rich table to satisfy one's hunger.

The *foie gras,* sausage from Morlaus, ham from Bayonne, Natural Chicken in Béarnaise Sauce, Ratatouille, and the Scrambled Eggs with Ham and Vegetables are truly provincial specialities found in this most cosmopolitan city.

Scrambled Eggs with Ham and Vegetables

2 large bell peppers
butter, as needed to sauté
2 - 3 onions, finely chopped
3 - 4 tomatoes
1 clove garlic
120 g (¼ lb) pork fillet (ham), diced
1 bouquet garni*
6 - 8 eggs
fine herbs, to taste

Peel and seed the peppers, slice them into thin slices, and sauté them in butter. Separately sauté the onions. Peel, seed, and cut the tomatoes into pieces, then add them to the onions and cook until their juices come out. Add the garlic and bell peppers, then add the diced pork fillet and bouquet garni. Simmer for 1½ hours. Beat the eggs, then scramble in a pan while adding the other mixture. When cooked, this new mixture should be soft and moist. Sprinkle with fine herbs and serve.

Serves: 2

Hostellerie de la Fuste

04210 Valensole, 04100 Manosque
Tel: (92) 72-05-95
Proprietor/Chef: Daniel Jourdan

Manosque is in the Haute Provence region of France, olive-growing country, and this restaurant is actually a little farmhouse set in the middle of a quiet park.

Daniel Jourdan, whose grandmother and father were chefs, has been with this restaurant for some 12 years now. His dishes (especially the Scrambled Eggs with Truffles) carry the taste of the Provence soil even when he goes in for variations such as his Beef Stew with Sweet Onion Purée in Sherry.

Scrambled Eggs with Truffles "Rabassaires" Style

3 very fresh whole eggs
60 g (2 oz) raw, washed, fresh truffles
2 tbsp olive oil
salt and pepper, as needed
1 tbsp fresh goats cheese

(Rabassaires are the professional truffle pickers in Haute Provence.)
Leave the eggs and truffles together in a closed container for at least 24 hours before using.

Shred the truffles, but not too finely, about 1 mm (.04 in) thick. Stew them for 5 minutes in ½ the oil in a covered pan. Scramble the eggs; season with a little salt and a large pinch of pepper. Whisk the cheese into a liquid cream to remove lumps, then add to the eggs. Add truffles and whisk lightly without mixing completely. Heat the remaining oil in a thick frying pan. When oil is hot, pour in the ingredients, stirring all the time with a fork to get a thick cream which is thicker in some parts than in others. Serve immediately.

Serves: 1

Au Bon Vieux Temps

3, Place de la Halle, 08200 Sedan
Tel: (24) 29-03-70
Proprietor: Jean-Claude Leterme • Chef: Guy Fourcart

M. Jean-Claude Leterme has been running this restaurant, with its reassuring name ("Good Old Times"), for 15 years. He and his chef, Guy Fourcart, have established a set of strict standards of quality upon which their customers have come to rely. It is, therefore, not unusual to find a marquis or a viscount or any person who appreciates high quality, dining at **Au Bon Vieux Temps.**

This intimate little room, with its old, rustic-style furniture, is the perfect setting for exploring such delicacies as Veal Sweetmeats "Brillat-Savarin" Style and Frogs Legs in Cream.

Frogs Legs in Cream

2.5 kg (5½ lb) frogs legs
2 litres (½ gal) double cream (whipping cream)
carcass of 1 chicken
700 g (1½ lb) chicken meat
500 g (1 lb) bacon fat
150 g (5¼ oz) fresh goose liver

200 g (7 oz) beef marrow
½ litre (1 pt) choux paste*
1 tbsp butter
salt and pepper, to taste
1 bunch chopped watercress, and as needed to garnish

Cook the frogs legs in the cream very gently for 15 minutes in a saucepan, then remove legs and remove the meat from the bones. Put the bones and the chicken carcass into the saucepan with the cream and gently cook another 25 minutes. Remove ½ litre (1 pt) of cream from the saucepan, thicken it with butter, then mix with the frog flesh. Discard the remaining liquid. Refrigerate 1 hour.

To prepare the stuffing: Mince the chicken meat and bacon fat very finely with the goose liver and beef marrow, then mix with choux paste in an electric mixer until the stuffing is smooth.

Butter 8 ramekins, then place a round piece of aluminum foil in the bottom of each with a brush and melted butter. Coat the ramekins with stuffing, 5 mm (¼ in) on the bottom and sides. Fill each ramekin with the meat from the frogs legs to 3 mm (⅛ in) from the top edge, then fill to the top with the remaining stuffing.

To complete sauce: Put the refrigerated cream mixture through a strainer, and thicken with butter. Season with salt and pepper. Mix in watercress and cook for 5 minutes.

Cook the ramekins in a bain-marie* in the oven at 325°F (160°C) for 25 minutes.

Unmould the ramekins on a base of watercress on a serving dish, coat with the sauce, and serve.

Serves: 8

La Bérangère

38860 Les Deux-Alpes
Tel: (76) 80-56-22
Proprietor: René Lherm • Chef: Patrick Lherm

Les Deux-Alpes is a modern paradise for winter sports. Located there is **La Bérangère** with its beautiful rooms, magnificent views, and . . . its restaurant. This hotel has been run by René Lherm since 1968 and is a favourite of amateur skiers. Patrick Lherm, who has studied with such chefs as Bocuse, Daguin, and Rostaing, is in the kitchen. Take note of his Rib of Beef "Reblochon," Leg of Pullet in Mushroom Sauce, Hazelnut Salad "Grenoble" Style, Frogs Legs in Pastry, and Ice Cream Pyramid with Bilberry (Blackberry) Sauce. They are wonderful.

The swimming pool and sauna will keep you from getting too fat from overeating, and the games rooms will help pass the time when the weather gets too bad.

Frogs Legs in Pastry and Green Butter

300 g (10½ oz) puff pastry dough*
100 g (¼ lb) butter, softened
60 g (2 oz) chopped parsley
1 clove garlic, chopped
50 ml (1½ oz) pastis (aniseed liqueur)
salt and pepper, to taste
juice of ¼ lemon
24 frogs legs, prepared for cooking
100 ml (½ cup) double cream (whipping cream)

Roll out six 10 cm (4 in) squares of dough and bake in oven at 350°F (180°C) for 10 minutes; keep hot.

To prepare green butter: Mix the softened butter with parsley, garlic, pastis, salt, pepper, and lemon juice, then warm.

Cook frogs legs in a steamer for 10 minutes or until tender, then mix with the green butter preparation, add cream, and cook for another 2 minutes.

Serve 4 legs on each pastry square coated with sauce.

Wine: *Sancerre white*   Serves: 6

La Dariole

49, rue du Colisée, 75008 Paris
Tel: 225-6676
Proprietor/Chef: Gilbert Drouelle

Gilbert Drouelle, a gentle giant of tough Burgundy stock, has just opened up in Paris (without giving up his other Dariole, a restaurant in Viry-Chatillon) in the Faubourg Saint Honoré. An almost spiral staircase leads up to a long, pleasantly modern room in which the menu is perhaps more stylish than the decor. Nevertheless, isn't what is on your plate the most important thing in a restaurant? Well, since Gilbert wishes us "a pleasant time," sit right down and taste his Mousse of Smoked Salmon with Cucumbers, his Calf Brains with Two Peppers, his Aiguillette in Jelly à la Nivernaise (a tribute to the neighbouring butcher store), his fine Stew of Lamb Sweetmeats in Brioche, his Goats Cheese with Cream, and his desserts.

Calf Brains with Two Peppers

400 g (14 oz) calf brains, cleaned and skinned
court bouillon,* as needed
60 g (2 oz) salted butter
3 eggs
200 ml (6 oz) double cream (whipping cream)
pinch of salt
2 garlic cloves, chopped
250 ml (1 cup) mixed herbs
7 g (¼ oz) pink peppercorns
10 g (⅓ oz) green peppercorns
1 bunch chopped chives
30 g (1 oz) finely sliced carrots
spinach leaves, as needed

Poach the calf brains in court bouillon for 10 minutes. Drain, then brown them very lightly in ⅓ the butter to remove all the liquid, then brown them further in the remaining butter. Add the eggs, ½ the cream, the salt, and garlic. Strain well. Add the mixed herbs, pink and green peppercorns, and chives. Blanch the carrots in salted water and add to the mixture.

Divide the mixture into 6 buttered ramekins, then cook in a bain-marie* in the oven at 350°F (190°C) for 45 minutes. Serve on a layer of spinach.

Wine: *Arbois red*   Serves: 6

Le Saintongeais

62, rue du Faubourg-Montmartre, 75009 Paris
Tel: 280-3992
Proprietor/Chef: Joël Girodot

The Saintonge, a small province in western France that is rich in the art of fine food, could wish for no better ambassador than Joël Girodot. Cooking in this region has kept its provincial and upright character, as well as the peculiar names for each speciality: "Cagouilles" (snails), "Bouilliture" of Eels (eels in thick sauce with wine and onions), and "Mouclade" (mussels in cream). This restaurant serves them all, plus other fine dishes such as Sausage Meat with Herbs. M. Girdot, who worked at the Plaza before taking his French cuisine to Tokyo and the Philippines, is home at last. He, his most charming wife, and the intimate and warm surroundings of **Le Saintongeais** all make this little restaurant a real haven for good, country style food.

Sausage Meat with Herbs

1 kg (2¼ lb) mixture of equal amounts of spinach and white-beet (Swiss chard) leaves
1 kg (2¼ lb) sausage meat
150 g (5¼ oz) thick, non-smoked bacon, cooked and diced
1 large onion, chopped
4 cloves garlic, chopped
1 bouquet chopped parsley
140 ml (4 oz) white wine
3 eggs, whisked
30 ml (1 oz) cognac
salt and pepper, to taste
1 sprig thyme
2 bay leaves

Blanch the spinach and beet (Swiss chard) leaves. Strain, squeeze out the liquid, and cut finely with a knife. Mix with the sausage meat and the bacon. Add onion, garlic, parsley, wine, eggs, and cognac. Season with salt and pepper. Place in an ovenproof casserole and place the thyme and bay leaves on top. Cook in a bain-marie* for 1 hour at 400°F (205°C). Let cool, slice, and serve cold.

Suggestion: Serve the slices covered with crushed nuts and surrounded with tomato slices, gherkins, and pickled onions.

Wine: *Muscadet, Gros Plant*

Serves: 6

Le Marcande

52, rue de Miromesnil, 75008 Paris
Tel: 265-7685
Proprietor/Chef: Jean-Claude Ferrero

The astounding Jean-Claude Ferrero came from Savoy to conquer Paris accompanied by his shining star, Mme. Andrée Ferrero. Elegant and distinguished describes the environment at **Le Marcande.**

As we enjoy ourselves, we observe Jean-Claude preparing his extraordinary dishes: Melon Soup Flavoured with Mint, Oxtail with Truffles in Crust, Young Rabbit with Rosemary, Seafood Assortment, Smoked Leg of Lamb, and many more absolutely divine treats. We also find beautiful desserts and a distinguished wine cellar, and for the gentlemen gourmands, there are lovely ladies in an endless parade of beauty to wait on you.

It is a real treat for the eyes and tastebuds when you dine at Le Marcande.

Smoked Leg of Lamb

15 litres (4 gal) water, and as needed
350 g (12 oz) potassium nitrate
350 g (12 oz) granulated sugar
3.2 kg (7 lb) rock salt
thyme and bay leaf, to taste
1 leg of lamb
resinous white pine wood (optional)
4 onions
10 cloves garlic, crushed
1 bouquet garni*
40 black peppercorns

To prepare the brine: Pour 15 litres (4 gal) water into a large pot. Add the next 5 ingredients. Add the leg of lamb and let it soak for 4-5 days. (Use a syringe to aid in saturating the lamb with brine.)

To smoke the lamb: Prepare a pit of resinous pine with 50% white wood. On a spit, cook the lamb over this burning wood for 12 hours (or cook in a rotisserie).

To poach the lamb: Put enough water in a large kettle to cover the leg of lamb. Add onions, garlic, bouquet garni, and black peppercorns. Bring the water to a boil. Add the lamb and cook for 2 hours. Turn off the heat and let the lamb stand for an additional hour. Remove the lamb from the kettle and refrigerate for 12 hours before serving.

Serves: 4-5

Hotellerie Beau Rivage

2, rue de Beau Rivage, 69300 Condrieu
Tel: (74) 59-52-24
Proprietor/Chef: Paulette Castaing

Veal Sweetbreads in Lettuce

2 large veal sweetbreads	1 large head lettuce
50 g (1¾ oz) white bread soaked in milk	2 chopped onions
100 g (¼ lb) veal fillet (veal loin)	2 chopped carrots
100 g (¼ lb) goose liver	1 sprig thyme
50 g (1¾ oz) sliced mushrooms	salt and pepper, to taste
150 g (5¼ oz) butter, and as needed	50 ml (1½ oz) port wine
2 eggs	200 ml (6 oz) veal stock*
chopped parsley, as needed	fresh butter, as needed

To prepare the stuffing: Clean, scald, trim, and remove sinews from the sweetbreads, then mix with bread, veal fillet, goose liver, mushrooms, 50 g (1¾ oz) butter, eggs, 1 bunch parsley, chives, and the heart of lettuce. Wrap in lettuce leaves. Prepare a braising stock with 100 g (¼ lb) butter, onions, carrots, thyme, and 1 handful parsley. Place wrapped sweetbreads in the stock, season with salt and pepper, and cook gently for 30 - 40 minutes, basting frequently. Remove sweetbreads and keep hot. Skim off fat, add port, and reduce to desired consistency. Add veal stock, swirl in a piece of butter, and strain through a fine mesh strainer. Serve the sweetbreads coated with sauce.

Wine: *Burgundy or Côtes de Rhône red wine*　　　　　　　　　Serves: 4

This restaurant sits on the beautiful banks (implicit in the French name) of the Rhône beside Condrieu, between Vienne and Valence — bargemen country. This is a dapper and perpetually young establishment of yesteryear with a sun-bathed terrace, several rooms, and a woman chef, who has owned this place since 1946.

Paulette Castaing learned her trade from several master chefs of the region, then she worked in the Lyon area where the recognition of good foods comes as second nature (or first!). That's where she unearthed many a secret, notably that of preparing pâté and Stew of Eels, Poached Poultry, Veal Sweetbreads in Lettuce, Pheasant with Cabbage — even a simple Scrambled Eggs with Crayfish can be sublime.

Bistro 121

121, rue de la Convention, 75015 Paris
Tel: 557-5290
Proprietor: The Moussié Family • Chef: André Jalbert

Hot Pâté "Wine-Grower" Style

1 small fillet of veal (veal loin)
1 kg (2¼ lb) cooked ham
4 large veal sweetbreads
butter, as needed
salt and pepper, to taste
200 ml (6 oz) cognac
750 g (1½ lb) puff pastry dough*
200 g (7 oz) duck liver, chopped
200 g (7 oz) topside (rump) of veal, chopped
egg wash, as needed

Cut the fillet of veal and ham into scallops, 2 cm (¾ in) thick and cut the sweetbreads into halves. Gently "stiffen" sweetbreads in butter without cooking them. Add salt and pepper, flame with ½ the cognac, strain, and let cool.

Roll out the dough into a large rectangle. Mix the chopped duck liver, remaining cognac, and chopped topside of veal together to make the stuffing. Place a thin layer of stuffing in the middle of the pastry, place a layer of sweetbreads on top, then a layer of veal, then a layer of ham, then another layer of stuffing etc. until all ingredients are used and stuffing is on top. Fold over the pastry, brush with egg wash, and decorate with scraps of dough. Put into a preheated oven at 350°F (175°C), then immediately reduce heat to 225°F (100°C) and bake for about 90 minutes.

Suggestion: Serve with mushrooms in cream or grapes and raisins in Périgourdine sauce.*

Serves: 10

Jean Moussié is an old hand in this business. Back in 1956, he decided to open his own establishment in the 15th *arrondissement* (district) of Paris with a warm, cosy atmosphere.

Jean has not forgotten the lessons of his apprenticeship in Cahors. He, his kitchen staff, and his daughter, Monique (who serves in the restaurant), pay great attention to a personalised regionalism with a touch of modern creativity. Jean calls this a restaurant "with the youth of a 25-year-old boy and the wisdom of a 50-year-man." There are real treats for you here: Raw Fillet in Three Kinds of Sauce, Stuffed Chicken Cooked in the Pot, Raw Fish "Tahiti" Style, and Hot Pâté "Wine-Growers" Style.

La Paix

Place de la République, 71 Chauffailles
Tel: (85) 26-02-60
Proprietor: Michèle Jury • Chef: Yves Jury

Hot Rabbit Pâté with Wild Thyme

250 g (½ lb) rabbit meat
125 g (¼ lb) spring peas
320 g (¾ lb) chanterelle mushrooms
2 pinches wild thyme (or thyme)
1 tbsp walnut oil
salt and pepper, to taste
1 pinch chopped chives
125 g (¼ lb) puff pastry dough*
200 g (7 oz) butter
juice of 1 lemon

Cut the rabbit meat into thin strips. Cook the peas and the chanterelles in boiling water for 15 minutes. Cool and drain. In a terrine, mix the rabbit meat, peas, chanterelles, 1 pinch thyme, walnut oil, salt, pepper, and chopped chives together. Fill 4 moulds with the dough, then fill the moulds with the mixture from the terrine. Bake in the oven at 400°F (205°C) for 15 minutes.

Reduce the butter, lemon juice, and remaining thyme in a saucepan and mix until smooth.

Unmould the pâtés onto 4 plates, cover with sauce, and serve.

Suggestion: Serve with a compote of onions and sautéed chanterelles.

Serves: 4

Michèle Guéneau-Jury was raised by a loving mother who also had a fabulous talent for cooking. Mme. Guéneau began cooking in 1911 in several bourgeois restaurants. Michèle has taken over her mother's position at **La Paix** and manages it with flair. This is a marvellous provincial restaurant located in the tranquil beauty of Provence. Yves Jury worked for Mère Brazier at Léon in Lyon before associating himself with Michèle. Chef Yves finds some fault with *la nouvelle cuisine,* but he would still rather serve light and delicate dishes. His dishes are all excellent, but if you can't decide, try the Saddle of Rabbit with Shallots and Mustard or Hot Rabbit Pâté with Wild Thyme, and for dessert, try the Raspberry or Fig Charlotte wth Beaujolais wine.

Le Totem

Flaine, 74300 Cluses
Tel: (50) 90-80-64
Proprietor: R. Giraud • Chef: M. Guillamou

Duck Livers with Apples

½ litre (1 pt) veal stock*
¼ litre (½ pt) port wine
salt and pepper, to taste
700 - 800 g (1½ - 1¾ lb) duck liver
4 Golden Delicious apples, 2 halved and 2 sliced
3 apricots, halved
5 tbsp double cream (whipping cream)
1 tbsp butter, and as needed to sauté

Boil ½ the veal stock with the port wine to thicken slightly. Salt and pepper the duck liver, then put it into the stock/port mixture and let it boil gently for 8 minutes. Take the liver out of the pot and set aside.

Put the remaining veal stock in a food processor. Add the 2 halved apples and the apricots and purée. Pour into a pot. Add cream, then slowly add 1 tbsp butter. Reseason if necessary and keep warm.

Brown the 2 sliced apples in a frying pan in butter. Finely slice the duck liver into ½ cm (¼ in) slices. Keep them warm in a pot containing ¼ of the duck liver cooking mixture.

To serve: Spread the slices of liver on a plate and cover with sauce. Decorate with sliced apples and serve hot.

Serves: 4

For a prestigious location, not much betters the Alps. A fabulous ski resort, Flaine, is there, and one of the most luxurious hotel-restaurants in Flaine is **Le Totem.** The restaurant's menu does not display high prices, yet it offers high class dishes such as Duck Livers with Apples, Duck with Fine Herbs, and Rabbit with Glazed White Onions.

Should you happen to have a sweet tooth, Le Totem offers an array of magnificent desserts such as the Millefueille with Raspberries and many divine pastries. If you eat at Le Totem once, you will definitely come again.

Hôtel Eychenne

8, avenue Paul-Laffont, 09200 Saint-Girons
Tel: (61) 66-20-55
Proprietor: Michel Bordeaux • Chef: Maurice Bordes

It makes no difference whether you are from the Champs Élysées or from out of town, the **Hôtel Eychenne,** for the past six generations, has welcomed the most finicky gourmets.

Here the cuisine is old-fashioned and tra-ditional, and one will find the variety in preparation as vast as the variety of foods. You must not forget to try the Raisin Quail, which cannot be surpassed, and the Duck Liver with Grapes. The Smoked Salmon is also an excellent feast.

Duck Liver with Grapes

1 fresh duck or goose liver
salt and pepper, to taste
100 ml (3 oz) cooking Sauterne
4 - 5 tbsp veal stock*
1 cluster of grapes, white seedless
Melba toast, to serve

Place the duck or goose liver in a pot, add salt and pepper, and cook over low heat, un-covered, for 10 minutes or until the juices are released. Skim off the grease. Add the cooking Sauterne and veal stock. Let cook for an additional 10 minutes.

Add grapes and let them poach slowly in the liquid for another 10 minutes. Cut the liver into thin slices and serve on Melba toast topped with poached grapes.

La Barrière Poquelin

17, rue Molière, 75001 Paris
Tel: 296-2219
Proprietor: Patrice Dard • Chef: Marc Besson

Patrice Dard has several restaurants to his name. He is the son of Frédéric Dard, the creator of San Antonio and the detective novels. Patrice hails from Lyon and has in-herited the gourmet taste one associates with that city of gastronomy. Having taken over **La Barrière Poquelin** in the rue Molière, he, together with his young chef, has made it into a most intimate restaurant/ bistro. The menu is dedicated mostly to sea-food, but it also offers many other fine dishes (especially the Foie Gras with Nuts).

The atmosphere here is amusing: a blend of Lyon wine corks and a refined elegance. There are quick meals before the show and delicate suppers after the show.

Foie Gras with Nuts

100 g (¼ lb) shelled hazelnuts
300 ml (9 oz) fruit liqueur (Pineau from Charentes is recommended)
400 g (14 oz) goose liver
salt and pepper, to taste

Marinate the nuts in the liqueur overnight. The next day, poach the goose liver in boil-ing water for 1 minute, then let cool. When cold, remove the sinews and dry with a cloth. Season with salt and pepper. Place the nuts on the liver and roll in a cloth into the shape of a long round sausage. Tie up the 2 ends. Refrigerate 4 - 5 days or longer.

Suggestion: Unwrap liver, slice, and serve with a green salad and green beans sea-soned with nut oil and vinegar.

Wine: *Pineau des Charentes liqueur*   Serves: 4

Chez Edgard

4, rue Marbeuf, 75008 Paris
Tel: 720-5115
Proprietor: Paul Benmussa • Chef: Jean-Jacques Moulinier

Foie Gras with Oranges

5 large oranges
750 g (1½ lb) duck liver
salt and pepper, to taste
1 tbsp cognac
10 large slices truffle
1 litre (1 qt) duck aspic (or gelatine)
60 ml (2 oz) Grand Marnier
parsley, to garnish

Halve the oranges, squeeze out the juice, and remove pulp. Reserve the empty halves of orange peel. Season the liver with salt, pepper, and cognac, then cook in an aluminum foil wrapping for 20 minutes at 350°F (175°C). Let cool.

Slice the liver into 10 pieces and put each piece into a reserved ½ orange peel. Place a slice of truffle on top of each liver cube, then fill to the top with duck aspic flavoured with the Grand Marnier. Sprinkle with parsley or other greenery and serve.

Wine/Liqueur: *Grand Marnier*

Serves: 10

Chez Edgard has, since 1969, been a sort of daily miracle worked in the realms of catering. Over the years, it has grown in size (salons on the first floor, "make-yourself-at-home" dining rooms, etc.) and has become a meeting place for many Parisians from the worlds of show business, the press, television, politics, etc. These Parisians come here to treat themselves to the cooking of Chef Moulinier, who hails from the Périgord region.

The Chez Edgard team, led by Paul Benmussa, is above all up with the times, but the right times. These circa 1900 rooms, echoing with the noisy clatter of knives and business chat, this array of seafood, and the busy, laughing waitresses make this restaurant quite unique — one-of-a-kind in Paris.

Restaurant Allard

41, rue Saint-André-des-Arts and 1, rue de l'Eperon, 75006 Paris
Tel: 326-4823
Proprietor/Chef: Mme. Allard

Truffled Chicken Liver Terrine

2 kg (4½ lb) chicken livers
800 g (1¾ lb) goose fat
2 eggs
1 tbsp double cream (whipping cream)
salt and pepper, to taste
pinch of nutmeg
50 ml (1½ oz) port wine
1 tbsp cognac
50 g (1¾ oz) truffles

Wash the chicken livers several times, then take out the hard parts, strain, and chop finely. In a large bowl, put eggs, cream, salt, pepper, nutmeg, wine, and cognac. Blend until mixture is thoroughly mixed.

Fill a terrine halfway with the mixture, place thinly sliced truffles on top, cover the terrine with aluminum foil, and place in a bain-marie* in a preheated oven at 400°F (205°C) for 45 minutes, then lower heat to 325°F (160°C) and bake another 15 minutes. When done, colour should be pink.

Place heavy weights on the terrine to firmly pack the mixture while it is cooling, then serve cool.

Serves: 8

This is, without a doubt, one of the most popular restaurants in all of Paris. M. Vincent Candre was the founder, M. Marcel Allard, his proud successor, and now Mme. Allard is the master chef. **Restaurant Allard** is clearly a family domain: even the wines are carefully chosen by a family member.

All of Paris, the true soul of Paris, have visited Restaurant Allard. They are enticed by such delicacies as Fresh Cucumber and Ham Salad garnished with snails from Burgundy, Truffled Chicken Liver Terrine, scallops cooked in the Allard's famous butter sauce, squid with delicately salted red beans, Duck Topped with Lentils and Olives, a green leaf lettuce salad garnished with lard, and a wondrous array of desserts; all are simply marvellous.

Le Moniage Guillaume

88, rue de la Tombe-Issoire, 75014 Paris
Tel: 327-0988 and 322-9615
Proprietor: Serge Lecerf • Chef: Raymond Archimbeaud

To say that at **Le Moniage Guillaume** the ocean is always honoured is redundant. To say that the oysters, shellfish, and crustaceans are fresh and plentiful is pleonastic.

To say that Serge Lecerf and Raymond Archimbeaud are attentive to their clients is also repetitious. To say that one feels good here, and that one can eat even better than one feels — that is simply the truth.

Terrine of Hermit Crab with Hazelnuts

8 kg (17 lb) hermit crabs
5 litres (5¼ qt) fish stock*
1.5 kg (3⅓ lb) brill (or any white fish), flesh only
salt, to taste
1 tsp cayenne pepper
100 g (¼ lb) hazelnuts
2 tsp butter

Wash the crabs and cook them in fish stock for 10 minutes. Drain, let cool, and shell. Purée the brill and the cooled crabmeat. Combine and season well with salt and cayenne pepper. Add the hazelnuts to this purée.

Butter a terrine and fill it with the purée. Put the terrine in the oven for 55 minutes at 400°F (205°C).

Suggestion: Serve the terrine cold with vinaigrette dressing* or cocktail sauce.

Serves: 10

La Croix Blanche

Lamotte-Beauvron, 41600 Chaumont-sur-Tharonne
Tel: (54) 88-55-12
Proprietor: Pierre Crouzier • Chef: Gisèle Crouzier

For two centuries, the kitchen of this restaurant has been monopolized by females. Today, it is run by Gisèle Crouzier, who is also the vice president of the Association of Women Restaurateurs and Chefs.

The atmosphere of this auberge is cosy, quaint, and retrospective. Here in these dining rooms, decorated in a style reminiscent of Louis XIII and XV, or sitting on the terrace adorned with flowers, one cannot help but reminisce.

La Croix Blanche epitomizes tender loving care in the preparation of fresh hams, truffles, seafood, and game. The desserts should be savoured slowly, as should the fine wines offered by M. Pierre Crouzier.

Seafood Delicacy with French Dressing

150 g (5¼ oz) fresh fillet of pike
150 g (5¼ oz) fresh fillet of carp
150 g (5¼ oz) fresh fillet of tench (sole)
4 eggs
6 tbsp double cream (whipping cream)
salt and pepper, to taste
pinch of paprika
2 crushed tomatoes plus 4 tbsp
4 stalks asparagus
2 tsp butter
4 tbsp strawberry vinegar
4 tbsp hazelnut oil
4 tbsp peanut oil
2 tbsp leeks, julienne
asparagus tips, to garnish

Mix the fish fillets with the eggs to obtain a smooth paste and until a foam forms. Add cream slowly, then add salt and pepper, paprika, 2 crushed tomatoes, and asparagus. Place ingredients in a buttered terrine. Cook in a bain-marie* for 25-30 minutes in the oven at 400-425°F (205-220°C).

To prepare French dressing: Mix strawberry vinegar, hazelnut oil, peanut oil, leeks, and 4 tbsp crushed tomatoes together well.

Take the terrine out of the oven, unmould onto a plate. Garnish with asparagus tips, pour French dressing over the mixture, and serve promptly.

Serves: 4

Chez Casimir

6, rue de Belzunce, 75010 Paris
Tel: 878-3253
Proprietor: Barthélémy Pujol • Chef: Bernard Prissette

Pike and Crayfish Terrine

1 kg (2¼ lb) pike (or perch) flesh
500 g (1 lb) salmon flesh
200 g (6 oz) butter
125 g (¼ lb) shallots
½ litre (1 pt) Chablis
60 crayfish (or small shrimps)
125 g (¼ lb) finely diced onions
125 g (¼ lb) carrots, diced
1 clove garlic, chopped
200 ml (6 oz) cognac
½ litre (1 pt) fish stock*
500 g (1 lb) tomatoes, peeled, seeded, and crushed
1 tsp thyme
1 bay leaf
1 handful parsley
salt and pepper, to taste
2 kg (4½ lb) spinach
10 egg whites
1 litre (2 pt) double cream (whipping cream)
1 pod grated nutmeg
125 g (¼ lb) fresh truffles, sliced

Brown the pike and salmon in ¼ of the butter with ½ the chopped shallots. Deglaze with the Chablis, leaving the fish in the pan. Cover and let cool for a few hours. Slice the salmon into thin scallops.

Wash the crayfish and remove the black, dorsal vein by pulling sharply on the central tail flap and gently draining the vein. Sauté the crayfish over high heat with the finely diced onions, carrots, garlic, and remaining shallots for 3 minutes. Flame with cognac. Moisten with the Chablis in which the fish have cooled and add the fish stock, tomatoes, thyme, bay leaf, parsley, salt, and pepper. Simmer for 10 minutes. Drain the crayfish; strain and reserve the cooking liquid. Remove the peel from the crayfish tails and keep to one side. Reserve 20 heads for the garnish.

To prepare crayfish sauce: Pound the remaining 40 crayfish heads in a mortar (or grind them), then strain them through a fine sieve, pressing to extract all the juice. Mix this juice into the reserved cooking liquid. Keep warm.

Wash the spinach. Cook it in boiling salted water for 3 - 4 minutes, then refresh it under cold running water. Drain and squeeze dry. Heat gently with 125 g (¼ lb) butter.

Sieve the pike flesh through a fine sieve or mince it finely in a food processor. Add the egg whites, two by two, mixing thoroughly with each addition. Place the bowl on crushed ice. When chilled, stir in the cream gradually. Season with salt, pepper, and nutmeg. Butter a rectangular terrine with some of the remaining butter. Line the base with a little less than half the pike mixture. Arrange the scallops of salmon, the crayfish tails, and the truffle slices on top, then surround with a line of spinach. Do not allow anything to touch the sides of the terrine or the pike will be difficult to cut neatly. Fill the terrine with the remaining pike mixture.

Cover the terrine with buttered greaseproof (wax) paper and bake for 1 hour at 325°F (160°C). Unmould and cut into thin slices. Serve on a bed of spinach, garnished with the reserved crayfish heads. Pour the crayfish sauce around the dish.

Serves: 10

Behind the Saint-Vincent-de-Paul Church, you will find **Chez Casimir**, a restaurant where you may taste a fine Pike and Crayfish Terrine or a Haunch of Young Wild Boar with Whortleberries (Huckleberries) — dishes fit for a king.

You may ask yourself whether the dining experience at Chez Casimir is dominated more by its hospitality or by its excellent cuisine. I suggest that to find out you must go there and let your senses decide.

Auberge de l'Argoat

27, avenue Reille, 75014 Paris
Tel: 589-1705
Proprietor/Chef: Marcel Goareguer

M. Marcel Goareguer is from the woods of Brittany, and that tells us all. His small auberge is hidden away deep in the heart of the 14th *arrondissement* (district) of Paris. This robust and diligent man, working alongside his family, is proud to serve his fine products from Brittany.

Ecologically, everyone should be happy, for here in M. Goareguer's domaine all ingredients are natural — from the bread, cheese, and wine to the very last pastry baked with honey and, of course, the Breton cider. Nature's best! The seafood arrives daily from Brittany so that the terrines may please, delight, and even surprise the palate. The fresh turtle, the scallops, the fish — everything here is an epicurean's delight!

Tunny (Tuna) Terrrine with Spinach

trimmings (bones, head, fins, etc.) of turbot
2 carrots
2 onions
2 shallots
2 leeks
2 branches thyme
bay leaf and rosemary, to taste
10 litres (2½ gal) dry white wine
1.5 kg (3⅓ lb) raw, fresh tunny (tuna), diced
500 g (1 lb) blanched fresh spinach
3 tbsp crushed apples
juice of 3 lemons
salt and pepper, to taste
6 eggs

In a large pot of boiling water, put the first 10 ingredients. Reduce to 2 litres (½ gal), then cool with ice. Strain the mixture and reserve the gelatine that is produced.

Mix the next 6 ingredients together by hand for a good length of time (about 10-15 minutes). Put this mixture in a terrine, heat on the stove on moderate heat, and cook for 50-60 minutes. When cooked and still hot, glaze it with the reserved gelatine mixture and serve.

Serves: 10

Le Petit Navire

14, rue des Fossés-Saint-Bernard, 75005 Paris
Tel: 354-2252
Proprietor/Chef: Jean-Claude Cousty

Before the First World War, this was the location of La Halle aux Vins. It was a Parisian and Rabelaisian province, and this street was full of enjoyable bistros. Now everything has changed, but at least one special bistro remains. Jean-Claude Cousty is now the owner of **Le Petit Navire**. The decor has the touch of the sea; it is definitely a naval man's paradise. The success of this fine earthbound "galley" is due mainly to the marvellous seafood dishes served here. Jean-Claude offers fish soup, grilled sardines, stuffed mussels, seafood plates, seafood salads, and seafood fricassees. But, don't discount the other dishes on the menu. The Tapenade, the cheeses, the desserts, and the wines are all delicious treats.

Tapenade

600 g (1⅓ lb) black olives, pitted
60 g (2 oz) capers
60 g (2 oz) anchovies in oil
1 pinch cayenne pepper
1 tbsp powdered rosemary
1 garlic clove, crushed

Grind the olives with the capers and crush the anchovies. Mix everything together until the mixture becomes very creamy. Add cayenne pepper and rosemary, then add the crushed garlic.

Suggestion: Serve with Melba toast, fresh butter, and lemon juice.

Wine: *A white Cassis*

Serves: 4-6

Clavel

44, rue Charles-Domerq, 33800 Bordeaux
Tel: (56) 92-91-52
Proprietor/Chef: Françis Garcia

Clavel, in Bordeaux, is the epitome of antiquity and reputation. Françis Garcia hasn't been here long, however his past record at Dubern in Bordeaux, Girgaglia in Port-Grimaud, and La Réserve in Bordeaux have marked him as a man destined for success.

He acquired Clavel in 1979 and totally transformed the place. Now, one finds Clavel a winter garden with spacious seating in which to experience the pleasures of comfort and ease while dining. The menu will appease, tantalize, and capture you with its classic delights so well prepared. The exquisite Flan Truffles with Black Sauce is just the beginning. There's also a splended selection of Bordeaux wines.

Flan Truffles with Black Sauce

125 g (¼ lb) fresh duck livers
125 g (¼ lb) white chicken meat, all sinew, nerves, and veins removed
150 g (5¼ oz) truffles, grated and boiled
100 ml (3 oz) white port wine
125 g (¼ lb) egg whites
300 ml (9 oz) double cream (whipping cream)

In a mixer, mix the duck livers, chicken, and truffles together until smooth and colour becomes black. Pour mixture into a saucepan, add wine, then let simmer slowly while stirring until liquid becomes very thick and smooth. Add egg whites and cream. Mix to a smooth consistency over moderate heat without curdling.

Pour the mixture into buttered moulds and place in a bain-marie.* Cover the pan and place in an oven at 375°F (190°C) for 20 minutes. Remove the moulds from the oven, turn the flan out of the moulds and onto plates, cover with sauce, and serve.

Serves: 10

Hôtel du Parc

24420 Savignac-Les-Églises
Tel: (53) 05-00-12
Proprietor/Chef: Jean Vessat

Hôtel du Parc is as much a traditional symbol of the area as are the ancient churches and cathedrals here. This old hotel belongs to a bygone era, the romantic days of the troubadours in Périgord.

Today, Hôtel du Parc features a quasi-religious atmosphere with traditional decor. While you are here, try the truffles; they are the most famous dish in the Périgord region.

Truffles Périgourdine

4 truffles, 45 g (1½ oz) each
300 ml (9 oz) port wine
salt and pepper, to taste
4 strips slightly salted lard
4 slices ham
150 g (5¼ oz) fresh goose liver, well mashed
750 g (1½ lb) puff pastry dough,* 10 cm by 8 cm by 4 mm (4 in by 3 in by ¹⁄₁₆ in), cut into 4 pieces
1 egg, beaten
400 ml (1½ cups) Périgourdine sauce*

Soak the truffles in water for a few minutes. Wash and scrub them. Gently cook them in a covered pan in the port for 20 minutes. Season with salt and pepper, let cool, then drain them.

Roll each truffle in a strip of lard. Cover each with a slice of ham and ¼ of the liver. Fold the pastry dough over each truffle and decorate into flower shapes. Brush with the egg. Let stand for 20 minutes in the refrigerator.

Bake the wrapped truffles in the oven at 475°F (250°C) for 25 minutes. Serve with Périgourdine sauce.

Wine: *Cahors Bergerac*   Serves: 4

La Taverne

1, rue Delpech, 46000 Cahors
Tel: (65) 35-28-66
Proprietor/Chef: Pierre Escorbiac

Between 1925 and 1952, Pierre Escorbiac travelled through France and overseas. Upon his return, he created **La Taverne**. Ever since, Pierre has remained in Cahors.

Surrounded by a rustic decor, Pierre devotes himself to preparing traditional cuisine from Quercy. You will be delighted with his Truffle Turnover, escargots, chicken in wine, and roasted duck.

In Cahors, the wine is worth tasting, and Pierre has one of the finest selections anywhere. Treat yourself to a sumptuous dinner and a fine bottle of wine at La Taverne.

Truffle Turnover

4 truffles, 60 g (2 oz) each
port wine, as needed to marinate
mirepoix,* as needed
120 g (4 oz) purée of goose liver
4 slices ham, each large enough to envelope a truffle
butter, as needed
puff pastry dough,* enough to envelope 4 truffles

Wash, brush, and marinate the truffles in enough port to cover them for 24 hours. Braise the truffles in a pan with some mirepoix and a little port wine from the marinade for 15 minutes.

On each slice of ham, spread a thin layer of goose liver purée flavoured with the marinade. Wrap each truffle in a slice of ham, fold it inside a buttered layer of puff pastry dough, and bake for 20-25 minutes at 350°F (176°C).

Suggestion: Serve with Périgourdine sauce.*

Serves: 4

Le Florence

43, boulevard Foch, 51100 Reims
Tel: (26) 47-35-36
Proprietor: Jean-Pierre Maillot • Chef: Jean-Luc Schvartz

What could be better than champagne for feasting and satisfying the gourmet? **Le Florence** is the place to do so. Situated in the centre of town, in a private hotel since the turn of the century, this restaurant is the perfect example of the patrician style, with its high sculptured ceilings trimmed in gold. For the past four years, M. and Mme. Maillot, with the help of Chef Jean-Luc Schvartz, have managed this aged establishment devoted to Italian cuisine with complete success. The cellars of this fine old place contain over a hundred distinguished brands of champagne. Even the vinegar is made from champagne. Here, the Sea Bream Pâté, Warm Sweetbread Salad, and the Snail Casserole are all marvellous.

Warm Sweetbread Salad

1 head escarole lettuce	**800 g (1¾ lb) veal sweetbreads**
1 head red leaf lettuce	**salt and pepper, to taste**
1 cucumber	**300 g (10½ oz) butter**
1 mango	**500 g (1 lb) chanterelle mushrooms**
zests* of 2 oranges	**2 shallots, finely chopped**
champagne vinegar and olive oil,	**1 bunch parsley, finely chopped**
as needed	**2 bunches chervil**
1 tbsp warm water	

Wash and separate the lettuce leaves. Peel the cucumber, remove the seeds, and cut it julienne. Peel the mango, remove the core, and cut it julienne. Slice the orange zest thinly. In a bowl, mix together 1 part vinegar to 3 parts oil to make a dressing, then add warm water.

Cut the sweetbreads into even parts, then sprinkle with salt and pepper. Sauté the sweetbreads in a pan with ¾ of the butter on low heat. In another pan, quickly fry the mushrooms in very hot remaining butter with the chopped shallots and finely chopped parsley. Season to taste.

Mix the lettuce with the cucumber, mango, orange zest, and dressing together on an ovenproof plate and place in a warm oven. On a serving plate, mix the sweetbreads and the mushrooms together. Decorate with chervil.

To serve: Take the warmed salad from the oven, place on a platter, and serve with the sweetbread mixture.

Wine: *A white Côteaux wine or Champagne Crémant*

Serves: 4

Chez Guyvonne

17, rue de Thann, 75017 Paris
Tel: 227-2543 and 755-8846
Proprietor/Chef: Guy Gros

Seafood Salad

400 g (14 oz) carrots, julienne
400 g (14 oz) turnips, julienne
800 g (1¾ lb) green beans, julienne
salt, as needed
16 large scallops
16 oysters
40 whole shrimps
96 mussels

1 litre (2 pt) white wine
1 shallot, chopped
60 ml (2 oz) double cream
  (whipping cream)
pepper, to taste
juice of ¼ lemon
3 tsp chervil, chopped
40 whole pieces chervil

Cook the carrots, turnips, and green beans in separate pots in salted water until tender. Cool and put aside.

Open the scallops, separate the insides from the shells and wash well. Remove the oysters from their shells. Take the shrimps out of their shells. Reserve 24 for decoration.

Clean the mussels, then cook them in white wine, chopped shallots, ½ the cream, salt, and pepper until they open. Remove mussels from shells and pour the cooking stock through a strainer into a pan. Slice the scallops and place them into the strained sauce. Add mussels, oysters, and the shelled shrimps. Bring to a boil and boil 3-4 minutes.

In a salad bowl, put the remaining cream, lemon juice, salt, pepper, and chopped chervil. Mix well. Add the vegetables and seafood to this preparation, decorate with whole chervil and the reserved shrimps, and serve.

Serves: 8

Guy Gros opened his *petite boîte* (small box) in 1969, and everyone was absolutely enchanted with it. Guy is from Ardéche and is devoted to fresh fish from Brittany, including Ray in a Nest of Kale, Turbot with Morel Sauce, Pike Back with Leek Fondue, Pork Sausage with White Beans, Kidneys in Red Ardéche Wine, Lamb Brains and Tongue on a Bed of Green Salad, Mutton Feet, and Seafood Salad.

Chez Guyvonne is a typical Parisian bistro, friendly and casual. Here, the art of dining is practiced as a religion.

Le Béluga

15, rue des Tonneliers, 64100 Bayonne
Tel: (59) 25-52-13
Proprietors: M. and Mme. Guedon • Chef: Jean-Claude Guedon

Winter Salad with Warm Scallops

50 g (1¾ oz) lamb's lettuce or corn salad (lettuce)
2 hearts of escarole
2 hearts of artichoke, sliced
10 tbsp olive oil
3 tbsp lemon juice
400 g (14 oz) scallops, shelled
heavily spiced court bouillon,* as needed
several leaves of chervil, chopped

Mix lamb's lettuce, escarole, and artichoke slices together in a salad bowl and season with olive oil and lemon juice. Spread onto 4 large plates.

Poach the scallops for 3 minutes, without boiling, in the court bouillon, then drain and arrange on top of the salad. Add a sprinkling of chervil and serve immediately.

Wine: *Sancerre rosé*

Serves: 4

Jean-Claude Guedon worked his way through Paris (Paul Chêne, Matignon, and Relais Alma) before returning home to Biarritz. Then he thought about setting up his own place, with his ever cheerful wife, Dany, in a 17th century building in Bayonne between Nive and Adour. That was in 1976. They had their own ideas in creating **Le Béluga**, notably to use an old-style decor with a wooden staircase and discreet lighting. They had ideas about cooking, too: to offer such dishes as Small Crab Soup with Scallops in Sorrel, Winter Salad with Warm Scallops, Braised Turbot in Mustard, Fricassee of Sole in Saffron, Braised Leg of Lamb, Confit of Leg of Duck, and hot and cold *foies gras*. They have reaped considerable success.

Laurent

41, avenue Gabriel, 75008 Paris
Tel: 359-1319 and 225-0039
Proprietor: M. Ehrlich • Chef: Marc Pralong

Sea Bream Salad

1 fresh pink sea bream (or perch) of 1 kg (2¼ lb)
1 large raddish, julienne
salt and pepper, to taste
fine herbs, to taste
125 g (¼ lb) algae (seaweed)
2 tomatoes, quartered
lemon juice, as needed
125 ml (½ cup) vinaigrette dressing,* prepared with 3 parts olive oil
**   to 1 part vinegar and 1 part mustard**
a few peppercorns, or to taste

Remove the fillets from the fish, slice them thinly, and keep cool. Spread the raddish slices on a plate and place the fillet slices over them. Season with salt, pepper, and fine herbs to taste.

Surround the sea bream with algae (seaweed) and tomato quarters on a serving plate. Squeeze some lemon juice over all, then pour vinaigrette dressing over all, add peppercorns, and serve.

Serves: 4

It was in 1842 that Hittorf, a well-known architect, built an elegant hotel near the Champs Élysées in the style of the Second Empire. Later it was to become the restaurant **Laurent**, which was the name of the original owner during *La Belle Epoch*. It is situated in La rue du Cirque, in the garden of the Champs Élysées.

With the assistance of Chef Marc Pralong, M. Ehrlich, the current owner, has nurtured the Laurent to success. Inside you will find magnificent salons, a piano bar, gardens, and circular dining rooms. You will also be treated to impeccable service. The menu offers Lobster Salad, Ratatouille, Sea Bream Salad, Veal Sweetbreads, Ravioles, and superb desserts.

L'Arc-en-Ciel

Tour du Crédit Lyonnais, 129, rue Servient — Part-Dieu Nord, 69003 Lyon
Tel: (78) 62-94-12
Proprietor: Frantel • Chef: Jean Fleury

Fillets of Sole Salad in Cream and Lemon

2 fillets of sole, 125 g (4 oz) each
butter, as needed
salt and pepper, to taste
125 g (¼ lb) blanched spinach leaves
½ litre (1 pt) court bouillon*
¼ litre (1 cup) double cream (whipping cream)
juice of 1 lemon
fine herbs, to taste

Place the fillets of sole on buttered aluminum foil; season with salt and pepper. Spread the spinach leaves on top. Using the foil, roll the fillets into little sausage-shaped rolls, then close both ends firmly and poach in court bouillon. Leave to cool. When cool, unwrap the fillets and cut them into very thin slices.

To prepare the sauce: Mix the cream, lemon juice, and herbs together. Coat the fillets with sauce and serve.

Serves: 2

Lyon, Capitale de la Gastronomie Français! — "Lyon, the Capital of French Gastronomy!" greets you on a billboard as you enter this metropolis of the Rhône. Jean Fleury is perhaps one of the best testimonies to that fact.

As the chef of this fine establishment, he has taken *cuisine Lyonnaise* to new heights. As a guest at **L'Arc-en-Ciel**, at the top of a skyscraper, you will surely be delighted, as well as enlightened, by the refinement of his cuisine.

Vanel

22, rue Maurice-Fonvielle, 31000 Toulouse
Tel: (61) 21-51-82
Proprietor/Chef: Lucien Vanel

I regard Lucien Vanel as one of the great chefs of France. He is an avid supporter of *la vrai cuisine* (the traditional French cuisine). This small man, with his charming southeastern accent, has come from Lacapelle-Marival to conquer Toulouse. His restaurant is very modern and very comfortable.

Lucien offers a "double cuisine:" the traditional dishes from Quercy, which include Pigs Feet in Cahors wine, and Omelettes with Crepes or Truffles; and dishes such as Spinach Salad with Livers and Truffles or Scrambled Eggs with Black Pudding and Pears, which are determined by the day's market choices.

Spinach Salad with Livers and Truffles

250 g (½ lb) fresh spinach
1 large truffle
150 g (5¼ oz) semi-salted lard
125 g (¼ lb) chicken livers, thinly sliced
125 g (¼ lb) fresh duck livers, thinly sliced
flour, as needed
1 tbsp wine vinegar
1 clove garlic, chopped
pepper, as needed

Wash spinach well, dry it, then place it in a salad bowl and keep warm. Slice the truffle into thin slices and set aside. Cut the lard into cubes and melt in a frying pan. Remove the cubes when the pan is well greased. Dust the sliced chicken and duck livers lightly with flour, then quickly fry them in the fat. Put the fried livers and truffles in the salad bowl on top of the spinach.

Remove pan from heat and add vinegar to the remaining grease in it. Put pan back on heat and boil for a few moments. Pour this mixture over the contents of the salad bowl, then add the chopped garlic clove and pepper. Mix well and serve.

Serves: 2

Lamazère

23, rue de Ponthieu, 75008 Paris
Tel: 359-6666
Proprietor: Roger Lamazère • Chef: Jacques Lagrange

Roger Lamazère is a magician. A real one. People will tell you he is one of a kind. He is from Toulouse and is a true *gourmand* as well as a magician. He did not want to give up magic, but he wanted more success, so in 1956 he became the proprietor of this Champs Élysées restaurant.

Here the colours are warm and passionate, and a refinement and flair are manifested in the Italian decor. The cuisine, without exception, is jewelry, and his creative dishes are diamonds. All the dishes are his inventions; the crepes, salads, fish, and cassoulets are matched only by the fine pastries and are exalted by the great wines and famous Armagnacs available.

Truffle Salad

1 truffle of 50 g (1¾ oz)
goose fat, for frying
butter, as needed
20 g (¾ oz) kernels of pine nuts
walnut oil, as needed
lemon juice, as needed
salt and pepper, to taste

Slice the truffle. Place the slices in a pan with the goose fat and let simmer.

In a buttered pan, lightly fry the kernels of pine nuts, then mix the truffle slices and pine nut kernels together in a salad bowl. Season with 2 parts walnut oil to 1 part lemon juice. Season with salt and pepper to taste. Serve this salad lukewarm.

Serves: 1

La Côte Saint-Jacques

14, Faubourg de Paris, 89300 Joigny
Tel: (86) 62-09-70
Proprietor/Chef: Michel Lorain

One cannot help but notice Michel Lorain; he's the one with the mustache. He is also a genius; he and those of his calibre form a group known as masters of gastronomy.

Strolling into **La Côte Saint-Jacques**, with its undeniably excellent delicacies, one cannot avoid the temptation to try the famous Truffles with Cabbage or the Veal Sweetbreads "Saint-Jean, Cap Ferrat" Style. It is bliss to eat here; everything is a delectable blend, a tantalizing mixture, of fine food and wine!

Your time here is also enhanced by the gracious welcome from Jacqueline Lorain and her expert advice on those famous wines of hers.

Truffles with Cabbage

10 truffles, 15 - 20 g (½ - ¾ oz) each, juice reserved
600 g (1¼ lb) breast of chicken meat, sliced into thin strips
20 - 30 leaves cabbage, blanched
10 pieces pork fat, each large enough to envelope a truffle
120 ml (4 oz) chicken stock,* reduced with port wine
1 tsp butter
chervil, to garnish

Wrap each truffle with a strip of chicken meat, then wrap each in 2 or 3 leaves of cabbage. Press to make a nice round shape of each. Cut a pocket into each piece of pork fat and place a wrapped parcel inside each. Braise for 30 minutes in the chicken stock in a tightly covered pan. Remove the parcels and set aside.

Let the cooking liquid reduce until it is of sauce consistency (thick enough to coat a spoon). Add the truffle juice and butter, pour over the parcels, garnish each with a few branches of chervil, and serve.

Serves: 10

Vettard

7, place Bellecourt, 69000 Lyon
Tel: (78) 42-07-59
Proprietor/Chef: Jean Vettard

For years, an old mark of distinction in Lyon was Le Café Neuf, and its fame had always been inseparable from its chef. When the establishment was put up for sale, Jean Vettard took it over. He kept the chef and changed the name to **Vettard**.

Inside this restaurant you will find a youthful decor, luxurious china, and classic meals, which include such dishes as the famous Pike Quenelles, Seafood Plate, Red Mullet Fillets with Tomato Sauce, Rabbit with Basil Sauce, and Chicken in Vermouth. The wine list is also very fine; the Rhône, Saône, Burgundy, and Bordeaux regions all supply Vettard's wine cellar. The dessert cart dazzles one with an exquisite display of sweets.

Seafood Plate

40 mussels
150 ml (½ cup) dry white wine
250 ml (1 cup) dry vermouth
3 shallots, chopped
12 large scallops
½ litre (1 pt) double cream (whipping cream)
2 plump tomatoes, peeled, seeded, and cubed
salt and pepper, to taste
few leaves tarragon
4 small scallops of catfish or sea perch fillet
4 small porgy or John Dory fillets
4 small sole fillets

Put the mussels, white wine, vermouth, and shallots in a pot. Heat until the mussels open, then remove their shells. On another burner, put the scallops in a pot and poach them quickly in ½ the stock from the mussels. Reduce the mixture by adding a bit of ice. Add cream and simmer until reduced to ¼ the original amount. Add the tomatoes and simmer until the sauce becomes very thick and rich. Season with salt, pepper, and tarragon. On a baking sheet, place the catfish scallops and fillets of fish, then add salt and pepper. Put the sheet into the oven at 300°F (150°C) and cook until the fish flakes easily. Reheat the mussels and scallops quickly.

To serve: Place the fish on a hot plate, put the scallops and mussels over them, then pour the very hot sauce over everything and serve.

Serves: 4

Au Chapon Fin

01140 Thoissey
Tel: (74) 04-04-74
Proprietor/Chef: Paul Blanc

A long time ago, in Vonnas, a Mme. Blanc had two sons. One of these sons was named Paul. After becoming of age, he left the family restaurant business to his brother and went off to set up shop at the crossroads leading to Bresse, the Beaujolais, and Dombes. That was way back in 1932, and ever since, Paul Blanc has reigned supreme over his **Chapon Fin** in Thoissey.

With the help of his assistant, Gilbert Broyer (who has been here for 20 years), Au Chapon Fin has become a most charming spot to stop. It has elegant rooms, a tranquil terrace filled with flowers, and offers a most succulent regional cuisine that includes Spring Vegetables "Val de Saône" Style, Quenelles "Nantua" Style, and Chicken in Cream.

Spring Vegetables "Val de Saône" Style

1 pike of 1 kg (2¼ lb)	¼ litre (1 cup) white wine
2 - 3 perch or pike perch	juice of 1 lemon
500 g (1 lb) carrots, sliced	1 kg (2¼ lb) crayfish
3 white onions, chopped	(or lobster tails), unshelled
1 bunch leeks	500 g (1 lb) peas
200 g (7 oz) turnips	500 g (1 lb) green beans,
1 head celery	cut with scissors
1 head fennel	1 tbsp double cream
2 sprigs basil	(whipping cream)
1 bunch parsley	300 g (10½ oz) butter, and as needed
3 litres (3 qt) water	chopped fresh parsley, to garnish
salt and pepper, to taste	

Fillet the pike and perch and cut into approximately 50 g (1¾ oz) each. Cook the carrots, onions, leeks, turnips, celery, fennel, basil, and parsley in the water. Add salt, pepper, wine, and lemon juice. Add crayfish to stock and cook for 5 minutes, then remove and shell. Remove vegetables and keep warm. Remove fish and keep warm. Steam the peas and beans until cooked, but still crisp (about 30 minutes).

To prepare sauce: Reduce the cooking stock to 100 ml (3 oz), then add cream. Whisk in butter, a piece at a time, but do not boil.

Arrange fish on 4 plates with vegetables and crayfish coated with sauce. Sprinkle parsley on top and serve.

Serves: 4

L'Auberge du Vert Galant

42, quai des Orfèvres, 75001 Paris
Tel: 326-8368
Proprietor/Chef: M. Bos

For a lover of Paris, there is no more moving a place than La Cité, the location of la Place Dauphine, le Pont Henry IV. And here on the first floor of an old building with tall windows is an old restaurant filled with the charm of things past. **L'Auberge du Vert Galant** seems to be frozen in time.

Also preserved is the tradition of preparing food whose primary virtues are freshness of the raw products and superb taste. Stewed Chicken "King Henry" Style is a fine example, as is the Raw Bass Marinated in Mint. All dishes are accompanied by wines proposed by a sommelier who is both knowledgeable and experienced.

Raw Bass Marinated in Mint

1 fresh bass of 1 kg (2¼ lb)
4 tbsp lemon juice
125 ml (¼ cup) olive oil
125 ml (¼ cup) peanut oil
2 shallots, chopped
zest* of one lemon, grated
1 tbsp chives, chopped
1 tsp fresh mint leaves, crushed
pinch of pepper
8 lemon quarters, to garnish
2 tomatoes, roughly chopped

Fillet the bass and cut it into very fine pieces.

Prepare a mixture of lemon juice, olive oil, peanut oil, chopped shallots, lemon zest, chives, mint leaves, and pepper. Put the pieces of bass in this sauce, stir, and serve immediately on a plate decorated with the lemon quarters and chopped tomato.

Serves: 4

Chiberta

La Tour d'Argent

Taillevent

La Poularde

Face au Casino, 42210 Montrond-Les-Bains
Tel: (77) 54-40-06
Proprietor: Joannès Randoing • Chef: Gilles Etéocle

La Poularde is a regular stopping place for gourmands. Joannès Randoing, an expert at his trade, is the master of the hotel. The expert in the kitchen is Gilles Etéocle. His menu will capture your attention with such dishes as Angler Fricassee with Anchovy and Wild Thyme, Turbot Stuffed with Pistachios, and Charolais Beef "Tonnelière" Style. The Cheese Gratin, prepared with white cheese from Forez, is absolutely delicious. The dessert menu leaves nothing to be desired; any sweet tooth can be satisfied here. Behind the austere façace of the building, there is a charming garden filled with cosy tables covered with pink tablecloths. Even the rooms are coordinated in pink colours.

Angler Fricassee with Anchovy and Wild Thyme

3 fresh anglerfish (monkfish or cod)
¼ litre (1 cup) water, and as needed
1 carrot, cubed
1 shallot, chopped
1 pinch wild thyme
¼ litre (1 cup) champagne
1 fresh anchovy
salt and pepper, to taste
1 tbsp double cream (whipping cream)
50 g (1¾ oz) butter

Fillet the angler and place the bones in a pot. Sweat* the fish bones in a little water with the carrot and shallot until the juices begin to come out. Strain and reserve the stock.

Soak the wild thyme in the champagne and ¼ litre (1 cup) water. Add to stock and cook over medium heat for 15 minutes. Simmer until liquid is ¾ of its original volume.

Cut the anchovy into thin strips and lay them alongside the angler in a pot. Season with salt and pepper, then cook for 7 minutes. Remove to a serving platter and keep warm.

To prepare the sauce: Add cream and butter to the fish stock. Reseason if necessary, then pour the sauce over the fish and serve.

Serves: 2

La Vieille Fontaine

8, avenue Gretry, 78110 Maisons-Laffitte
Tel: 962-0178
Proprietors: Manon Letourneur, François Clerc • Chef: François Clerc

For the past ten years, Manon and François have occupied this old house, which has been turned into a restaurant. It is located in a beautiful park in Maisons-Laffitte.

For as many years as François had been in business, he had not succeeded in keeping a good chef. Therefore, he decided he would put on an apron and at last have a good chef he could count on keeping. Now the menu offers precisely what he wants — original and elegant dishes such as Caviar-Filled Crepe Pouches.

This small but charming restaurant in Maisons-Laffitte is dedicated to creatively preparing all the delicious food served by the charming hostess, Manon Letourneur.

Caviar-Filled Crepe Pouches

100 ml (3 oz) milk
4 tbsp flour
3 whole eggs
25 g (¾ oz) melted butter
50 ml (1½ oz) beer
1 pinch of salt
200 g (7 oz) caviar
50 g (1¾ oz) double cream (whipping cream)
2 small bunches chives

To prepare the crepes: Combine the first 5 ingredients, then fry 30 small crepes in a small pan (they should be very thin). Let cool for 15 minutes.

In the centre of each crepe, spoon in ½ tsp of caviar and ½ tsp of cream. Fold the sides of each crepe up and fasten each with a strand of chive to form small pouches. Just before serving, pop the pouches into the oven for a couple of minutes at medium heat (350°F or 175°C).

Suggestion: These bite-size appetizers can be served with vodka.

Serves: 6

L'Olivier

12, rue Boieldieu, 34000 Béziers
Tel: (67) 28-86-64
Proprietors: William Druet, Michel Roque • Chefs: Michel Roque, Angel Yagues

Clams with Morels

4 egg yolks
2 whole eggs
10 g (⅓ oz) dried morel mushrooms, soaked in 100 ml (3 oz) water overnight
salt, pepper, and nutmeg, to taste
½ litre (1 pt) milk
butter, as needed
1 shallot, finely chopped
1.5 kg (3⅓ lb) clams
30 ml (1 oz) dry vermouth
30 ml (1 oz) double cream (whipping cream)

In a mixing bowl, mix the egg yolks and whole eggs together. Strain the mushrooms and reserve their juice. Add the drained mushrooms, salt, pepper, and nutmeg to the egg mixture and mix for 3 minutes. Pour the mixture evenly into a salad bowl and mix in the milk. Divide the mixture evenly among 10 buttered flan (custard) moulds. Cook in a bain-marie* in the oven at 400°F (205°C) for 30 minutes.

In a frying pan, sauté the finely chopped shallot in butter. Wet the clams with vermouth and 50 ml (1½ oz) of the reserved mushroom juice. Add clams to the shallot pan and let cook, uncovered, until the clams open. Remove the clams from the pan, shell them, and keep them warm.

Reduce the clam stock remaining in the pan by ½, then add cream to the sauce and check the seasoning. Simmer for 3 minutes.

To serve: Invert the contents of each mould onto a plate, surround with clams, and pour the sauce over everything. Serve hot.

Serves: 10

In 1969, William Druet, a retired head steward from Air France, became associated with Chef Michel Roque, and together they opened a restaurant in Béziers, city of wine, which was not endowed with any fine restaurants at the time. Today, **L'Olivier** with its luxurious decor and intimate ambiance has changed that.

The menu features Michel Roque and Angel Yagues preparations, fine meals fit for a fine table. There are also eminently modern and exquisitely served L'Olivier specialities including Salad of Salmon with Green Beans and Artichokes, Clams with Morels, Lamb Sweetbreads with Preserved Onions, and Duck Breast in Red Wine, and remarkable sorbets (sherbets).

La Terrasse

Hôtel Juana, Avenue Georges-Gallice, La Pinède, 06160 Juan-Les-Pins
Tel: (93) 61-08-70
Proprietor: The Barache Family • Chef: Alain Ducasse

Crayfish with Champagne Butter

40 medium-sized crayfish
(40 large shrimps)
salt, as needed
16 small cocktail (cherry)
tomatoes, seeded
100 ml (3 oz) olive oil
2 long courgettes (zucchini)
1 aubergine (eggplant)
¼ litre (1 cup) dry champagne
300 ml (9 oz) double cream
(whipping cream)
250 g (½ lb) butter
1 egg yolk (optional)
pepper, as needed

Cook the crayfish in salted boiling water for 2 minutes. Take out and cool. Crush the tomatoes. Cook for 2 minutes in 1 tbsp olive oil and salt. Take off heat and let cool. Slice the 2 long courgettes 3 cm (1¼ in) thick. Cut the aubergine 5 cm (2 in) thick. In a pan, heat 2 tbsp olive oil and sauté the aubergine and courgette slices. Season with salt. Remove after 2 minutes, put on a dish, and let cool. Shell the crayfish and cut the tails lengthwise. In 4 moulds, arrange layers as follows: 1 slice of aubergine, a layer of crayfish, a layer of tomato, a layer of courgette slices, and so on. End with a slice of aubergine on top. Cook the moulds in a bain-marie* for 5 - 8 minutes in a medium oven at 350°F (175°C).

To prepare the sauce: Reduce the champagne to ½ over high heat. Add ⅔ of the cream with a whisk. Add butter, little by little, while bringing mixture to a slow boil. Take off heat; correct the seasoning. (To lighten the sauce, mix remaining cream with an egg yolk and add slowly.) Unmould the moulds onto a plate. Season well with pepper and cover with sauce.

Suggestion: Arrange 4 steamed courgette flowers and steamed tomatoes on the plates, sprinkle with chervil, and serve hot.

Serves: 4

Hôtel Juana, in Juan-Les-Pins, has its own private beach, which is only a part of a very lovely piece of property owned by the Barache family. The Baraches were fortunate to find Alain Ducasse, a chef of many talents. According to Jacques Maximin, the chef of the famed Chantecler and a man who knows his cuisine, Alain has made **La Terrasse** one of the best restaurants in France. The menu offers Foie Gras, cooked the traditional way, Terrine of Squab from Bresse in Gelatine, Crayfish with Champagne Butter, and much more for the discriminating palate. This restaurant is called La Terrasse because you are encouraged to eat out on the terrace when the weather allows.

Pernollet

Place de la Victoire, 01300 Belley
Tel: (79) 81-06-18
Proprietor/Chef: Ernest Pernollet

It all started back in 1821 when Claude Pernollet and his wife, Jeannette, bought a restaurant in Belley. Maybe it really all started when Brillat-Savarin published *Physiologie du Goût* after having dined with friends here at **Pernollet** in the late 1820s. Brillat-Savarin was one of the first *culinographers,* and his memory still lives on in Belley.

Today, Ernest, the great grandson of Claude Pernollet, continues the family tradition with such fine dishes as Gâteau Foies Blonds, Morels in Cream, and Crayfish Tails Timbale.

In this rustic provincial setting, the quality of the cuisine remains unchanged. The dinners are rich in flavour and are a true gastronomic experience.

Crayfish Tails Timbale

1 medium-sized onion, sliced
6 shallots, sliced
6 cloves garlic, chopped
1 branch thyme
1 branch parsley
2 cloves
1 litre (2 pt) dry white wine
salt and cayenne pepper, to taste
4 kg (8¾ lb) crayfish tails (or lobster tails)
250 g (½ lb) butter
1 tbsp flour
½ litre (1 pt) plus 2 tsp double cream (whipping cream)
3 egg whites

In a saucepan, place the sliced onion, shallots, and garlic; add the thyme, parsley, and cloves. Pour over the white wine. Bring to a boil and reduce by ½. Season with salt and 3 sprinkles of cayenne pepper. Add the crayfish, turn the heat up to high, and cover the pan. After 4 minutes stir the crayfish. Continue cooking for 4 minutes more, by which time the crayfish should be uniformly scarlet. If necessary, stir and cook another minute.

Pour the crayfish into a bowl and leave to cool for 1 hour, stirring frequently. Drain them and reserve the cooking liquid. Peel the tails.

Put the butter in a wide saucepan and turn the heat up to high. When the foam of the hot butter begins to subside, add the crayfish tails, a handful at a time, shaking the pan constantly. Turn down the heat. When the crayfish have lost their excess moisture, stir in the flour and cook gently for 3 minutes. Moisten with ½ the cooking liquid. Bring to a boil, stirring constantly, and simmer for 10 minutes. Add the ½ litre (1 pt) cream and bring back to a boil. If the sauce is too thick or not tasty enough, add some more liquid and cook for another 3 minutes.

Prepare a mixture of 3 egg yolks and remaining cream. Add this to the pan contents, stirring carefully. Allow to come to a boil, stirring all the time. Remove from the heat and continue stirring for another minute. Pour the sauce into a heated bowl and serve separately with the crayfish.

Wine: *Roussette Seyssel or Pouilly Fumé*   Serves: 8

Auberge du Clou

30, avenue Trudaine, 75009 Paris
Tel: 878-2248
Proprietor/Chef: Jean-Robert Chelot

Jean-Robert Chelot is something of an imposing figure — imposing when it comes to taste and imagination, energy, and invention. He is very creative. For example, his Pâté of Crab in Ricard Liqueur is creamy and soft enough to make anyone's mouth water. And he is always offering new discoveries. His Hot Crayfish "Parish Priest" Style is a recipe taken straight from the Middle Ages!

As you regretfully leave this little restaurant (you'll soon be back for more), well-nourished and content, don't forget to stop and look at the curious little apparatus invented by Courteline; its presence here is one of the numerous little pranks of Chef Jean-Robert, who is full of talent and ideas.

Hot Crayfish "Parish Priest" Style

125 g (¼ lb) onions
125 g (¼ lb) carrots
1 stick celery
175 g (6 oz) butter
2 tbsp oil
salt and pepper, to taste
48 small to medium-size crayfish (or small shrimps)
dash of cayenne pepper
20 ml (½ oz) cognac
2 pinches thyme
½ bottle Muscadet white wine
1 litre (2 pt) double cream (whipping cream)
6 egg yolks
1 tbsp freshly chopped tarragon

Chop the first 3 ingredients together finely, then put in a saucepan with 25 g (¾ oz) butter, oil, salt, and pepper. Cook over low heat for 15 minutes without browning.

In a thick frying pan, stir fry the crayfish, then add salt, pepper, and cayenne pepper. Flame with cognac. Add the vegetable mixture and thyme. Add wine to pan and cover. Cook on very hot heat for 10 minutes (the wine should be almost totally evaporated). Add cream and bring to a boil, then remove crayfish. Mix the egg yolks with the remaining butter, then add to cream mixture. Pass the sauce through a strainer and reseason if necessary. Place crayfish back into sauce, sprinkle with tarragon, and serve.

Suggestion: Serve with rice pilaff.

Wine: *Meursault*   Serves: 4

Les Claires

Rue William Bertrand, 17560 Bourcefranc
Tel: (46) 85-08-01 and 85-07-01
Proprietor/Chef: Michel Suire

Viva **Les Claires**! — It is as enchanting as the ocean is plentiful, with bountiful "fruits from the sea." Michel Suire obviously has an affinity for seafood. Whether it be Bass with Lime Juice, or Lobster in Pastry, or Langoustines "Les Claires" Style, the gastronomic man shall be conquered.

Michel also exhibits his inexhaustible energy in the dining room where his flair and indisputable exuberance prove his masterful dominance.

Langoustines "Les Claires" Style

1 tbsp oil
1 kg (2¼ lb) langoustines
100 ml (3 oz) cognac
90 g (3 oz) shallots, chopped
500 ml (1 pt) double cream (whipping cream)
1 pinch curry
salt and pepper, to taste

In an ovenproof frying pan, heat the oil, then fry the langoustines for 2-3 minutes. Flame with cognac, then add the shallots and fry them. Then add the cream, curry, salt, and pepper.

Put the pan in the oven at 400°F (205°C) for 7 minutes. Remove from oven. Remove the langoustines to a warmed plate.

Simmer and reduce the sauce in the pan. Reseason to taste (no flavour should dominate another). Pour the sauce over the langoustines and serve hot.

Wine: *Sancerre*   Serves: 4

Le Relais Brenner

Route de Lézardrieux, 22500 Paimpol
Tel: (96) 20-11-05
Proprietors: M. and Mme. Gabriel Brenner • Chef: Gabriel Brenner

Grilled Mussels in Butter

70 mussels
150 g (5¼ oz) blanched almonds
225 g (½ lb) butter
chopped garlic, to taste
chopped parsley, to taste
bread crumbs, as needed

Place 10 mussels into each of 7 small soufflé moulds. Pound the almonds in a mortar to make a paste, then mix with the butter, garlic, and parsley. Add the mixture to the moulds. Sprinkle bread crumbs over each mould. Bake in the oven at 450°F (230°C) for 10 minutes, then serve hot.

Serves: 7

After serving his apprenticeship, Gabriel Brenner settled in Lézardrieux, where he opened a small auberge. Business was excellent, but its size soon became inadequate, so Gabriel decided to expand — he did, and quite extravagantly; he constructed a panoramic restaurant in this hotel, and he embellished **Le Relais Brenner** with elegance and comfort, as designed by Jean-Louis Brenner, his son.

Gabriel works to perfect everything, especially his cooking. He offers such delicacies as Grilled Mussles in Butter, Veal with Avocados, and Fish Soup, and there are Honey Crepes for dessert. People from Brittany make no mistake about food. They will travel for delicacies. Some even cross the Channel to discover this refuge.

Chez Tante Louise

41, rue Boissy-d'Anglas, 75008 Paris
Tel: 265-0685 and 265-2829
Proprietor/Chef: M. Fiorito

Mussels au Gratin

2.5 kg (5½ lb) mussels
2 chopped shallots
1 bouquet garni*
2 cloves garlic, chopped
70 ml (2 oz) dry white wine
250 ml (1 cup) milk
100 ml (3 oz) double cream (whipping cream)
salt and pepper, to taste
125 g (¼ lb) grated Swiss or Gruyère cheese

In a saucepan, place mussels, shallots, bouquet garni, garlic, and white wine. Leave in saucepan over medium heat until mussels open. Remove mussels from pan, let cool, then remove mussels from shells. Set aside.

To prepare the sauce: Slowly add milk to the liquid in the pan and mix very well with an egg beater or whisk. Let sauce colour slightly, then bring to a boil. Add the cream and leave to thicken (about 3 minutes). Season with salt and pepper.

Put the mussels into an ovenproof dish, pour the sauce over. Spread the cheese over the mussels. Place in the oven at 450°F (230°C) until the cheese is golden. Serve hot.

Wine: *Sancerre white*

Serves: 6

Forty years ago, an authentic "chef" from the Franche-Comté region, Aunt Louise, with her art of the bourgeoisie and serenity, created this durable restaurant. In spite of many changes of ownership over the subsequent years, **Chez Tante Louise** never ceases to retain its originality.

Part of its air of distinction is that everything here, from the menu to the wine list, is the very best.

Chef Fiorito's favourite recipe is his Fillets Tante Louise made with wine from Jura. I also recommend his remarkable *foie gras* (a cabbage salad with smoked goose liver), his Fricassee of Sole with Mussels, and his Mussels au Gratin. Even the desserts are as distinguished as the place in which they are served.

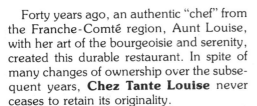

Chez Michel

10 rue de Belzunce, 75010 Paris
Tel: 878-4414
Proprietor/Chef: Michel Tournissoux

M. Curnonsky, or the "Prince of Gastronomy" as he is known to some, called **Chez Michel** "a quaint little box" — not in any way referring to the size, but rather to its ambiance — one of intimacy, with a dash of provincialism.

Michel Tournissoux reigns happily, with his wife, over this perennial nest. By choice, not habit, the regulars always return for his delectable treats such as Stuffed Mussels and for other elegant and succulent dishes that would please even the most finicky epicurean. The Veal Sweetbreads "Vallée d'Auge" Style and the Chicken with Morels "Alexandre Dumaine" Style are plates of incomparable classicism, which never cease to whet any appetite.

Stuffed Mussels

3 kg (6½ lb) mussels
100 ml (3 oz) dry white wine
4 cloves garlic, crushed
12 g (½ oz) shallots, chopped
125 g (¼ lb) parsley, chopped
200 g (7 oz) ham
200 g (7 oz) almonds, sliced thinly
500 g (1 lb) white mushrooms, sliced
250 g (½ lb) butter
25 g (¾ oz) salt
10 g (⅓ oz) pepper
pinch of nutmeg

Wash the mussels very well; let drain. Place them in a large cooking pot with the wine and let cook until they open. Remove the mussels from the shells and set aside. Reserve the shells.

Blend the garlic, shallots, and parsley together; then heat on low heat and stir twice in the pan. Add ham and almonds. Stir in the mushrooms and mussels slowly. Stir all the ingredients a few times in the pan, then let them simmer to absorb all the excess moisture. Add butter and mix well. Add salt, pepper, and nutmeg, and stir again.

Once the mixture is smooth, spoon a teaspoonful into each mussel shell. Place the filled shells on an aluminum baking sheet and bake for 10 minutes at 350°F (175°C). Serve hot.

Wine: *A dry white Loire wine*   Serves: 6

Le Bretagne

56230 Questermbert
Tel: (97) 26-11-12
Proprietor/Chef: Georges Paineau

A few rooms of the greatest comfort looking out onto an indoor Breton style garden are quite enough to justify any stop-off here. And if you add to that the very personalised cooking of Georges Paineau . . .

In a decor which is almost too aristocratic for the local colour, this inspired chef opted for a brilliant menu featuring Fillet of Lamb in Cream of Garlic, Oysters in Packets, Escalope of Turbot with Ginger, and Duck in Peppers, to name just a few. Add to that the very fine desserts, well-selected wines (direct from the growers), and even a "low calorie" menu for those who believe they will be unable to restrain themselves. With wooden beams very much to the fore, the decor is worthy of the food, which in turn is worthy of the service.

Oysters in Packets

24 large spinach leaves
4 dozen oysters
1 pinch salt
1 pinch cayenne pepper
300 g (10½ oz) butter
juice of 1 lemon

Wash the spinach leaves and set aside.

Open the oysters, filter their juice (reserve), and rinse the oysters. Wrap the oysters in the spinach leaves to form 6 little packets, 2 oysters per leaf.

Place the leaf packets in a thick frying pan and moisten with the filtered oyster juice. Bring to a boil, add salt and cayenne pepper, then bake the packets in the oven at 475°F (250°C) for 2 minutes.

Serve the oysters, well strained and very hot, with a little lemon-flavoured butter.

Wine: *A dry, white but fruity wine*   Serves: 4

Pétrus

114, avenue de Villiers and 12 place du Maréchal-Juin, 75016 Paris
Tel: 380-1595
Proprietors: Monique André, Jean Berneau • Chef: Gilbert Dugast

This once was a restaurant-café in a small square named Péreire. The square has been renamed Maréchal-Juin, and it is a favourite meeting place of the older Parisian generation. In 1976, Monique André arrived on the scene and transformed the old restaurant into a seafood café.

Since then, Monique has been joined by Jean Berneau, and together they have made **Pétrus** into a quality restaurant with a comfortable ambiance. It is a place where you can treat yourself to all the wonderful seafood dishes you ever dreamed about. Scallops with Roquefort Cheese, Clams Rockefeller, Oyster Sausage in Brioche, and Salmon and Stuffed Shellfish with Kale are only a few of the many offerings. There is also a delicious Chocolate Soufflé available here; it is very special.

Oyster Sausage in Brioche

10 g (¾ oz) yeast
70 ml (2 oz) water
30 g (1 oz) sugar
300 g (10 oz) flour
15 g (½ oz) plus 1 pinch salt
3 eggs
120 g (¼ lb) butter, softened
36 oysters
500 g (1 lb) fillet of pike
250 g (½ lb) fillet of eel
3 egg whites
1.2 litre (2¼ pt) double cream (whipping cream)
3 g (small pinch) pepper
strained fish stock,* as needed
1 egg yolk, beaten
50 g (1¾ oz) butter
chopped chervil and chives, to taste

To prepare the brioche: Activate the yeast in the water with a little sugar. Mix flour, pinch of salt, and remaining sugar in a bowl; place on a cold work surface and make a well in the centre. Put whole eggs and yeast in the well. Mix everything gradually to obtain a soft dough. Cover and allow to rise until doubled in bulk. Punch dough down. Knead it energetically, beating it against the table, until it is elastic and no longer sticky. Work in the *softened* butter, a piece at a time, incorporating each piece before adding the next. Cover the dough and refrigerate for at least 6 hours or overnight.

To prepare the sausage: Open the oysters in a hot oven. Remove from shells and reserve.

To make a fish mousse: Finely mince the pike and eel flesh in a processor. Mix in the egg whites thoroughly and chill. Work in 1 litre (2 pt) cream gradually until thoroughly incorporated. Season with salt and pepper.

Spread a muslin (cheesecloth) on the table; cover it with a sheet of greaseproof (wax) paper. Spread a strip of fish mousse over this and arrange 18 oysters upon it. Cover with some more mousse, place the remaining oysters on it, and finish with the rest of the mousse. Roll the sausage in the muslin and greaseproof paper. Tie it tightly at the ends. Pour enough fish stock to cover the sausage into a sufficiently large saucepan. Bring it to the simmering point and poach the sausage in it for 20 minutes. Drain carefully, leave to cool, then remove wrappings.

Punch down the brioche dough. Roll it out on a cold surface and carefully roll up the sausage in it. Place on a baking sheet with the seam side down and brush it with egg yolk. Let it rise for 20 minutes. Bake it for 15 minutes at 425-450°F (220-230°C).

To prepare the sauce: Reduce ¼ litre (1 cup) of the poaching liquid. Add the remaining cream, reduce a little more, and whisk in the butter. Add the chopped herbs just before serving, then serve.

Wine: *Chablis, Meursault, or Pouilly Fumé*   Serves: 6

Le Vieux Logis

24510 Tremolat
Tel: (53) 61-80-06
Proprietor: Mme. Giraudel-Destord • Chef: Didier Gelineau

Salmon Scallops with Julienne Courgettes (Zucchini)

3 courgettes (zucchini),
  250 g (½ lb) each
2 red plump tomatoes
1 shallot, chopped
100 ml (3 oz) olive oil
salt and pepper, to taste
3 tbsp fish stock,* prepared

¼ litre (½ pt) double cream
  (whipping cream)
butter, as needed
juice of 1 lemon
50 ml (1¾ oz) peanut oil
60 g (2 oz) salmon roe (or red caviar)
6 scallops of salmon

Wash and dry the courgettes but do not peel. Cut off the ends, then cut them into lengthwise strips of 8 cm (3¼ in) each, then cut the strips into thick julienne strips.

Blanch the tomatoes, peel them, then remove the seeds and crush them. Over low heat, simmer the chopped shallot in 3 tbsp of olive oil, then add the crushed tomatoes and season with salt and pepper to taste. Set aside, but keep warm. Season the julienne courgettes with salt and pepper, then quickly fry them for 5 minutes.

Combine the fish stock, cream, a bit of butter, salt, pepper, lemon juice, and peanut oil in a pan. Stir and heat until mixture reaches sauce consistency. Add the salmon roe and keep warm.

Sparingly oil the salmon scallops with remaining olive oil and season with salt and pepper. Fry the salmon scallops without additional oil or butter in a pan (the skin of the salmon is now greasy enough) for 3 minutes.

To serve: Place one salmon scallop in the centre of each of 6 plates. Place a portion of courgettes around each salmon scallop and spoon some tomato mixture over the courgettes. Spoon some sauce over each salmon scallop and serve.

Serves: 6

In this region of a thousand castles, Mme. Giraudel-Destord has hers. Inside these old carved walls, covered by an old-fashioned tile roof, and filled with antique furnishings, lives an expression of incomparable taste for traditional cuisine.

Didier Gelineau serves such fine dishes as Veal with Truffle Crepes, Seafood Salad with Lime, Langoustine Fricassee with Cucumbers, Scallops of Salmon with Julienne Courgettes, Mignonnettes of Lamb, and desserts with Armagnacs.

Though the cooking is home-made and traditional, it still pleases the gourmets of today.

La Sologne

8, rue de Bellechasse, 75007 Paris
Tel: 705-9866
Proprietor/Chef: Christian Guillerand

Sardine Crepes with Sorrel

6 sardines
1 large bouquet sorrel
60 g (2 oz) plus 3 tbsp butter
salt and pepper, to taste
1 dash raspberry vinegar
2 egg whites
6 crepes,* prepared

Remove the bones from the sardines.

Chop the sorrel and cook it gently in butter until wilted. Season with salt and pepper and add just a touch of vinegar.

Beat the egg whites firmly and spread on the crepes. Stuff the sardines with the buttered sorrel, place 1 stuffed sardine in the middle of each crepe, and fold the crepe over it. On top of each crepe, place ½ tsp butter. Bake for 4-6 minutes at 400°F (205°C) and serve hot.

Serves: 6

Sologne is the land of hunting and fishing, grey skies, forests, and small auberges. **La Sologne** is a soothing and comfortable restaurant dedicated to this region but located right in the heart of Paris. It is presided over by Christian Guillerand, and his cuisine is faithful to the restaurant's name.

During the hunting season, game is the main dish, but there are other wonderful meats and freshly caught fish served here. Each dish is made with the finest ingredients, and the menu doesn't hesitate to hail the freshness of the Sardine Crepes with Sorrel, Sea Bream with Fennel Mousse, Anglerfish with Apple Cider, and Pike with Beer. After your regal feast, top off your meal with Christian's wonderful Caramel and Walnut Ice Cream.

Les Hirondelles

52, avenue Jean Mermoz, 06290 Saint-Jean-Cap-Ferrat
Tel: (93) 01-30-25
Proprietor/Chef: Marie Venturino

Marie Venturino, or Madame Marie as she is called by the fishermen of this tiny port, has been cooking almost since she was born . . . as naturally as a bird starts singing! She has been cooking for her friends since 1935, and in this little restaurant in the Riviera sun, all her customers are her friends. **Les Hirondelles** is a chic restaurant with a rustic style decor that is both warming and intimate, credit for which must be given to Marie's daughters, Monique and Véronique, who help her. Here, fish jump straight from the sea into the frying pan, or so it seems, and Marie Venturino, at 70 years of age, still insists on picking her own *herbes de Provence,* and she lets nobody else prepare her bouillabaisse, stuffed sardines, mussels, and sea bream.

Stuffed Sardines "Hirondelles" Style

5 sardines
2 cloves garlic, chopped very finely
few sprigs parsley, chopped very finely
pinch of salt and pepper
Provence herbs, to taste
2 fresh tomatoes, sieved and juice reserved
2 eggs, slightly beaten
10 g (⅓ oz) butter

Remove the scales from the sardines, cut off the heads, open them, and remove the backbones.

To prepare the stuffing: Mix garlic, parsley, salt, pepper, herbs, sieved tomatoes, and eggs together in a bowl. Slightly butter an ovenproof tray. Fill the sardines with the stuffing, then close them.

Place sardines on the tray, separating each one with the reserved tomato juice and bake in the oven at 275°F (135°C). Watch the cooking carefully; it will only take about 10 minutes. Serve warm.

Wine: *Vin de Bellet, Blanc des Blancs*   Serves: 1

Le Chanzy

8, rue Chanzy, 62000 Arras
Tel: (21) 21-02-02
Proprietor: Robert de Troy • Chef: Hervé Mit

Jean de Troy bought a little bistro in 1944 and created **Le Chanzy** restaurant. His son, Robert, joined him in 1950, and the establishment grew in size and stature. Then Robert de Troy quit the family business to go and discover how the rest of the world lived; he left for work in the United States but returned to the family cradle to help make Le Chanzy what it is today — a kind of fishing boat anchored right in the middle of Arras, with a room for tourists and another for gastronomy, all located around an indoor garden. It is a restaurant *rôtisseur* with really great cooking and a wine cellar containing about 100,000 bottles and 1,000 labels. Also, there is the regional side of things; do taste the Chitterlings "Arras" Style and the Rillettes of Scallops.

Rillettes of Scallops

200 g (7 oz) butter
125 g (¼ lb) chopped shallots
300 g (10½ oz) roughly chopped tomatoes
1 bouquet garni*
few sprigs parsley
1 crushed garlic clove
2 kg (4½ lb) fresh, large, shelled scallops
100 ml (3 oz) dry vermouth
salt and pepper, to taste
100 ml (3 oz) double cream (whipping cream)

In a thick frying pan, melt ½ the butter without browning it, then add shallots, tomatoes, bouquet garni, parsley, and garlic. Cook gently without covering the pan. Remove the herbs and pour the preparation into a bowl and set aside.

In another thick frying pan, melt the remaining butter, add scallops, and stir very gently for 3-4 minutes. Add vermouth and cook gently, without covering, for another 3 minutes. Whisk to beat the scallops into a kind of *rillettes* (a ground mixture). Add salt and pepper and the reserved preparation in the bowl. Add the cream, whisking all the time. Check the seasoning. Let cool, then serve in an earthenware bowl.

Suggestion: Serve on warm, soft toast.

Wine: *Pouilly Fumé, Burgundy white, or Sancerre white*   Serves: 8

Flavio

1 and 2, avenue du Verger, 62520 Le Touquet
Tel: (21) 05-10-22
Proprietor: Flavio • Chef: Guy Delmotte

Ah! Flavio — who could miss him — that dynamic 50-year-old who exudes life. After Paris, London, Dorchester, Mayfair, Coq d'Or, and Monte Carlo, what else is there? Well, for Flavio, there was something else; he decided to create the "Club de la Forèt" on the Champs Élysées of Le Touquet.

Ah! Flavio — at his side is the remarkable Guy Delmotte, and there is no sphere they cannot conquer. Because of Flavio's dynamism and Guy's notable talent, we can now enter the land of culinary wonder by entering this restaurant. Who can resist their Raw Salmon or Scallops in Ginger or Boiled Lobster in Tarragon? No one! If people cross the English Channel for these delectable delicacies, why not the Atlantic?

Scallops in Ginger

300 ml (9 oz) double cream (whipping cream)
100 ml (3 oz) Chablis
3 kiwi fruit
juice of 1 lemon
24 large scallops
1 tbsp ginger
½ tsp curry
1 tomato concasse*

In a copper pan, simmer the cream and Chablis together. Peel the kiwi fruit; slice thinly. Wet the kiwis with lemon juice and set aside.

Cut the scallops into 3 parts each, then add them to the cream mixture. Simmer. Add ginger and curry to the sauce. Heat the ingredients to a rich creamy consistency, then remove the scallops and place them on a hot plate. Put the tomato over the scallops, place pieces of kiwi fruit on the tomato, then cover all generously with the cream sauce and serve.

Serves: 4

La Ferme d'Argenteuil

2, bis, rue Verte, 95100 Argenteuil
Tel: (3) 961-0062
Proprietor/Chef: Claude Rivière

Argenteuil was once a land of grape vines and asparagus plants. They both flourished all over this sleepy countryside. Today, the vines have all but disappeared and asparagus is no longer as plentiful, but this delicious vegetable can still be found at **La Ferme d'Argenteuil**, cooked to perfection by Chef Claude Rivière in a variety of special dishes. This is a modest establishment, not grandiose or luxurious, but every dinner is prepared from the heart and with delicacy. Claude takes deep pride in the preparation of fine food; he wants this small town tavern to be known for its excellent cuisine. Dishes such as Anglerfish in Sauterne, Chicken with Crayfish, and Scallop Ragout with Asparagus should assure his restaurant's reputation.

Scallop Ragout

250 g (½ lb) fresh asparagus
1 litre (2 pt) salted water
150 g (5 oz) double cream (whipping cream)
300 g (10½ oz) butter
1 kg (2¼ lb) fresh large scallops
1 tbsp chives, finely chopped
salt and pepper, to taste

Poach the asparagus in salted boiling water. Remove the asparagus. Reduce the cooking liquid from the asparagus. Add the cream, then continue to simmer slowly. Add the butter, then add the scallops. Continue to cook for 3 minutes, then add the chives and season with salt and pepper.

Cut the asparagus into 2 cm (¾ in) pieces and add to the mixture. Adjust the seasoning and serve warm.

Wine: *Sancerre white*

Serves: 6

Le Bristol

112, rue du Faubourg Saint Honoré, 75008 Paris
Tel: 266-9145
Manager: Robert Chauland • Chef: E. Tabourdiau

This is one of the great establishments of Paris — a sumptuous hotel on the eternally aristocratic thoroughfare of Faubourg Saint Honoré. It's also one of the most modern of hotels, with its own parking places for cars, its winter garden, its swimming pool on the roof, and its incomparable restaurant. The cuisine of Chef Tabourdiau is, at the same time, youthful and classical, and always as distinguished as this most marvellous *maison* requires. Robert Chauland will guide you through this exotic menu of tasty specialities that you might not recognize. You see, here the oysters are coated with a very unexpected and most subtle sauce, the lamb is accompanied by a purée of sweet garlic, and the scallops are served with a Beluga caviar and cream sauce.

Scallops with Caviar

10 large scallops with coral
3 egg yolks
400 ml (12 oz) chilled double cream (whipping cream)
salt and pepper, to taste
125 g (¼ lb) butter, and as needed
200 ml (6 oz) truffle juice
1 chopped shallot
100 ml (3 oz) champagne
juice of ¼ lemon
50 g (1¾ oz) caviar, Beluga preferred
1 bunch fresh chives

Press 6 scallops through a strainer, add egg yolks, and mix in ½ the cream. Season with salt and pepper. Butter 4 small moulds and fill with the mixture. Let poach in a bain-marie* for about 15 minutes in a medium, 350°F (175°C), oven. Remove and keep warm.

Slice the remaining scallops and cook them gently with the coral, truffle juice, and a few knobs of butter for 4 minutes. Reserve. Sweat* the shallot in butter, deglaze with champagne, and reduce until almost dry. Add the reserved scallop mixture and the remaining cream. Let cook for 1 minute, then thicken with remaining butter. Add a few drops of lemon juice, and mix in the caviar.

To serve: Place the moulds in the centre of each of 4 plates, surround each mould with sauce, garnish all with chives, and serve.

Wine: *Champagne*   Serves: 4

Fouquet's

99, Champs Élysées, 75008 Paris
Tel: 723-7060
Proprietor: Maurice Casanova • Chef: Pierre Ducroux

This year we are all commemorating the 80th birthday of **Fouquet's** — the most Parisian of Parisian restaurants with its most international clientele. The bars and terraces are overrun with flowers in celebration. Fouquet's shows no sign of antiquity but, rather, everlasting life and sparkle.

Pierre Ducroux's cuisine is youthful and classic and is complemented by wines served by André Georges and M. Vonnick, under the direction of Pierre Lafferière. It is they who have contributed to the incomparable perpetuity of Fouquet's and have made this restaurant a part of the eternal youthfulness that is Parisian life.

Scallops with Saffron

20 large whole scallops, in thin shells
200 g (7 oz) carrots
3 stalks celery
10 small white onions
water, as needed
100 ml (3 oz) dry white wine
1 sprig thyme
salt and pepper, to taste
pinch of saffron
1 bunch parsley
50 g (1¾ oz) butter
300 g (10½ oz) puff pastry dough,* cut into 4 pieces
2 leeks, whites only

Open the scallops, keeping the coral, and clean them carefully. Cut the carrots and celery julienne, keeping the parings. Cut the onions into thin slices. Make a stock with the scallop coral by wetting with water and white wine and flavouring with the vegetable parings. Add thyme, salt, pepper, saffron, and some parsley and simmer for 20 minutes. Pass the stock through a cloth strainer to remove the large particles. Mix the butter, julienne vegetables, strained stock, and onions together and bring to a boil. Season to taste. Divide the scallops into 4 ovenproof bowls, then pour vegetable and stock mixture over each. Sprinkle remaining parsley on top. Cover each bowl with the puff pastry dough and bake in the oven at 450°F (230°C) for 15 minutes. Serve straight from the oven.

Wine: *Burgundy, Aligoté, 1976*   Serves: 4

Le Pré Catelan

Route de Suresnes, Bois de Boulogne, 75016 Paris
Tel: 524-5558
Proprietors: Gaston and Colette Lenôtre • Chef: Patrick Lenôtre

Sea Urchin Soufflé

20 sea urchins, 125 g (¼ lb) each
300 g (7 oz) fillet of whiting
salt and pepper, to taste
6 egg whites
1 egg yolk
100 ml (3 oz) juice from the sea urchins

Using scissors, open the sea urchins. Using a spoon, take out the insides. Wash the shells and put them in a hot oven for 1 minute to dry.

Blend the whiting in a mixer with salt and pepper, 1 egg white, and 1 egg yolk until smooth. In a bowl, mix the whiting mixture together with the sea urchin insides and season. Whip 5 egg whites to soft peaks. Add to seafood mixture. Fill the sea urchin shells with the mixture and place them on a thick-bottomed plate. Place plate on a bain-marie,* cover with aluminum foil (to prevent a crust from forming on the soufflés), and bake in the oven at 425°F (220°C) for 5 minutes. Serve hot.

Serves: 10

"Come let us go to the woods," is Colette and Gaston Lenôtre's invitation to **Le Pré Catelan**. Here, the pleasures of dining take place in an enchanting atmosphere of marvellous gardens. And here, the art of cooking is a fine art.

Everything is a feast for your eyes and your palate. Try the warm Langoustines, the Sea Urchin Soufflé, the Poultry à l'Étuvée, and the delicious desserts. You will be tempted to prolong your stay, just as one wants to prolong all such moments of bliss.

Les Armes de Bretagne

108, avenue de Maine, 75011 Paris
Tel: 320-2950
Proprietor: P. Boyer • Chef: M. Boucheret

Snail Cassolettes with Nuts

2 shallots
3 cloves garlic
1 handful parsley
7 large white mushrooms
130 g (4½ oz) butter
salt and pepper, to taste
4 dozen snails, shelled
30 g (1 oz) shelled hazelnuts
50 g (1¾ oz) peeled white seedless grapes
2 tbsp capers
200 ml (6 oz) Muscadet wine

To prepare snail butter: Chop the shallots, garlic, parsley, and 3 mushrooms; mix together well. (Cut remaining mushrooms julienne.) Add 100 g (3½ oz) butter, salt, and pepper; mix well.

In a large frying pan, melt the remaining butter. When butter is brown, add snails. Stir snails a couple of times in the pan, add hazelnuts, grapes, capers, and the 4 julienne mushrooms. Season with salt and pepper, then add wine. Cook all ingredients until wine has evaporated. Add snail butter mixture slowly, blending all together. Reseason if necessary. Serve hot in 4 cassolettes or ramekins.

Wine: *Chablis*

Serves: 4

Even though this restaurant is exquisitely decorated in the exuberant style of Napoleon III, the decor does not surpass the excellence of the cuisine. The quality and variety of seafood are of the highest calibre.

The lobster from Brittany is roasted with sorrel and the haddock is poached "English" style. And do not forget about the excellent meats served here! Even the most finicky gourmet will be satisfied at **Les Armes de Bretagne.** Be sure to start your meal with the Snail Cassolettes with Nuts. It's indicative of all the wonderful things to come.

Hôtel de la Côte-d'Or

2, rue d'Argentine, 21210 Saulieu
Tel: (80) 64-07-66
Proprietor/Chef: Bernard Loiseau

Snails in Nettle Sauce

50 g (1¾ oz) nettles
125 g (¼ lb) butter
salt and pepper, as needed
4 dozen snails, not in shells
1 tbsp lemon juice

Blanch the nettles for 3 minutes. Put through a strainer, then mix in the butter. Let mixture rest for 3 minutes. Season with salt and pepper.

Heat the snails in boiling water with lemon juice and a pinch of salt. Remove the snails from pot, then add them to the nettle sauce that has sat for 3 minutes. Mix the sauce and snails gently together. Reseason if necessary and serve hot.

Wine: *Chablis*   Serves: 4

While passing through Saulieu in 1677, Mme. de Sévigné would treat herself by dining here. Colette stayed at this hotel before the war. This was the grandiose *maison* of the great chef Alexandre Dumaine. Naturally, his successor had to be particularly deserving to follow in this gentleman's footsteps. The young Bernard Loiseau has brought the **Hôtel de la Côte-d'Or** back to life.

Bernard mastered and refined his creative art under the tender guidance of Claude Verger at La Barrière. One only needs to savour his Sliced Duck Breast with Peaches and his Snails in Nettle Sauce to be convinced of Bernard's talent. This restaurant is filled with a tempting and unique selection of dishes.

La Gratienne

17113 Mornac-sur-Seudre
Tel: (46) 22-73-90
Proprietor: Mireille Forgerit • Chef: Paul Forgerit

Aran Scallop Soup

2 tbsp lard
80 g (2¾ oz) thick, diced smoked bacon
300 g (10½ oz) firm potatoes in large dice
1 packet seaweed, about 120 g (4 oz), thinly sliced
1½ generous litres (6½ cups) hot water
salt, pepper, parsley, and thyme, to taste
1 bay leaf
1 large onion
500 g (1 lb) fresh cod
16 large whole scallops with coral

Heat the lard in a thick-bottomed saucepan then brown the bacon in it on medium heat. When brown, and no more, let it sweat* gently for 15-20 minutes with the pan covered. Add potatoes and seaweed and cook for 6-7 minutes. Moisten with very hot water, then add salt, pepper, herbs, and onion and let boil gently for 40 minutes. Clean the cod and scallops. Cut cod into large dice. Split scallops in half and remove coral. Simmer the cod for 10 minutes, the scallops for 6 minutes, and the coral for 5 minutes in the prepared liquid. Be careful: the scallops and coral should remain firm and hold all their flavour.

Suggestion: Lightly skim the soup and serve with croutons fried in lard.

Wine: *A dry white wine*   Serves: 4

Paul Forgerit is an astonishing man, born and bred in the Charente district, who left the sea for frying pans and friends. To see him through his retirement, he and his daughter Mireille took over a little restaurant. **La Gratienne** in Mornac-sur-Seudre is an antique shop, a tea shop, and, at meal times, a restaurant that is a venue for lovers of beef stew and mussels. A Paul Forgerit dish is poetry. Just whisper to him that you know that in Ireland they used to prepare a scallop soup or that Dodin-Bouffant had, in Adèle, a servant and cook of the greatest inspiration, and he'll be off to prepare his Aran Scallop Soup or his Black Pudding "Adèle" Style, both with his own personal touch; they are both masterpieces.

Hiély-Lucullus

5, rue de la République, 84000 Avignon
Tel: (90) 86-17-07
Proprietor/Chef: Pierre Hiély

Fisherman's Broth

1 clove garlic, crushed
1 carrot, thinly sliced
1 onion, thinly sliced
2 sprigs thyme
pinch of saffron
1 bay leaf
12 mussels poached in ½ litre (2 cups) water
fish stock,* as needed
¼ litre (1 cup) double cream (whipping cream)
1 fillet of anglerfish of 250 g (½ lb)
1 fillet of sole of 250 g (½ lb)
12 cheese flavoured croutons, as needed

In a pan rubbed with garlic, gently cook the carrots and onions until they are golden brown. Add thyme, saffron, and bay leaf. Add ⅓ of the liquid the mussels were poached in, an equal amount of fish stock, and the cream. Reduce until thick.

Thinly slice the anglerfish and sole and add to the mixture. Poach slowly in the reduced mixture.

Place the mussels on croutons and pour the hot mixture over. Serve.

Serves: 4

At **Hiély-Lucullus**, we find Pierre Hiély presiding over the destiny of this old family enterprise. He has most conscientiously set a reasonable fixed price for the high quality, French cuisine appearing on his menu.

Located on the first floor of an old building in this historic city, the service is managed with a feminine touch by the lovely Mme. Hiély, who is originally from Brittany. She has also decorated the restaurant in a simple, unpretentious way, inspired by the love of life and youth for which Brittany is known.

In the same spirit, her husband prepares Fisherman's Broth, Mussels Wrapped in Spinach, Ragout with Noodles, Sole with Clams, and Guinea Fowl with Peaches.

Via Veneto

13, rue Quentin-Bauchart, 75008 Paris
Tel: 723-7684
Proprietor/Chef: Jacques Simon

Fish Soup

1 kg (2¼ lb) onions
1 large clove garlic
few sprigs thyme
few bay leaves
1 bunch parsley
200 ml (6 oz) olive oil
1 kg (2¼ lb) tomatoes
salt and pepper, to taste
1 tsp saffron
3 kg (6½ lb) striped bass or any Mediterranean rock fish (scorpion fish, red gurnet, conger eels), cut into pieces
5 litres (5⅓ qt) water
aniseed, as needed

Brown the onions, garlic, thyme, bay leaves, and parsley in olive oil on hot heat for 10 minutes. Add tomatoes, salt, pepper, and saffron and let reduce for 10 minutes. Add fish and leave on heat for 20 minutes. Add water, bring to a boil, and let boil on medium heat for 45 minutes. Put the preparation through a vegetable grinder with a large mesh, then through a fine mesh. Bring back to a boil, add a little aniseed, and let boil on medium heat for 15 minutes.

Suggestion: Serve soup with croutons (crusts removed), mayonnaise with pimento, and Parmesan cheese.

Wine: *White or Rose Vin de Provence*

Serves: 6

Jacques Simon was the steward of His Highness the Prince Aga Khan and, later, of his son Aly Khan. With them he learned a style of living that one could call *la dolce vita*. Later (some 20 years ago), when he wanted to set up a restaurant business, he chose this brilliantly promising name, **Via Veneto**, and with his young wife, Hélène, he made this unknown spot on an unknown street into a sort of all-Parisian venue for the pleasures of life. With such a name, half the menu just has to be Italian. In a decor of Roman frescoes, vines from Asti, pretty, singing colours in the evening with candelabras and the strumming of guitars, the Via Veneto is a most pleasant restaurant with a remarkable fish soup, tasty *pasticciatas*, and *zabaglione*.

La Table de Jeannette

12, rue Duphot, 75001 Paris
Tel: 260-0564
Proprietor/Chef: Jeanne de Bouteiller

Garbure (Cabbage Soup)

200 g (7 oz) white beans
1 kg (2¼ lb) potatoes
250 g (½ lb) leeks
300 g (10½ oz) carrots
1 medium-sized onion
200 g (7 oz) smoked bacon
1 tsp chopped garlic
125 g (¼ lb) salt
600 g (1⅓ lb) green cabbage
3 - 4 sprigs thyme

Soak the beans for 12 hours in 5 litres (5⅓ qt) of water, then boil the beans. During this time, wash and peel the potatoes, leeks, carrots, and onion, then cut them into 1 cm (½ in) slices. Boil these vegetables and the beans together with the smoked bacon, garlic, and salt for 45 minutes. With a fork, mash the contents of the pot together. This will make the preparation chalky in colour.

Cut the cabbage into large pieces. Put the cabbage pieces into the mashed vegetable-bean preparation; add the thyme. If mixture is too stiff, add a bit of boiling water. Adjust the seasoning. Cook for 20 minutes more at medium heat, stirring occasionally.

Wine: *A red Bordeaux or Cahors*

Who would bother going so much out of their way to find a table to have dinner? Well, go to the end of rue Duphot and you will discover Jeannette's restaurant nestled in a large courtyard. It is a darling little house, feminine and meticulous down to the last detail. Parisians don't hesitate coming to Jeannette's because her unique personality and this enchanting little place make for a wonderful dining experience. Jeannette is a chef with a delicate touch, as is evidenced by her Warm Turnip Salad, Garbure, Snow Eggs, and Sole Meunière Wrapped in Parchment Paper.

Frankly, people do not come to Jeannette's only to dine; there is something very special here that makes sitting down to a drink or espresso very enjoyable.

Lous Landès

157, avenue du Maine, 75014 Paris
Tel: 543-0804
Proprietors: Georgette and Jean-Pierre Descat • Chef: Georgette Descat

---

Garlic and Onion Soup

3 tbsp goose fat
10 garlic cloves, sliced
1 onion, peeled and chopped
1 litre (2 pt) water
salt and pepper, to taste
1 egg
1 tsp wine vinegar
4 slices French bread

In a large pot, melt the goose fat, then add garlic and onion and sweat* for 5 minutes. Add water, salt, and pepper, bring to a boil, then lower heat and simmer for 10 more minutes to make soup.

Beat the egg and vinegar together. Place the bread in a soup terrine, pour the soup over, and slowly add the egg and vinegar mixture. Serve.

Wine: *Bordeaux*   Serves: 4

Georgette and Jean-Pierre Descat started not too far from here in a tiny country house. Georgette, a jolly woman with a strong accent, and Jean-Pierre, her son, are now in a new location, but the decor is the same as the old house and features an unusual collection of bric-a-brac from *la Belle Epoch*.

Jean-Pierre serves the marvellous dinners prepared by his mother. Georgette offers *foie gras* and *confit* (a native treat), Salad of Haddock, superb Garlic and Onion Soup, Tortillions of Sole, and Fish Gelatine with Mint. Everything at **Lous Landès** is served with the warmth of a home.

Gaston et Gastounette

7, quai Saint-Pierre, 06400 Cannes
Tel: (93) 39-49-44
Proprietors: M. and Mme. Cassin • Chef: Michel Corbet

In the south of France, Cannes to be exact, there is a fabulous little restaurant called **Gaston et Gastounette**. This restaurant is known to everyone in town and may be the most recommended spot to tourists.

It is quaint and comfortable and serves a traditional menu, which is much appreciated by the older clientele. M. and Mme. Cassin offer a light and delicious variety of seafood prepared by Chef Michel Corbet. The Soupe au Pistou, Mussel Soup, and Stuffed Mussels, Grilled Mussels, and Poached Mussels are all excellent. Being so close to Italy, they also offer lasagna and other traditional Italian dishes. To accompany your dinner, try the wine from Provence; it is perfect!

Mussel Soup

2 shallots, chopped
2 cloves garlic
125 g (¼ lb) leeks, whites only
2 carrots, chopped
2 tomatoes, concasse*
2 tbsp oil
100 ml (3 oz) fish stock*
1 litre (2 pt) cooked mussels, liquid reserved
3 tbsp double cream (whipping cream)
125 g (¼ lb) grated Gruyère cheese
10 g (⅓ oz) bread crumbs

Sauté the shallots, garlic, leeks, carrots, and tomatoes in hot oil. Add the fish stock and liquid from mussels and let cook on medium heat for 20 minutes. Add the mussels and cream and stir gently.

Pour the mixture into ovenproof bowls. Cover each with grated Gruyère and bread crumbs. Put in a hot oven at 450°F (230°C) until the cheese becomes brown.

Wine: *Blanc de Blanc Ott or Côte de Provence*   Serves: 3

Les Célébrités

61, quai de Grenelle, 75015 Paris
Tel: 575-6262
Proprietor: Jean-Marie Leclerq • Chef: Joël Robuchon

"Under the Mirabeau Bridge flows the Seine." You will sing this refrain at the new **Les Célébrités**, a beautifully decorated restaurant with an intimate and comfortable atmosphere. Joël Robuchon is one of the best culinary talents around, and he is always full of pleasant surprises. Three of his latest creations are Calf's Head in Ragout, Shellfish Court Bouillon with Mushrooms, and Fillet of Lamb in Basil Cream Sauce; they are outstanding, as is everything else appearing on the menu. Incidentally, the menu changes with the seasons.

Here you will dine with the politicians as well as theatre, television, and movie personalities who come here often to enjoy the excellent cuisine and wines.

Shellfish Court Bouillon with Mushrooms

60 g (2 oz) leek whites, julienne
150 g (5¼ oz) butter
salt, as needed
125 g (¼ lb) pleurotus mushrooms
25 g (¾ oz) ginger root, julienne
1.5 litre (3 pt) chicken stock*
6 large lobsters, shelled
12 large scallops, cut into thirds
6 medium oysters
pepper, as needed
3 pinches chervil

Put the julienne of leek into a saucepan with 80 g (2¾ oz) butter and a pinch of salt. Sweat* for a few minutes, stirring with a fork. Add mushrooms, cut in 4-5 pieces; cover and stew for 5 minutes. Add ginger and chicken stock and bring to a boil. Check the seasoning.

Pour mixture into 6 cups or bowls. Add 1 lobster, 2 scallops (cut into thirds), 1 oyster, ⅙ of the remaining butter, and a sprinkling of pepper to each bowl. Bake, uncovered, in a bain-marie* in the oven at 475°F (250°C) for 8 minutes. At the last minute, add chervil and serve.

Wine: *Sancerre Rouge, Lucien Crochet*   Serves: 6

La Couronne

31, place du Vieux-March, 76000 Rouen
Tel: (35) 71-40-90
Proprietors: The Dorin Brothers • Chef: Jean Fouquet

Sole Consommé with Shrimps

4 tsp oil
2 carrots
2 onions
½ leek
200 g (7 oz) mushrooms
1.5 kg (3⅓ lb) sole in fillets, bones reserved
400 ml (12 oz) white wine
3 litres (¾ gal) water
2 bouquets garni*
2 stalks celery
salt, as needed
12 peppercorns
24 baby shrimps
100 ml (3 oz) double cream (whipping cream)

To prepare the first fish fumet: Mix ½ the oil, 1 carrot, 1 onion, ¼ leek, ½ the mushrooms, and ½ the bones from the sole together, then sweat* in a saucepan until the juices are released. Add ½ the white wine and all the water. Add 1 bouquet garni and 1 stick celery and bring to a boil. Salt to taste and add ½ the pepperecorns. Boil, uncovered, for 45 minutes. Strain and reserve the juice.

Prepare the second fish fumet the same way with the same amounts of ingredients, only do *not* add any water.

Mix the two fish fumets together and heat; then add the fillets of sole and the shrimps and cook them in the stock. Add cream and serve hot.

Without a doubt, **La Couronne** is the oldest tavern in France, present since 1345. Behind this ancient façade lies the culinary dynasty of the Dorin family who began working here in 1919. This establishment has been renowned for fine cuisine for decades, and the Dorin brothers have continued the tradition. Jean Fouquet, the chef, prepares *la grande cuisine,* the epitome of culinary perfection that time cannot erase. It, like the Norman-Gothic decor of the restaurant, is staunch and sturdy. Here the food is succulent and can please even the most delicate of tastes. The Sole Consommé with Shrimps and the Fillet of Sole "Normandy" Style are two dishes on their way to becoming legends, as the Pink Duck served in rosé wine already has.

Le Récamier

4, rue Récamier, 75007 Paris
Tel: 548-8658
Proprietor/Chef: Martin Cantegrit

Beef Bourguignon

1.8 kg (4 lb) neck of beef (chuck)
150 g (5¼ oz) bacon cubes semi-salted
salt and pepper, to taste
2 tbsp oil
125 g (¼ lb) carrots, sliced
125 g (¼ lb) shallots, chopped
200 g (7 oz) large onions, cut into cubes
4 - 5 tbsp flour
1 clove garlic, crushed
red wine, as needed
1 bouquet garni*
1 bunch parsley

Cut the pieces of beef into squares of 3 cm (1¼ in). Season the bacon cubes with salt and pepper, then sauté them in oil in a skillet.

In another skillet, sauté the carrots, shallots, and onions, then pour them over the meat. Dust the meat with flour, season with salt and pepper, and cook in the oven at 350°F (175°C) for 5 - 10 minutes until the flour colours a bit. Add the garlic. Wet the preparation with red wine, add the bouquet garni and the parsley, and cook for 30 minutes. Add a little water (enough to reach the level of the meat) and cook for another 1½ hours in the oven at the same temperature as before.

Serve the meat with vegetables and bacon cubes on the side.

Wine: *Santenay, 1976*

Serves: 6

The name **Le Récamier** is very suitable for this marvellous restaurant found in the 7th *arrondissement* (district) of Paris. In the image of that celebrated lady of the Empire, Mme. Récamier, Martin Cantegrit unites a brilliant society at his tables. Ask Martin to tell you about his farm (that's where the freshest possible produce comes from daily — at 4 a.m.). He loves to chat with his customers. I'm sure you will hesitate a moment while trying to choose among the Roast Young Partridge on Toast or Beef Bourguignon or Veal Kidney "Santenay." Ask Martin for advice. He will also charm you with his greeting and his precious stories. You will quickly discover that dining at Le Récamier is definitely one of the more interesting experiences available to you in the capital.

Les Trois Marmites

215, boulevard Saint-Denis, 92400 Courbevoie
Tel: 333-2535
Proprietor / Chef: Robert Daubian

Beef Stew à la Charentaise

2 kg (4½ lb) neck of beef
  (chuck), cubed
4 tbsp oil
3 large onions, sliced
500 g (1 lb) carrots, sliced
80 g (2¾ oz) flour
2 bottles red wine
salt and pepper, to taste
1 bouquet garni*
5 tomatoes

1 clove garlic
250 g (½ lb) lard
1 tsp butter
juice of 1 lemon
400 g (14 oz) white mushrooms
250 g (½ lb) small onions
50 g (1¾ oz) sugar
toasted croutons and chopped
  parsley, to garnish

Sauté the meat cubes well in hot oil, then place the meat in a cooking pot. Sauté the carrots and onions until onions are golden, then mix in with the meat. Heat the contents of the pot gently, dust the meat with flour, and bake in the oven for 10 - 15 minutes at 325 - 335°F (165 - 170°C). Mix frequently until the meat is brown. Add the red wine, salt, pepper, bouquet garni, tomatoes, and garlic; mix and cover. Place back into the oven and let cook for 3 hours at the same temperature. (Check cooking now and then to be sure that all liquid has not evaporated. Add water if necessary.)

To prepare the garnish: Cut the lard into small cubes, blanch them, drain, and reserve. In a saucepan with some water, butter, and lemon juice, cook the mushrooms for 10 minutes; drain. In another saucepan, cook the small onions in water and sugar; let reduce until the remaining moisture at the bottom of the pan forms a glaze; reserve.

Take the cooking pot out of the oven and put the contents of all the pans onto a large platter. Top with toasted croutons and sprinkle with parsley.

Wine: *Burgundy or Beaujolais*

Serves: 6 - 8

Unfortunately, the original owners of this small furnished house, transformed into a restaurant, were not inspired enough to make a success of the place. Two years later, however, Robert Daubian acquired the establishment and prospered. Now, **Les Trois Marmites** has become a stopping place for gourmands.

Robert uses only the freshest ingredients to prepare the terrines and pastries, which he makes himself. The excellent Smoked Salmon and the Stewed Beef à la Charentaise are authentic traditional dishes.

Here you will dine in intimacy and beauty, for the decor is delicate and romantic. The gracious Mme. Daubian will tend to all your needs throughout your dinner.

Chez Georges

273, boulevard Péreire, 75017 Paris
Tel: 574-3100
Proprietor: Roger Mazaquil • Chef: M. Merle

Beef Ribs

1.4 kg (3 lb) beef ribs
100 ml (3 oz) oil
3 pinches coarse salt
100 ml (3 oz) water
salt and pepper, to taste

Fasten the ribs together so the meat doesn't separate. Protect the bones sticking out with aluminum foil. Coat the meat with oil and sprinkle with salt.

Put the ribs on a roasting pan and place into the oven. The oven should be very hot (500°F or 260°C) so the meat can sizzle for 30 minutes. After 15 minutes, lower the heat to 400°F (205°C). Baste the meat frequently with the grease. Take the meat out of the oven and let stand 15 minutes.

Remove the grease, add water to the pan, and scrape the bottom of the pan to collect the meat drippings. Season to taste.

Pour the drippings over the meat and serve hot.

Serves: 6

In 1926, M. Mazarquil created his bistro. Meanwhile, Roger, his son, was attending a hotel and restaurant school so that one day he could take over his father's business. Since 1960, Roger has managed his father's bistro. There have been a few changes made since. For one, he has redecorated, most agreeably, I must say, without disfiguring the original style. For another, it is no longer a bistro. Rather, it is a restaurant that serves bourgeois dinners: solid and hearty portions of fine Leg of Mutton with Flageolets (green kidney beans). Beef Ribs, Steak with Gratin Dauphinois, Pickled Sole with Choux Paste, and Pot-au-Feu with Vegetables. For the past 30 years, **Chez Georges** has remained a restaurant of high calibre. Here you will discover fine cuisine.

Le Clovis

Hôtel Frantel Windsor, 14, rue Beaujon, 75008 Paris
Tel: 563-0404
Proprietor: Frantel • Chef: Pierre Larapidie

The Frantel organisation should be proud of its wisdom in choosing the right locations and the best chefs for its restaurants. **Le Clovis** has an ambiance of modern luxury and flowered verandas. Pierre Larapidie will make you forget that just a few steps away is the commotion of traffic circling around the Arc de Triomphe.

This young chef doesn't lack imagination. He has a flair for blending subtle spices with exotic spices to flavour his fabulous Terrine of Duck Confit, his "Pithivier" of Lamb, and his Filet Mignon. You will enjoy your visit to Le Clovis.

Filet Mignon

1 fillet of beef (tenderloin) of 1 kg (2¼ lb)
1 kg (2¼ lb) chard
125 g (¼ lb) butter
salt and pepper, to taste
250 g (½ lb) mushrooms, sliced and seasoned
2 egg yolks
½ litre (1 pt) double cream (whipping cream)
1 bunch chervil, chopped
100 ml (3 oz) port wine

Trim the fillet, cut into 8 equal parts, and flatten. Blanch the chard and cut the leaves into 2 cm (¾ in) strips. In a pan, sizzle the leaves in butter without thoroughly cooking them. Add the meat strips to the pan and cook, but keep meat rare. Season with salt and pepper to taste. Remove everything from the pan. Place the pieces of meat on the chard and cover with slices of mushrooms. Form small parcels by folding the leaves over the meat and mushrooms. Make a sauce by mixing the egg yolks, cream, and chervil together. Spread this sauce over the fillets and glaze them in a salamander or under a broiler. Add port wine to the juices from the meat and reduce to a good gravy consistency.

Place the meat parcels on a hot plate, pour the reduced gravy and port mixture over them, and serve.

Serves: 4

Le Procope

13, rue de l'Ancienne-Comédie, 75006 Paris
Tel: 326-9920
Proprietor: Michel Déroussent • Chef: Alain Camus

It is wonderful to be able to enjoy a meal in a most historic place. **Le Procope** is the oldest café in Paris; it dates from 1686. Diderot, Bonaparte, Verlaine, Benjamin Franklin, and many other famous people have stopped to have dinner at Le Procope.

Michel Déroussent renovated this café and offers wonderfully tasty cuisine. Taste the marvellous Fillet of Beef with Chervil, but remember: the menu includes many other surprises. Rich and abundant is the image of Le Procope — rich in history and character and fine cuisine.

Fillet of Beef

600 g (1⅓ lb) fillet of beef
  (tenderloin)
salt and pepper, to taste
1 litre (2 pt) good red wine
200 g (7 oz) carrots, cut into strips
200 g (7 oz) minced onions
200 g (7 oz) tomatoes,
  cut into pieces
2 cloves of garlic, unpeeled
1 bouquet garni*
100 ml (3 oz) vinegar
peppercorns, to taste
75 g (2½ oz) butter
100 ml (3 oz) cognac
2 croutons

Trim the fillet and cut it into tournedos.* Season with salt and pepper. Marinate for 3-4 days in the red wine, carrots, onions, tomatoes, garlic, and bouquet garni.

To prepare pepper sauce: Remove the vegetables from the marinade to a skillet with oil and lightly sauté them. Wet with the vinegar and reduce until liquid has evaporated. Add ⅔ of the marinade and cook for 45 minutes on medium heat, mixing frequently. Put peppercorns into the preparation 10 minutes before the end of cooking. Pass the sauce through a fine strainer. Add a little more marinade and let cook until you obtain desired sauce consistency. Once again, pass the sauce through a fine strainer.

Dry the tournedos; season again with salt and pepper. Sauté the tournedos in ⅔ of the butter on very high heat, then flame with cognac. Take the tournedos out of the pan, put the rest of the marinade into the pan, and add the pepper sauce and remaining butter. Adjust the seasoning. Cover the tournedos with the sauce and serve hot.

Serves: 2

Moissonnier

28, rue des Fossés-Saint-Bernard, 75005 Paris
Tel: 329-8765
Proprietor / Chef: M. Moissonnier

With a suitcase filled with delicious gastronomic recipes, M. Moissonnier, from Lyon, came to Paris to capture the Parisians with the *grand cuisine Lyonnaise*. He succeeded, not by "beating a drum" to get publicity but with his recipes: dishes such as Lyonnaise Salad, Marinated Beef Rumen, Sautéed Tripe, and many others, all served with excellent Beaujolais wines.

M. Moissonnier prepares good and simple dishes that are neither too fancy nor too plain.

Marinated Beef Rumen

6 portions beef rumen (stomach or paunch), 15 cm by 15 cm (6 in by 6 in) each
100 ml (3 oz) water
3 tbsp mustard
1 litre (2 pt) dry white wine
200 ml (6 oz) sauce anglaise*
1 loaf white bread, in crumbs
salt and pepper, to taste
4 tbsp oil
15 g (½ oz) butter
mayonnaise, as needed
1 tbsp capers, chopped
1 tbsp gherkins, chopped

Boil the pieces of rumen in water until soft (about 5 minutes). Drain. Prepare a marinade by mixing the mustard and white wine together. Soak the rumen in the marinade for 24 hours. Drain the rumen, then dunk each into sauce anglaise, roll in the bread crumbs, and season with salt and pepper. Sauté the rumen in a skillet with the oil and butter for 5 minutes on each side.

Serve the rumen with mayonnaise, capers, and gherkins on the side.

Suggestion: Serve with sautéed potatoes.

Wine: *Beaujolais*   Serves: 6

Le Champs de Mars

17, avenue de La Motte-Picquet, 75007 Paris
Tel; 705-5799
Proprietor / Chef: Jacques Gelle

Mars, the Roman god of war, is here as Mars, a god of gastronomy. It is Jacques Gelle who is the deity in this restaurant.

Jacques serves his fortunate customers such culinary delights as Turbot and Rhubarb, Fricassee of Chicken "à l'Angevine," Onglet au Roquefort, and Calf's Head in Gribiche Sauce (a cold sauce made with hard-boiled eggs, oil, vinegar, mustard, capers, chervil, parsley, and tarragon).

You will be conquered by the cuisine here.

Onglet with Roquefort Cheese

50 g (1¾ oz) crushed almonds
50 g (1¾ oz) Roquefort cheese
50 g (1¾ oz) butter
2 tbsp oil
4 *onglets* (beef shortribs or top of skirt), 250 g (½ lb) each
125 g (¼ lb) double cream (whipping cream)
salt and pepper, to taste

Pound the almonds, cheese, and butter to a paste in a mortar. Sauté the *onglets* in oil; remove and keep warm. Deglaze the pan with cream. Add the almond mixture, season, and reduce the sauce, whisking frequently, until the consistency is smooth and creamy. Serve the *onglets* napped* with sauce on a hot plate.

Wine: *Bourgueil, 1976, or Cahors, 1976*   Serves: 4

Pic

285, avenue Victor-Hugo, 26001 Valence
Tel: (75) 44-15-32
Proprietor/Chef: Jacques Pic

A century and a half ago, there was a restaurant named L'Auberge du Pin that was tended by Chef Sophie Pic. Her son, André, later succeeded her and founded **Pic** in Valence, where it flourished in the middle of the gardens beside Nationale 7.

Since 1936, Pic has been synonymous with refined cuisine that is both sensibly priced and sumptuous. Jacques Pic, grandson of Sophie, succeeded his father and continues the family tradition, just as his son, Alain, expects to do someday.

And what a tradition! The Pheasant Salad wth Small Onions, John Dory with Snails, Lamb Brains, Oxtails Dauphinoise, Game with Thistles, and Pullet from Bresse with Lobster Medallions and Artichokes are all quite savoury.

Oxtails Dauphinoise

500 g (1 lb) oxtails
1 litre (2 pt) white wine
125 g (¼ lb) lean bacon, boiled and cubed
6 large chestnuts
20 small white onions, cooked in 125 g (¼ lb) butter

Cut the oxtails into pieces and braise in white wine for 1 hour. Place the pieces of oxtail in covered casserole with the boiled cubes of bacon, chestnuts, and the small cooked onions, and cook for 3 hours at 350°F (175°C).

Remove the cooking liquid, strain, then, in a pan, reduce it to sauce consistency. Serve over contents of casserole.

Serves: 2

Anglard et du Cerf

Super-Lioran, 15300 Murat
Tel: (71) 49-50-26 and 49-50-27
Proprietor/Chef: Jean-Pierre Anglard

In this atmosphere of fresh air and romance, both athletes and lovers will find **Anglard et du Cerf** very inviting. Auvergne, no matter what time of year, is appealing and beautiful. Auvergne has a special charm about it; it is picturesque and the perfect setting for a storybook fantasy.

Jean-Pierre will prepare for you Salted Beef Mignonnettes or a *truffade* cooked to perfection. You will certainly enjoy this rustic restaurant set in the beautiful and clean country of Auvergne where life is slow and simple. Here, the simple pleasures are the only pleasures, and that is enough.

Salted Beef Mignonnettes

700 g (1½ lb) beef fillets (tenderloin)
salt and pepper, to taste
4 tbsp green peppercorns, crushed
80 g (2¾ oz) butter
100 ml (3 oz) Bourgueil wine
1 tbsp aspic or gelatine
50 ml (1½ oz) Armagnac

Cut the beef fillets into 4 thick pieces, then season with salt and pepper to taste. Roll the fillets gently in crushed peppercorns. In a pan with 15 g (½ oz) butter, sauté the fillets, but keep the meat rare. Once sautéed, keep the fillets warm.

In a skillet with another 15 g (½ oz) butter, fry the shallots until soft. Deglaze the pan with Bourgueil wine. Add the aspic and the rest of the butter and reduce to obtain a thick sauce. Flame the sauce with Armagnac.

Suggestion: Pour the flambed sauce over the meat and serve the fillets with sautéed potatoes or steamed potatoes.

Wine: *Bourgueil*

Serves: 4

Abbaye Saint-Michel

89700 Tonnerre
Tel: (86) 55-05-99
Proprietor / Chef: Daniel Cussac

Tournedos with Ratafia Sauce

6 beef tournedos,* 180 - 200 g (6½ - 7 oz) each
salt and pepper, to taste
100 ml (3 oz) ratafia (any fruit liqueur)
200 ml (6 oz) veal stock*
4 tbsp double cream (whipping cream)

Sauté the tournedos over high heat, but keep rare, then season with salt and pepper. Add the ratafia, reduce by ¼, then remove meat from pan and keep warm.

Add the veal stock and the cream to the pan. Boil until the sauce is reduced to ½ the original amount.

Put the tournedos back into the sauce. Let cook for a few minutes, then serve hot.

Wine: *Bouzy Rouge*   Serves: 6

In 1964, Daniel Cussac created this restaurant that is situated within the walls of a Benedictine monastery founded n the 10th century. These are the same historic walls in which Joan of Arc found refuge in 1429. Who would have imagined that five centuries later gourmand travellers would be savouring Avocado Pastry, Quail Soufflé with Prunes, Tournedos with Ratafia Sauce, Veal Sweetbreads with Oranges, and Avocado, and a delicious Cassis and Pear Soufflé with Chablis and Sabayon in this same place?

Assisting Daniel in the kitchen are two young cooks who help him create these delightful dishes, which he serves with his wines from Tonnerre, port from Burgundy, and others.

Le Petit Coin de la Bourse

16, rue Feydeau, 75002 Paris
Tel: 508-0008
Proprietor / Chef: Guy Girard

Kid Goat Bouillabaisse with Fresh Fennel

1 young goat, cut into pieces
salt and pepper, to taste
2 cloves garlic
1 g (very small pinch) saffron powder
200 ml (6 oz) olive oil
5 onions
4 leeks, white part only
2 tbsp tomato paste
½ litre (1 pt) white wine
water, as needed
1 bouquet garni*
2 Chinese anise flowers
1 heart of celery, julienne
2 fennel bulbs, julienne
3 carrots, julienne
50 g (2 oz) butter
250 g (½ lb) double cream (whipping cream)

Season the pieces of goat meat with salt and pepper, then leave in a pan with 1 clove garlic, saffron, and a little olive oil for 3 hours.

Slice the onions, slice the white of the leeks, grind 1 clove garlic, and place all in the pan with the meat and remaining olive oil. Cover and let the whole preparation sweat* on low heat, stirring occasionally. Add tomato paste and wine, then reduce for a few minutes.

Moisten the bouquet garni and anise flowers with enough water to almost cover ingredients; add to the meat pan. Check the seasoning and cook very gently for about 1 hour.

In a separate pan, sweat the white of leeks, celery heart, fennel, and carrots in butter and a little water.

When the goat meat is cooked, remove the bones and cut up the meat into small pieces. Add the meat to the cooking vegetables (leeks, celery, etc.). Pour the cooking juices from the meat over all, then add cream. Bring to a boil, cool, then serve in soup dishes.

Serves: 12

This restaurant is owned by the astonishing M. Girard, a jolly, grey-haired figure, who looks very much like one of Snow White's seven dwarfs, with a beard suggestive of both wisdom and invention. After 40 years of working just about everywhere, he ended up in this establishment which is over 100 years old. Guy has changed nothing of the outdated decor except for the addition of a bit of life and soul.

The dishes he prepares are quite extraordinary. For example, his Fish Sauerkraut, Fricassee of Small Grey Snails with Wild Mushrooms, and Bouillabaisse of Kid Goat with Fresh Fennel first amaze then delight.

Ile-de-France

32, avenue de New York, 75016 Paris
Tel: 723-6021
Proprietor: François Benoist • Chef: Benoît Fava

Rump of Kid "Ile-de-France" Style

60 ml (¼ cup) oil
60 ml (¼ cup) vinegar
120 ml (½ cup) dry red wine
salt, pepper, coriander,
  and rosemary, to taste
1 rump of kid goat of 1 kg (2¼ lb)
3 tbsp olive oil
½ litre (1 pt) double cream
  (whipping cream)

20 g (¾ oz) butter
4 small pears
½ litre (1 pt) Bordeaux wine
40 g (1½ oz) sugar
10 g (⅓ oz) cinnamon stick
1 kg (2¼ lb) pippin apples,
  peeled and sliced

To prepare the marinade: Mix the first 3 ingredients together and season with salt, pepper, coriander, and rosemary to taste. Trim and pare the rump and place in the marinade for 3 days in a cool place. Turn it twice a day.

Cut the rump into 6 pieces and brown the pieces in the olive oil. Add 2 tbsp of the marinade, salt to taste, and the cream. Bring to a boil, then place in a moderately hot oven at 375°F (190°C) for 30 minutes. Baste the pieces 3 times during the cooking period. Reconstruct the pieces on a serving dish and keep warm.

Reduce the cooking liquid to the desired consistency, then add butter and adjust the seasoning.

Cut the pears in half and cook them in the Bordeaux wine with ½ the sugar and the cinnamon. In a separate pan, cook the apples into an apple sauce with 100 ml (3 oz) water and the remaining sugar. Serve the rump with pears and apples.

Wine: *A red Burgundy*

Serves: 6

François Benoist, formerly of Chez Les Anges, demonstrated his creativity when he turned a barge into a floating restaurant on the Seine.

The floating **Ile-de-France** features a beautiful dining room with very exotic colours. It also has reception rooms and a huge kitchen with an interior that is quite modern. The charming Isabelle Benoist will greet you and see to your comfort while you dine in view of the majestic Eiffel Tower that will surely remind you that you are in Paris.

La Régalido

Rue Frédéric-Mistral, 13990 Fontvieille
Tel: (90) 97-73-67
Proprietor/Chef: J.-P. Michel

Garlic Flavoured Lamb

1 leg of lamb of 3.5 kg (7¾ lb)
100 ml (3 oz) olive oil
salt and pepper, to taste
20 cloves garlic, unpeeled
few sprigs thyme
50 g (1¾ oz) butter
2 tbsp water

Cut the lamb into slices of 300 g (10½ oz) each. Heat the olive oil in a pot. When the oil is hot, sauté the lamb well on each side over high heat. Season with salt and pepper. Add the unpeeled garlic, thyme, and butter. Let cook in pot at medium heat until the meat is slightly pink.

At the end of cooking, increase the heat and add 2 tbsp water. Cover for a moment, then serve.

Serves: 10

Fontvieille is the place where Daudet wrote *Lettres de mon Moulin*. It is the same *moulin* (mill) that J.-P. Michel transformed into an inn of excellent quality in 1967. **La Régalido**, as the name implies, offers a regal cuisine. J.-P. and his son will graciously welcome you to their comfortable inn and no doubt will serve you as impeccably as they did the Queen of England when she came to dinner. Their menu offers local dishes, such as Anise Flavoured Mussels and Snails, Gratin of Mussels with Spinach, Ventoux Thrush with Raisins, Angler Scallops with Puréed Leeks, Casserole of Sliced Leg of Mutton, Garlic Flavoured Lamb, plus many other classic items.

Le Vivarois

192, avenue Victor-Hugo, 75016 Paris
Tel: 504-0431
Proprietor/Chef: Claude Peyrot

You must ignore the unfinished dining room, the decorations that are still being coordinated, and an incomplete menu, because you will enjoy dining at **Le Vivarois**. The chef, Claude Peyrot, has *carte blanche* here because he is also the owner. Trust him; he will choose for you the best he offers. The decor of Le Vivarois might be incomplete but the cuisine is not. If you enjoy natural and fresh treats, then try the Oysters Curry and the Clams en Vessie; they are both excellent, as are the Lamb Blanquettes, a hearty and delicious surprise.

Le Vivarois has received numerous accolades and proves it deserves them each time a dinner is prepared and served. For those who enjoy delicacy and fabulous gourmet dishes, Le Vivarois will accommodate you.

Lamb Blanquettes

1 shoulder of lamb of 2 kg (4½ lb)
4 mutton feet (or calves feet), blanched
500 g (1 lb) onions
5 cloves garlic
500 g (1 lb) carrots
1 bouquet garni*
200 ml (6 oz) double cream (whipping cream)
1 egg yolk
2 tbsp Dijon mustard
salt and pepper, to taste

Remove the fat and cut the shoulder of lamb into stew meat sized pieces, then blanch them. Put mutton feet in a pan with the pieces of lamb and the onions (pierced with the garlic cloves), carrots, and bouquet garni. Simmer about 1 hour or until meat is tender. Remove the meat from the pan, but keep warm.

Reduce the remaining liquid, whisk in the cream, then mix in the egg yolk and mustard. Adjust the seasoning to taste.

Suggestion: Put the preparation on a platter and serve with green beans or green kidney beans.

Serves: 6

Le Grand Véfour

17, rue de Beaujolais, 75001 Paris
Tel: 296-5627
Proprietor: Raymond Oliver • Chef: Yves Labrousse

Raymond Oliver, truly a master of great cuisine, a giant among chefs, is held in great esteem by the many chefs whom he has taught. M. Oliver is too great for anything less than outstanding surroundings, which is why he chose **Le Grand Véfour**. One cannot describe Le Grand Véfour easily. It dates from 1760 and is situated in the gardens of the Palais-Royal, so loved by Louis XIV as a child. Jean Véfour was the proprietor around 1810 and made it fit for a restaurant. Here, the most illustrious of visitors were attracted: Brillat-Savarin, Cambacérès, Balzac, Jean Cocteau, Colette, etc. Le Grand Véfour reflects the ultimate in fine dining, not only because of its stately decor and fine food, but because of the genius of Raymond Oliver.

Lamb Chops à l'Albarine

12 thick lamb chops, suitable for stuffing
salt and pepper, to taste
150 g (5¼ oz) veal kidneys
125 g (¼ lb) butter
125 g (¼ lb) goose liver, sliced
200 g (7 oz) pork fat
125 g (¼ lb) flour
2 onions, finely chopped
200 ml (6 oz) dry white wine
½ litre (1 pt) double cream (whipping cream)

Pare the lamb chops and reserve the bones. Make an incision into the thickness of the meat to create a cavity. Season the lamb with salt and pepper. Sauté the kidneys in ½ the butter. Fill the openings in the lamb with the kidneys and slices of goose liver. Close the chops, coat them with pork fat, dust them in flour, and fry them in a skillet for 8 minutes. Remove from heat and keep warm.

To prepare Smitane sauce: Sauté the finely chopped onions in the remaining butter. Add dry white wine and reduce. Add cream and cook over low heat for 15 minutes.

Season the sauce to taste, then pass through a very fine strainer. Serve the sauce with the stuffed lamb chops.

Wine: *Saint-Estephe*   Serves: 10-12

Le Crocodile

10, rue de l'Outre, 67000 Strasbourg
Tel: (88) 32-13-02
Proprietor/Chef: Emile Jung

Lamb Gâteau with Tomatoes and Artichokes

200 g (7 oz) chicken breasts, skinned and boned
125 ml (½ cup) double cream (whipping cream)
3 eggs
butter, as needed
400 g (14 oz) leg of lamb
150 g (5 oz) roughly chopped tomatoes
2 artichoke hearts, cubed
200 g (7 oz) veal stock*

To prepare chicken mousse: Purée the raw chicken breasts, cream, and eggs together in a food processor. Refrigerate.

Cut the lamb into cubes and sauté in butter. Remove when the cubes are still rare. Cool the lamb. Fill 6 moulds with the chopped tomatoes, cubes of lamb, and the artichoke hearts.

Simmer the veal stock and 3 tbsp butter together in a pan. Pour 1 tbsp of this mixture into each mould. Top each mould with 1 layer of mousse.

Poach the moulds in a bain-marie* in the oven for 25 minutes at 265°F (130°C). Unmould and serve.

Wine: *Pinot Noir d'Alsace or Pouillac*   Serves: 6

For the past century and a half, **Le Crocodile** has been a celebrated trademark of the cuisine from Alsace. For the last ten years, M. and Mme. Emile Jung have managed this old pub, which they have transformed into an elegant, coquettish, fresh, and flowered restaurant. "All this is my inspiration for working," says the chef, who is a prime example of discretion and modesty. The menu reminds us that we are in Strasbourg, with its *foies gras,* Frog Soup, Lamb Gâteau with Tomatoes and Artichokes, Fish Stew, Gosling with Sauerkraut, and game in season. These are only some of the specialities, however there are many others, all with the sublime sauces that mark a great chef. All is done to perfection, even the service under the supervision of Monique Jong.

Pierre Traiteur

10, rue de Richelieu, 75001 Paris
Tel: 296-0917
Proprietor: Guy Nouyrigat • Chef: M. Faucheux

Lamb Stuffed with Grapes

450 g (1 lb) lean pork
350 g (¾ lb) pork fat
80 g (2¾ oz) bread, soaked in milk
parsley, as needed
1 chopped onion
3 eggs
200 g (7 oz) Smyrne grapes or French prune plums
1 pinch salt
1 pinch pepper
1 pinch nutmeg
1.7 kg (3¾ lb) lamb breast or brisket

To prepare the stuffing: Grind the pork, pork fat, bread, parsley, and onion together. Mix in the 3 eggs. Add the grapes, salt, pepper, and nutmeg, and mix together well.

Take the bones out of the breast of lamb. Sew one side to the other with the skin on the inside, but leave an opening. Fill the opening in the lamb with the stuffing and complete sewing the lamb shut. Roast in an ovenproof casserole in the oven for 1½ hours at 325°F (160°C) and serve.

Serves: 8

The Nouyrigats established themselves at Palais Royal in the late forties and, after 35 years, have remained in the same neighbourhood. Today, Guy, their son, is in charge of the business and serves many of his parents' clients.

The tradition and cuisine haven't changed, which explains why, for years now, the regulars always come back for the Stewed Meat or Fish, Lamb Stuffed with Grapes, Beef "Ficelle Ménagère," Black Pudding Biscuits, Snow Eggs, etc. They can count on the wines and the cuisine being up to their usual high standards.

Pierre Traiteur is the place where Parisians dine when they want to be alone and unnoticed and still have an excellent dinner.

La Réserve

Avenue du Bourgailh, 33600 Pessac
Tel: (56) 45-13-28
Proprietors: R. and C. Flourens • Chef: J. Aguirre

Lamb with Cèpe Mushroom Sauce

750 g (1½ lb) noisettes of lamb (round, thick fillets from the rib or loin)
salt and pepper, to taste
2 tbsp oil
500 g (1 lb) fresh cèpe (boletus) mushrooms, sliced
2 tbsp double cream (whipping cream)

Trim and slightly flatten the noisettes, season to taste, and sauté in hot oil in a skillet for 2-3 minutes per side. Place the noisettes around the edge of a serving plate and keep warm.

In a skillet, sweat* the sliced mushrooms. Add the cream and reduce to ½ the original amount.

Place the mushrooms covered with sauce in the middle of the serving plate surrounded with the lamb and serve.

Serves: 2

Pessac is the doorway to Bordeaux. It is also the site of **La Réserve**, with its elegant dining rooms filled with lush greenery and tiny lamps that softly illuminate the beautiful orange decor, fine porcelain dishes, and crystal glasses.

Chef Aguirre has specialised in, and mastered, authentic traditional cuisine. Try the Garbour Landaise (a cabbage, ham, bacon, and pickled goose soup), Chicken in Graves Wine, Lamprey à la Bordelaise, Lamb with Cèpe Mushroom Sauce, and Foie Gras with Honey or Raisins; they are all sumptuous dishes. Choose a Bordeaux to enhance your meal; Michel Betzer would like your opinion on it since he makes the selections for the wine cellar.

Trianon Palace

1, boulevard de la Reine, 78000 Versailles
Tel: 950-3412
Proprietor: J.-P. Marcus • Chef: Alain Bayle

Lamb with Thyme Flowers

2 kg (4½ lb) saddle* of lamb, bone removed
salt and pepper, to taste
300 g (10½ oz) clarified butter
125 g (¼ lb) shallots, sliced
20 g (¾ oz) thyme flowers
250 ml (1 cup) double cream (whipping cream)
100 ml (3 oz) veal stock*

Remove the fillets from the meat and cut into 24 rounds of 60 g (2 oz) each (4 per person). Add salt and pepper and sauté on high heat for 2-3 minutes per side in butter. Remove the lamb, then add shallots. Let sweat* a little, then add the thyme, cream, and the veal stock. Reduce until thick. Serve the lamb on a hot plate coated with the sauce.

Suggestion: Serve with green beans, cooked in butter, and carrots and turnips.

Wine: *Graves red wine, Pierre Coste, 1979*

Serves: 6

Versailles! Here are the "Trianons" of Marie Antoinette, of course, but also this **Trianon Palace**, which is almost as rich in history. (Was it not here on May 7, 1919, that Clémenceau, in the presence of Lloyd George and Woodrow Wilson, laid down the terms for a peace treaty to the German delegation? And did not General Eisenhower stay here from September 1944 until March 1945?)

In this very beautiful hotel, in the midst of an aristocratic garden and just a few steps away from the park and Trianons of the Queen, Alain Bayle gives of his best and adds his own creations to classical dishes. Turbot in Honey and Orange, Lamb with Thyme Flowers, and Fricassee of Poultry with Green Tomatoes are examples.

L'Oursinade

Rue Neuve-Saint-Martin, 13001 Marseilles
Tel: (91) 91-91-29
Proprietor: Frantel • Chef: René Allion

In the heart of the Marseilles we have **L'Oursinade**, *clef d'or* (the golden key) of French gastronomy. Inspired by many great cooks, René Allion never hesitates to use dishes from far away places. He specialises in cooking with exotic spices and herbs which give his dishes a most unique taste and savoury fragrance.

Dining at L'Oursinade is a peacefully enjoyable treat. You can feel the delicate ocean breeze as you look out over the old port of Marseilles. You will love the Scorpion Fish Mousse with Pistachio covered in sauce and the Mutton Feet with Basil and Anchovies.

Mutton Feet with Basil and Anchovies

24 mutton feet (calves feet)
3 litres (6 pt) bouillon
500 g (1 lb) carrots, sliced
300 g (10½ oz) white mushrooms
500 g (1 lb) celery, sliced
500 g (1 lb) turnips, sliced
200 g (7 oz) butter
100 ml (3 oz) cognac
200 ml (6 oz) Madeira wine
¼ litre (1 cup) double cream (whipping cream)
¼ litre (1 cup) veal stock*
125 g (¼ lb) anchovies, puréed
10 g (⅓ oz) basil, chopped
whole basil, to garnish

Cook the mutton feet in the bouillon until tender. Once the feet are cooked, remove the bones and cut the meat into cubes. Stew the carrots, mushrooms, celery, and turnips in a little water until tender but crisp. In butter, stew the mutton cubes. Flame the cubes with cognac, then with Madeira wine. Add cream, veal stock, anchovy purée, and chopped basil.

To serve: Add the stewed vegetables to the mutton cubes, garnish with whole basil, and serve immediately.

Wine: *Château Vignelaure, 1978*   Serves: 12

Abbaye de Sainte-Croix

Route du Val de Cuech, 13300 Salon-de-Provence
Tel: (90) 56-24-55
Proprietor/Chef: Jean-Pierre Cario

In the valley of Cuech near Provence, with its beautiful panoramic view, we have another ancient abbey. This one dates from the 12th century. It has been intelligently and richly transformed into a comfortable and beautiful inn.

At the **Abbaye de Sainte-Croix**, you will enjoy a peaceful solitude, interrupted only by the singing birds, that is most conducive to relaxing and dining. The dinners are carefully prepared and elegantly served. Specialities are Mutton Stew, Anglerfish Flan, Lamb Stew, and the simple braised or grilled fish and meats, all served with fine regional wines. Dine with candlelight and relax in this tranquil medieval building.

Mutton Stew

60 ml (¼ cup) oil
60 ml (¼ cup) vinegar
120 ml (½ cup) dry red wine
salt, pepper, coriander, and rosemary, to taste
4 kg (8¾ lb) leg of mutton, cubed
2.5 kg (5½ lb) shoulder of mutton, cubed
250 g (1½ lb) onions, sliced

4 shallots
200 ml (6 oz) oil
100 ml (3 oz) champagne
1 calf's foot, blanched and cubed
1 pinch paprika
1 garlic clove, crushed
stewed tomatoes, to taste
300 g (10½ oz) blanched lard
200 g (7 oz) mushrooms

To prepare the marinade: Mix the first 3 ingredients together and season to taste with salt, pepper, coriander, and rosemary. Marinate the cubed leg and shoulder of mutton for 1 week, then drain the meat and reserve the marinade. Gently sauté the onions and shallots. Sauté the meat in extremely hot oil in a pan, then add meat to the pan containing the onions and shallots. Flame the meat with champagne. Wet the meat with the reserved marinade, then add the cubed calf's foot, paprika, crushed garlic, and tomatoes. Cook slowly in the oven at 175°F (80°C) for about 1 hour or until meat is tender. (You may baste the meat with some lard.) Take the meat out of the oven, strain the sauce, and let cool. Add mushrooms, blanched lard, sautéed shallots and sautéed onions. (This mixture should look like brown gelatine.) Pour the sauce over the meat and serve very hot.

Suggestion: Serve with noodles.

Wine: *Châteauneuf du Pape*   Serves: 12

Relais de la Poste

14220 Thury-Harcourt
Tel: (31) 79-72-12
Proprietor/Chef: Jean Mouge

Thury-Harcourt, the doorway to Normandy, is a city of quaint charm and the site of **Relais de la Poste**, an adorable restaurant-hotel that was created by Jean Mouge. Jean is assisted by his wife, who has been under his tutelage for more than 10 years. Together, they prepare a marvellous Angler and Morel Casserole, Brill with Leeks, Noisettes of Lamb "Normandy" Style, and for desserts, fresh fruits, sorbets (sherbets), and their famous Agen Plums with Lime Juice.

The rooms here are comfortable, and the walk in the Valley d'Orne, passing by the church and the chateau, is very pleasant. A few miles away you can enjoy the pleasures of the sea.

Noisettes of Lamb "Normandy" Style

8 medium-sized loin lamb chops, boned
6 tbsp butter
2 kg (4½ lb) lamb and veal bones, chopped
1 carrot, quartered
1 onion, quartered
1 litre (2 pt) cold water
1 bouquet garni*
100 ml (3 oz) cider
2 tbsp double cream (whipping cream)
20 ml (½ oz) Calvados
salt and pepper, to taste

Sauté the lamb until medium rare in 4 tbsp butter over brisk heat. (Turn them halfway through cooking.) Set on a platter and keep warm.

To prepare the stock: Roast the bones, carrot, and onion until brown, turning occasionally. Place in a saucepan with water and bouquet garni. Cover and cook 2 hours, skimming frequently. Allow to reduce by ⅔, then strain.

To prepare the sauce: Remove excess fat from the lamb cooking pan and deglaze with cider. Reduce until nearly dry. Add the stock and add cream. Bring to a boil, add Calvados, and correct the seasoning with salt and pepper. Nap* the lamb with sauce and serve.

Suggestion: Serve with caramelised baked apple quarters.

Serves: 4

La Réserve

91, boulevard de la Plage, 06170 Cros-de-Cagnes
Tel: (93) 31-00-17
Proprietor/Chef: Loulou Bertho

Cagnes is a vacation city with beaches, open air theatres, and Loulou Bertho. The creative intelligence of Loulou makes **La Réserve** one of the best places for dining in the area. Loulou has been preparing delicious dinners for the past 25 years. He has a special rapport with all of his customers, who, for the most part, have become his friends.

Loulou has a fresh selection of fish every day and a special dish for each day. He also owns an authentic bakers oven in which he prepares his delicious hot apple tarts that are served generously covered with his own chantilly cream. His Rack of Lamb is always a favourite item on the menu.

Rack of Lamb

6 medium-sized potatoes, sliced
100 ml (3 oz) water
salt and pepper, to taste
1 tbsp thyme, chopped
1 tbsp rosemary, chopped
1 tbsp crushed bay leaf
1 tbsp savory, chopped
4 racks of lamb, 300 g (10½ oz) each

Line a roasting pan with aluminum foil. Spread the slices of potato in the pan and add the water, salt, and pepper. Sprinkle lightly with ½ the herbs and place the racks of lamb on top. Sprinkle with the remaining herbs.

Bake in the oven for ½ hour at 500-550°F (250-290°C). Turn over twice during cooking. Separate the lamb from the potatoes. Spread the potatoes on a platter, top with meat, and serve.

Wine: *St. Émilion or Bellet Rouge*

Serves: 4

Hostellerie du Grand Saint-Antoine

17, rue Saint-Antoine, 81000 Albi
Tel: (63) 54-04-04
Proprietor: Jacques Rieux • Chef: Francis Combes

Roast Leg of Lamb with Juniper Berries

1 leg of lamb of 1.4 kg (3 lb)
100 ml (3 oz) juniper berries
125 g (¼ lb) bacon fat

Make small incisions in the leg of lamb and push the juniper berries into these. Let rest for 2 days.

Roast the lamb on a roasting spit. Baste it with bacon fat and turn it frequently. Roast until pink.

Crush the juniper berries into the pan juices and mix to make a gravy.

Serve the lamb with gravy.

Serves: 4

Albi is an old city that also houses the famous Toulouse-Lautrec Museum. The Hostellerie Saint-Antoine was founded in 1734. At that time, the chef was serving cabbage soup with bacon bits, and Francis Combe still serves it that way today. The Hostellerie Saint-Antoine is an institution in Alby, and Jacques Rieux manages it with complete success.

Because this hotel and its restaurant have been in the business of serving people for so many years, naturally they have accumulated a nice collection of signatures on their guest register: Juarez, Pompidou, Paul Emile Victor, Calder, and Pierre Benoit, to name just a few. The restaurant's cuisine will satisfy even the most delicate gourmand.

Auberge de la Belle Route

R.N. 202, 06670 Saint-Martin-du-Var
Tel: (93) 08-10-65
Proprietor/Chef: Jean-François Issautier

Rump of Lamb with Glazed Vegetables

500 g (1 lb) small onions
800 g (1¾ lb) yellow carrots, julienne
3 small artichokes, trimmed
  and quartered
olive oil, to sauté
salt, to taste
1 bay leaf
3 cloves garlic
800 g (1¾ lb) courgettes
  (zucchini), trimmed
3 rumps of lamb, 300 g (10½ oz) each

100 ml (3 oz) oil
125 g (¼ lb) butter, and as needed
freshly ground pepper and nutmeg,
  to taste
1 shallot, finely chopped
100 ml (3 oz) dry white wine
100 ml (3 oz) wine vinegar
300 ml (9 oz) meat gravey
1 basil leaf, crushed
2 tomatoes, concasse*

Brown the onions, carrots, and artichokes in hot olive oil. Put vegetables in a pot with salt, bay leaf, and 1 clove garlic, and add enough water to cover all. Cook until liquid is almost evaporated. Add courgettes and cook until liquid is gone.

Put rumps of lamb into a casserole with oil and 125 g (¼ lb) butter. Season with salt, pepper, and nutmeg. Roast in the oven at 400°F (205°C), basting frequently, for about 15 minutes. Remove the lamb and keep warm. Remove excess fat from pan, add a small piece of butter, and sweat* the shallots in this. Deglaze with wine and vinegar. Add meat gravy and reduce to sauce consistency. Add 2 crushed garlic cloves, basil, and tomatoes at the last minute. Carve lamb into thin slices, arrange the vegetables around them, and pour the sauce over.

Wine: *Rouge or Rosé de Provence*

Serves: 6

Saint-Martin-du-Var (27 kilometres from Nice) is a small village set amongst hills and cliffs. It is here that Jean-François Issautier, a young man, cooks with love and intelligence.

The Sorrel Salad, Lobster with Tarragon, Roast Lamb with Glazed Vegetables, Lamb with Pistou (a thick Italian soup with vegetables and vermicelli), grilled meats, and the wide variety of desserts are all excellent.

The atmosphere here is nostalgic and the service is most attentive. This really is the **Auberge de la Belle Route** because it leads to a most beautiful place — Nice.

La Marée

1, rue Daru, 75008 Paris
Tel: 763-5242 and 227-5932
Proprietor: Marcel Trompier • Chef: M. Rouillard

Saddle of Lamb in Crust

600 g (1⅓ lb) meat from 2 saddles* of lamb, ½ the panoufle
  (underpart of the top of the saddle), reserved
1 handful of herbs from Provence: savory, thyme, and ½ bay leaf
oil, to sauté
400 g (14 oz) puff pastry dough*
1 sprig tarragon

Sprinkle the inside of the meat with the herbs. Roll them into cigar shapes and sew together. Sauté in oil in a skillet for 5 minutes, then let cool. Roll out the dough into 2 round circles. Put the meat between them, and seal the ends well. Decorate the dough using a knife.

Bake the preparation in the oven at 400°F (205°C) for 15 minutes (for rare) or 20 minutes (for lightly pink).

Gently heat the reserved ½ of the panoufle to release its juices (about 15 minutes). Skim the grease from the juice and add the tarragon, but do not stir.

Serve the lamb on a plate with the second preparation served separately.

Wine: *Pauillac*   Serves: 2

As the son and grandson of wine growers, it is no surprise that Marcel Trompier developed a passion for wine. What better way is there to enjoy your passion than by serving it? So Marcel became a restaurateur and master of fine wines. He first opened Anne de Beaujeu (named after the patron saint of Beaujolais) in Paris, then in 1963, he created **La Marée**. La Marée is a dining room of elegance, an ambiance reminiscent of the 18th century with Flemish tapestries on the wall and hand-painted china.

The dishes are perfect examples of traditional cuisine. Saddle of Lamb in Crust and Heavenly Fish, are just two of the famous dishes. The cuisine of Chef Rouillard is exactly correct, neither too conservative nor too modern.

La Petite Alsace

4, rue Taine, 75012 Paris
Tel: 343-2180
Proprietor/Chef: M. Rosenblatt

Baeckoffe

500 g (1 lb) neck of beef (chuck)
200 g (7 oz) chine of pork (spare ribs or pork loin chops)
500 - 700 g (1 - 1½ lb) shoulder of lamb
1.2 kg (2½ lb) bacon
2 litres (½ gal) Riesling wine
1.2 kg (2½ lb) onions, sliced
salt and crushed peppercorns, to taste
800 g (1¾ lb) white of leeks, sliced
1 bouquet garni*
butter or oil, to sauté
3 kg (6½ lb) potatoes
400 g (14 oz) flour
100 ml (3 oz) water

Marinate the first 4 ingredients for 24 - 48 hours in a marinade made by combining the wine, sliced onions, salt, crushed peppercorns, white of leeks, and bouquet garni. Drain and reserve the marinade.

Separate the meats from the onions and whites of leeks. Sauté the onions and leeks until lightly gold in colour; drain. Wash, peel, and slice the potatoes into 80 mm (3¼ in) strips.

In the bottom of a terrine, spread half of the potatoes, onions, and the whites of the leeks, then spread the meats on top. Cover with the remaining onions, leeks, and potatoes. Wet the preparation with the reserved marinade and close the terrine. Seal the lid with a paste made by mixing the flour and water together. Cook in the oven for 3 hours at 300°F (150°C).

Wine: *Riesling*   Serves: 8

Most often Alsatian cuisine brings to mind choucroute (sauerkraut) because it's the most popular speciality of that region. In the 12th *arrondissement* (district) in Paris you will find a little piece of Alsace. In **La Petite Alsace**, with its personnel dressed in red, its textured walls, and its chandeliers, you will find authentic choucroute and much more. Since 1965, when he opened this restaurant, M. Rosenblatt has not been satisfied with merely serving choucroute, therefore, he presents a well-rounded cuisine, characteristic of Alsace, with dishes such as Smoked Trout, Vol-au-Vent (puff pie), Chicken with Riesling, Tarts with Leeks or Onions, and Baeckoffe, a dish combining beef, pork, and mutton.

Château d'Artigny

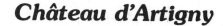

Montbazon, 37250 Veigne
Tel: (47) 26-24-24
Proprietor: Alain Rabier • Chef: Jacques Niqueux

Château d'Artigny is a dream. It is one of many chateaux in Touraine, but it is not like the others. This chateau was built after World War II in the image of the *Grand Siècle* (grand century), as if the proprietors were expecting they would one day be welcoming the Queen of England and other illustrious people. Reigning over these multicoloured marble columns and stones, is Alain Rabier who, along with his team headed by Jacques Niqueux, the chef, has created a "Palace of 1001 Nights." Everything on the menu (the wines, entrées, desserts, coffees, teas, and eaux-de-vie) is there to tempt you. Here, you will eat as well as you might in other fine restaurants, but this chateau offers an ambiance that you might not find elsewhere.

Pot-au-Feu "Touraine" Style

1 chicken of 1.4 kg (3 lb)
1 calf's tongue
800 g (1¾ lb) veal sweetbreads
1 oxtail cut into 8 pieces
300 g (10½ oz) chicken wings
500 g (1 lb) fillet of beef
  (tenderloin), cubed
500 g (1 lb) fillet of veal, cubed
1 chicken gizzard
250 g (½ lb) bone marrow, cut in slices
juice of 2 lemons
300 g (10½ oz) peeled carrots
300 g (10½ oz) peeled turnips
300 g (10½ oz) peeled rutabaga

300 g (10½ oz) celeriac (celery root)
8 small leeks
1 large onion
300 g (10½ oz) small onions
250 g (½ lb) green beans
1 head green cabbage
4 tomatoes, peeled, seeded, and
  squeezed into balls
600 g (1⅓ lb) truffled pork sausage
125 g (¼ lb) morel mushrooms
30 g (1 oz) salt
10 peppercorns
2 cloves
1 bouquet garni*

Place the first 10 ingredients in a bowl of water and ice and leave for 2 hours. Cut the carrots, turnips, rutabaga, celeriac, and leeks into oval shapes. Blanch *all* the vegetables. (Do not blanch tomatoes or mushrooms.) Place the ingredients from the bowl of water in a large pot of boiling water (enough to cover all). Bring back to a boil, skimming frequently. Add the blanched vegetables to that pot, starting with those that need the most cooking. Let the contents simmer for about 2 hours. Halfway through the cooking time, add the remaining ingredients (tomatoes, pork sausage, etc.). Check the seasoning just before the cooking time is up. Arrange the meats around the chicken on a platter with the vegetables surrounding all. Serve.

Wine: *Gamay de Touraine Mesland, 1976*   Serves: 8-10

La Bourgogne

6, avenue Bosquet, 75007 Paris
Tel: 705-9678
Proprietors: Christian and Jean-François Julien • Chefs: Christian Julien, Jean-Jacques Mothe

There is an obligation that comes with naming a restaurant "La Bourgogne," for "Burgundy" implies that one will eat wholesome, hearty dishes that will accompany the marvellous Burgundy wines. This restaurant meets that requirement.

Created by Robert Monassier in 1947, **La Bourgogne** was saved from oblivion by Christian Julien in 1980. He manages it with his family and is assisted by Jean-Jacques Mothe in the kitchen. The decor is neat, cosy, and impeccable, and you may eat a few things here that aren't very common anymore: Pork with Parsley in Stuffed Cabbage, Chicken in Chambertin with Morels, Stewed Beef with Pasta, and Truffled Chicken, and all are accompanied by Burgundy wine, of course.

Stuffed Cabbage "Burgundy" Style

3 green cabbages, blanched in
  salted water
600 g (1⅓ lb) breast of veal
600 g (1⅓ lb) chine of pork
  (spare ribs or pork loin chops)
600 g (1⅓ lb) hindquarters of rabbit
flour, to dust
125 g (¼ lb) butter
300 ml (9 oz) oil
200 ml (6 oz) truffle juice
500 g (1 lb) small onions
500 g (1 lb) carrots

1 bouquet garni*
6 shallots, coarsely chopped
2 garlic cloves, coarsely chopped
1 bunch parsley, coarsely chopped
3 tbsp double cream
  (whipping cream)
3 eggs
1 tbsp flour
salt and pepper, to taste
pinch of nutmeg
3 cubes of bacon
3 strips of pork fat

Gently spread out each cabbage leaf to flatten the cabbages. Remove bones from all meats. Cut meats into small pieces, flour them and brown them in butter and oil. Moisten with some truffle juice; add onions, carrots, and bouquet garni. Simmer gently 30-40 minutes.

Mince the meats coarsely with shallots, garlic, and parsley. Arrange in a mound with a well in the centre. Put cream, eggs, flour, remaining truffle juice, salt, pepper, and nutmeg in the centre. Mix well. Form this stuffing into balls and place on centre of each cabbage leaf. Reform each cabbage, pressing hard. Spread a layer of stuffing on the outsides and finish shaping. Place a cube of bacon on each cabbage. Wrap each cabbage in a strip of pork fat; squeeze each cabbage in a cloth and tie with string. Arrange cabbages in a casserole surrounded by cooked carrots and onions. Bake at 300°F (150°C) for 1-1½ hours. Remove the cloth and string and serve.

Wine: *Burgundy*   Serves: 8

La Tassée

20, rue de la Charité, 69002 Lyon
Tel: (7) 837-0235
Proprietor: Roger Borgeot • Chef: Jean-Paul Borgeot

Black Pudding (Blood Sausage) with Apples

500 g (1 lb) puff pastry dough*
125 g (¼ lb) minced shallots
150 g (5¼ oz) butter
300 ml (9 oz) white wine
300 ml (9 oz) double cream (whipping cream)
450 g (1 lb) boudin noir (black pudding or blood sausage)
5 apples, peeled, cored, and diced
3 pinches of minced chervil

Roll out the dough and cut it into 4 sheets, 15 cm (6 in) long by 5 cm (2 in) wide. Fold each sheet over once to make a pocket. Seal edges. Bake them in an oven at 425°F (220°C) for 10 minutes or until they puff up.

To prepare the sauce: Simmer the shallots in some of the butter, wet them with white wine, and reduce by half. Add the cream and let simmer for a few minutes.

Sauté the boudin noir with the apples. Take the pastry out of the oven. Open each pocket and fill with the apples. Place the boudin noir over the apples, then close pockets. Add the remaining butter mixture to the sauce, adjust seasoning and add chervil. Cover pockets with sauce and serve.

Wine: *Vin Blanc de Condrieu or Givry Blanc*   Serves: 4

Roger Borgeot, one of the best sommeliers in France and a devoted Beaujolais drinker, opened **La Tassée** in Lyon. He welcomes his friends to this tavern, which also serves some of the finest cuisine found in this city. Jean-Paul, his son, prepares gastronomic delights such as Tripe, Hot Salami, and Lion's Tooth Salad (dandelions, herring, and hard-boiled eggs), Black Pudding with Apples, Duck with Peaches, and Medallions of Angler with Sorrel; they are all gourmet pleasers.

La Tassée is the place to come for a crowd, a superb wine cellar, fabulous service, and excellent food.

Au Pied de Cochon

6, rue Coquilliere, 75001 Paris
Tel: 236-1175
Proprietor: Clément Blanc • Chef: Albert Jézéquel

Grilled Pigs Feet

4 pigs feet, front feet preferred
2 litres (½ gal) water
300 ml (9 oz) white wine
salt and pepper, to taste
1 bouquet garni*
1 pinch oregano
250 g (½ lb) lard
125 g (¼ lb) bread crumbs

Clean the pigs feet well and wrap them in a thin cloth. Place them in a metal pot with water and white wine flavoured with salt, pepper, bouquet garni, and oregano. Bring to a boil, simmer for 4 hours, then leave overnight off the heat. The next day, remove the pigs feet, unwrap, and dry them.

Grease the pigs feet with the lard. Spread them on a greased cooking sheet, cover with ½ the bread crumbs, and broil them. Once they are well browned, turn them over, cover the other side with bread crumbs, and grill again.

Suggestion: Serve the pigs feet with Béarnaise sauce,* French fries, and cress.

Serves: 4

Au Pied de Cochon is located near Les Halles, on one of the most exciting and tumultous streets in Paris. It is especially exciting at night when the lights dazzle you as they illuminate the city.

You should definitely stop in to dine at Clément Blanc's restaurant. He will treat you to many culinary delights. When dining in this Blanc family bastion, Grilled or Stuffed Pigs Feet is a must.

Chantecler (Négresco Hotel, Nice)

L'Oustau de Baumanière

La Tupina

Cazaudehore

1, avenue du Président-Kennedy, 78100 Saint-Germain-en-Laye
Tel: 973-3660
Proprietor: Pierre Cazaudehore • Chef: Jacques Rochard

Preserved Pork

4 pork fillets (tenderloin)
salt and crushed peppercorns, as needed
garlic, to taste
125 g (¼ lb) pork fat, and as needed

Salt the fillets of pork very well and pepper well with the crushed peppercorns. Stack the fillets on a cooking sheet and set aside for 24 hours.

Wipe the fillets with a cloth to remove all the salt. Tie groups of 4 fillets together with a thin string and insert some cloves of garlic.

Melt the pork fat and place the fillets in the grease. Cook them over low heat, moving them around in the pan occasionally, until done. Take the pan off the heat and put the fillets on a plate to cool.

Remove the grease from the pan the pork was cooked in and put this warm grease in a covered container. Immerse the fillets in this grease and seal the container. (Be sure there are no air bubbles.) The next day, put more grease on top of the fillets.

To serve: Take out the fillets whenever you desire (they are well preserved in the container) and cut them into slices. Serve them cold or hot.

Suggestion: Accompany with a green leaf salad with garlic or sautéed potatoes sprinkled with parsley and garlic.

In 1928, M. Cazaudehore, *homme de salle* in a great Parisian restaurant, was asked to build a cynodrome (greyhound racing track) and a refreshment stand. As it turned out, the cynodrome was never built, but the restaurant was, and it blossomed into a restaurant and hotel. Today, **Cazaudehore** dominates the thick forest of Saint-Germain, 15 minutes from Paris, and is run by M. Cazaudehore's son, Pierre, and Pierre's wife, Christine, a fine interior decorator. Their hotel-restaurant is the one stopping place outside of Paris that everyone knows about. Cazaudehore offers a menu specialising in the family's famous recipes and specialities from Béarn — all enticing. The wine cellar equals the very good cuisine.

Chez Françoise

Aérogare de Invalides, 75007 Paris
Tel: 705-4903
Proprietor: Guy Demessence • Chef: Marcel Vilaseca

Chez Françoise is an underground restaurant. In Paris, there seems to be a whole different world underground. Beneath the streets of Paris, you will find shops, boutiques, hair salons, cafés, and even restaurants. Here at Les Invalides, we have Chez Françoise, which was the first underground restaurant. It was created in 1949 by Turenne Rousseau. Amidst the noisy crowds and the metros coming and going, there is a unique ambiance at Chez Françoise that makes it worth stopping by to see. Since 1975, Guy Demessence has owned Chez Françoise. He has kept the original menu, but now he also offers a simple, yet robust, dinner at a low fixed price. The specialities include Black Pudding with Two Kinds of Apples, Rabbit in Sherry Wine Vinegar, and Pigs Feet.

Rabbit in Sherry Wine Vinegar

1 rabbit of 1.2 kg (2½ lb)
100 ml (3 oz) oil
1 large onion, sliced
1 carrot, sliced
2 cloves garlic
2 tbsp flour
150 ml (4½ oz) sherry wine vinegar
200 ml (6 oz) veal stock* or bouillon
1 bouquet garni*
salt and pepper, to taste
fine herbs or parsley, to garnish

Cut the rabbit the following way: 2 parts from each thigh, 2 from the back, 2 from the front legs, and cut the ribs in 2 — lengthwise. In a pot with some oil, sauté the rabbit pieces with the onion, carrot, and garlic until the rabbit is golden brown. Pour off the excess grease. Sprinkle the rabbit pieces with flour and, with a spatula, turn all the ingredients a few times. Pour in 100 ml (3 oz) of vinegar and add the veal stock or bouillon. Add the bouquet garni, salt, and pepper, and let simmer for 40 minutes. Remove rabbit pieces and keep warm.

Reduce the liquid to sauce consistency. Strain. Add remaining vinegar and boil once more for 1-2 minutes.

Pour the sauce over the rabbit, sprinkle with fine herbs or parsley, and serve.

Serves: 6

Les Trois Marches

Hôtel de "Gramont"
3, rue Colbert, 78000 Versailles
Tel: 950-1321
Proprietor/Chef: Gérard Vie

Roast Rabbit in Saupiquet Sauce

1 rabbit of 1.3 kg (2¾ lb), liver reserved
salt and pepper, to taste
1 clove garlic, crushed
250 ml (1 cup) wine vinegar
1 rabbit liver
1 egg yolk
250 ml (1 cup) olive oil

Season the rabbit with salt and pepper. Roast the rabbit in the oven at 450°F (230°C) for 30 minutes.

To prepare the sauce: Put the garlic and vinegar in a saucepan and reduce. While the vinegar is reducing, put the rabbit liver into a blender and purée. Add puréed liver, 1 egg yolk, olive oil, salt, and pepper to the vinegar mixture and mix to the consistency of mayonnaise.

Suggestion: Serve the rabbit with the sauce separately and accompanied by potatoes sautéed in butter.

Serves: 6

Versailles, a royal city, is deserving of a restaurant with royal elegance. After stays at Lucas-Carton, Lapérouse, the Plaza Athénée, and the Carlton Tower, Gérard Vie decided to open the royal and elegant **Trois Marches**. Today we find Gérard in an 18th century hotel facing the Château de Versailles.

M. Vie has decorated the restaurant with 14th century furniture and delicate paintings. Not only does Gérard have a refined taste for decorating, he also possesses a magnificent talent for preparing culinary delicacies. Everything here is superb: the entrées, salads, and desserts (such as the mousses, the chestnut ice cream, . . .). Even the coffees and teas are especially chosen for Gérard.

Les Maritonnes

71570 Romaneche-Thorins
Tel: (85) 35-51-70
Proprietor/Chef: Guy Fauvin

Saddle of Hare in Cream Sauce

1 saddle* of hare of 1 kg (2¼ lb)
1 carrot
2 shallots
1 sprig thyme
½ bay leaf
salt and pepper, to taste
1 tbsp mustard
⅓ litre (1½ cups) white wine
100 ml (3 oz) cognac
¼ litre (1 cup) double cream (whipping cream)
julienne truffles, to garnish

Pare the membrane from the back of the saddle. Chop the shallots and the carrot. Place them in a casserole or terrine just large enough to hold the saddle. Add the thyme, bay leaf, salt, pepper, and mustard. Put the saddle on top of these and pour the white wine over. Leave to marinate for 12 hours.

Drain the saddle. Simmer the marinade in a small saucepan 5 minutes or until it is no longer bitter. Brown the saddle in a shallow pan. Cover the pan and cook for 12-15 minutes. The saddle should be cooked medium to remain tender. Remove the saddle. Detach the meat from the bone and place on a serving dish.

Deglaze the pan with the cognac. Flame the cognac, then add 100 ml (3 oz) of the marinade. Reduce to a syrupy consistency. Add cream and allow to reduce to a creamy sauce consistency. Adjust the seasoning. Strain the sauce over the saddle, garnish with truffles, and serve.

Wine: *Côtes de Nuits or an old Burgundy*

Serves: 2

Located in the heart of the wine country, on five acres of land in a beautiful park-like garden, Guy Fauvin manages his family enterprise. Guy has been here since 1963. Prior to that he was an apprentice for his father and worked in Lyon.

Les Maritonnes features a few lovely rooms overlooking the vineyards, and downstairs you may dine in a rustic dining room, bright with sunshine.

The cuisine at Les Maritonnes is very *beaujolaise,* which means it's delicious. Featured are Saddle of Hare in Cream Sauce, Gratin of Sole "Newburg," Escalop of Turbot "Nantanaise," chicken from Bresse, and wine from Burgundy. Let Guy Fauvin orchestrate your meal.

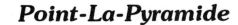

Point-La-Pyramide

Avenue Fernand-Point, 38200 Vienne
Tel: (74) 53-01-96
Proprietor: Mme. Point • Chef: Guy Thivard

When speaking of cuisine, one must speak of "Sacha" Guitry, otherwise known as Fernand Guitry, who opened this restaurant just after World War I. For years, **Point-La-Pyramide** has been instrumental in forming the talents of many now-famous chefs such as Bocuse and Alain Chapel. And now Guy Thivard is here, continuing the tradition.

There are prestigious dishes on the menu: Fresh Foie Gras Loaf, Veal Sweetbreads Feuilleté, Oysters in Champagne, Crayfish Tail Cassoulet, Saddle of Hare with Grapes, Ragout of Squab from Bresse, Gratin Dauphinois, Green Beans and Grey Chanterelle Mushrooms, appetising cheeses, sweet marjoram, gâteaux, fruits, ices . . . It's hard to decide what to order.

Saddle of Hare with Grapes

1 saddle* of hare of 4 kg (8¾ lb)
100 ml (3 oz) red wine
100 ml (3 oz) wine vinegar
1 onion, chopped
2 carrots, chopped
1 sprig thyme
200 g (7 oz) lard, cut in thin strips
salt and pepper, to taste
70 ml (2 oz) cognac
100 ml (3 oz) double cream (whipping cream)
1 tbsp butter
peeled and seeded white grapes, to garnish

Pare the membrane from the saddle and marinate the saddle for 2 days in a mixture of red wine, vinegar, onion, carrots, and thyme.

Insert a strip of lard through the surface of the meat using a larding needle, ice pick, or thin knife. Roast the saddle in the oven at 400°F (205°C) for 15-20 minutes. Remove the saddle and keep hot.

To prepare the sauce: Remove the fat from the roasting pan and deglaze it with the cognac and the marinade. Reduce to a syrupy consistency. Add the cream. Boil and remove from the heat. Whisk in the butter and adjust the seasoning.

Pour the sauce over the saddle, garnish it with the peeled and seeded grapes, and serve.

Serves: 6

Les Frères Runel

27, rue Maguelone, 34000 Montpellier
Tel: (67) 58-43-82
Proprietor/Chef: Georges Runel

Since 1933, **Les Frères Runel** has been a landmark for a gourmet cuisine. This is not a grand, luxurious restaurant, but rather, it is a large dining room with warm colours. Mme. Runel's warm greeting makes up for whatever, if anything, may be missing.

Her son helps her husband in the kitchen and together they prepare an admirable Saddle of Hare with Saupiquet Sauce, a remarkable *foie gras*, Gratin of Sole and Langoustines, and beautiful desserts. The wine cellar is rich in fine bottles. The cuisine here is classic and delicately prepared, and you will be served with style.

Saddle of Hare with Saupiquet Sauce

2 hares, 2 kg (4½ lb) each, blood drained and reserved
salt and pepper, to taste
175 g (6 oz) lard
150 g (5¼ oz) Prosciutto ham
250 g (½ lb) onions, chopped
3 cloves garlic
200 ml (6 oz) wine vinegar
½ litre (1 pt) red wine
1 bouquet garni*

Cut the saddles* from the hares (remove head, legs, ribs, and tail). Trim them and remove the membrane with a sharp knife. Season with salt and pepper. Chop the livers and kidneys and reserve. Place the saddles in a roasting pan with 125 g (¼ lb) lard. Roast in the oven at 450°F (230°C) for 10 minutes (rare), 15 minutes (medium rare), or 20 minutes (medium).

To prepare Saupiquet sauce: Sauté the ham, onions, garlic, kidneys, and livers in the remaining lard until the onions brown slightly. Deglaze with vinegar and reduce to ½. Add the wine and bouquet garni and simmer for 20 minutes. Purée the mixture in a blender, then bring to a boil. Remove the pan from the heat and stir in the blood. The sauce should thicken. If not, place the pan over the heat for a few seconds and stir, but do not allow sauce to approach the boiling point or the blood will coagulate. Adjust the seasoning.

Remove the hare from the oven, slice the meat, cover with Saupiquet sauce, and serve.

Wine: *An old Châteauneuf du Pape*

Serves: 12

Pujol

21, avenue Général-Compans, 31700 Blagnac
Tel: (61) 71-13-58
Proprietor/Chef: Marcelin Pujol

Saddle of Hare with Saupiquet Sauce "Pujol" Style

1 hare of 1.5 kg (3⅓ lb)
1 large onion, sliced
1 carrot, chopped
3 - 4 crushed garlic cloves
1 bouquet garni*
60 ml (¼ cup) oil
60 ml (¼ cup) vinegar
120 ml (½ cup) dry red wine
150 g (5¼ oz) onions

50 g (1¾ oz) flour
50 g (1¾ oz) garlic, sliced
1 bouquet garni*
2 litres (½ gal) red wine
50 g (1¾ oz) onions, chopped
crushed peppercorns, as needed
50 ml (1½ oz) vinegar
50 ml (1½ oz) white wine

Remove the saddle* from the hare. Pare it completely; reserve bones, liver, trimmings, and blood, (purée the liver). Stir the next 7 ingredients together to make a marinade. Place the salad in a casserole, cover it with the marinade, and leave it to marinate for 2 - 3 days. Remember to turn it regularly.

To prepare the game sauce: Brown the bones, trimmings, and 150 g (5¼ oz) onions and sliced carrots. Sprinkle with flour and toss a few times. Add the garlic, bouquet garni, and red wine. Bring to a boil, then cook in the oven at 300°F (150°C) for 2 hours. Strain.

Drain the saddle. Sauté it over high heat, but do not cook it more than rare. Remove the saddle and keep hot. Pour off the fat from the pan. Add the chopped onion and a few crushed peppercorns. Deglaze with the vinegar and white wine. Let this reduce to ¼ of its original volume. Pour in the strained game sauce. Reduce to the desired amount and adjust the seasoning. Thicken the sauce with the puréed liver and the blood. Serve the saddle with sauce on the side.

Wine: *A Pomerol or a Pommard*   Serves: 6

La Ciboulette

141, rue Saint-Martin, 75004 Paris
Tel: 271-7234
Proprietor: Jean-Pierre Coffe • Chef: Claude Segal

Sliced Saddle of Rabbit

500 g (1 lb) chard
130 g (4 oz) butter, and as needed
300 g (10½ oz) onions, finely sliced
salt and pepper, to taste
1 pinch mustard seeds
30 g (1 oz) shallots, chopped
50 g (1¾ oz) champagne vinegar
200 ml (6 oz) dry white wine
1 tsp French mustard
4 saddles* of rabbit
oil, as needed
200 g (7 oz) spinach, coarsely chopped

Peel the chard and cut it into 5 cm (2 in) pieces. Cook for 10 - 15 minutes in boiling water. Leave to cool. Melt 80 g (2¾ oz) butter in an ovenproof saucepan. Add onions and season with salt and pepper. Stew in the oven at 400°F (205°C) for 15 minutes. Purée the mustard seeds and chopped shallots in a blender with the vinegar and white wine. Bring to a boil in a small sauté pan. Reduce to a paste and allow to cool. Whisk in stewed onions over low heat. Remove from heat and check seasoning. Stir in a spoonful of mustard. Strain the chard. Stew it gently in a shallow pan with almost all the remaining butter.

Roast the saddles of rabbit in a little oil for 10 minutes at 450°F (230°C). Allow to rest in a warm place. Add chopped spinach, onion mixture, and a little butter to the chard. Cook for 1 minute; correct the seasoning. Slice the rabbit thinly, arrange slices on top of the vegetables in a serving dish, and serve.

Serves: 4

Toulouse is the metropolis of the southwest of France. Since 1970, Marcelin Pujol has followed his family's restaurant tradition, which began some 40-odd years ago. Marcelin is a classic chef who prepares food with the utmost finesse.

The dining room at **Pujol** features rustic elegance and is comfortably bourgeois. The main attractions on the menu are the Cassoulet Touloussain, confits, *foies gras*, Fresh Duck in Port Wine, Grilled Magret of Duck en Papillote , and Saddle of Hare with Saupiquet Sauce.

Pujol is a regular stopping place for businessmen and gourmets from Toulouse who always find what pleases them on the menu. At Pujol, tradition is upheld.

Jean-Pierre Coffe is a man of taste, a literary talent (his book, *Gourmandise au Singulier,* is very amusing), a comedian, a decorator, and a chef by passion. He has two successful restaurants and has recently opened a third one.

La Ciboulette is an 18th century hotel that has been transformed into a ravishing restaurant. There is a beautiful garden off the terrace, as well as a mezzanine, a foyer, and two large dining rooms. The restaurant is gaily decorated, in excellent taste, with a collection of beautiful *objets d'art.*

Claude Segal, the chef, has composed a great wine list and a delicious menu. The philosophy at the new Ciboulette is "This is going to be the best Parisian restaurant of the year," and it shows.

Le Petit Pré

1, rue Bellevue, 75019 Paris
Tel: 208-9262
Proprietor/Chef: Christian Verges

It took a lot of courage for an inexperienced self-taught chef to open a restaurant in Belleville in the 19th *arrondissement* (district) of Paris. It happened back in 1976, and Christian Verges admits, "There were a lot of mistakes at the beginning but . . . I love eating!" His appetite was a good starting point. Now this little restaurant has become a very good one.

I am pleased that his cooking is inspired by old recipes (albeit somewhat lighter ones), rather than new-fashioned concoctions, and that he is always looking for top quality products. You'll enjoy the Avocado Gâteau with Prawns, the sliced Rabbit with Thyme, the Sardine Fillets "Sailor" Style, the Pigs Feet Stuffed with Fresh Pasta, the Tart Tatin, and the Cream of Lemon and Orange Soup.

M. Verges and his wife, Jacqueline, the food fanatics, have brought Belleville back to life. Bravo!

Sliced Rabbit with Thyme

1 young rabbit of 2 kg (4½ lb)
1 large sliced onion
1 carrot, sliced
150 g (5¼ oz) butter
100 ml (3 oz) olive oil
1 tbsp flour
1 bottle dry white wine
salt and pepper, to taste
2 kg (4½ lb) fresh tomatoes, peeled and halved
1 bouquet garni*
1 stalk celery
2 cloves garlic, crushed
1 sprig fresh thyme
½ bunch chives, chopped
½ bunch tarragon, chopped
½ bunch chervil, chopped
1 kg (2¼ lb) spinach, blanched and cooked in butter

Remove the bones from the rabbit legs and back, remove the gristle from each fillet, tie up the thighs with string, and put them and the liver aside. Crush the bones and brown them with the onion and carrot in ⅓ the butter and ½ the olive oil. Remove the fat, sprinkle the flour on top, add the wine and a little salt, and begin to heat it.

Remove the seeds and juice from ½ the tomato halves and add to the crushed bone preparation along with the bouquet garni, celery, and 1 garlic clove. Add a little water (if necessary) and let simmer for 45 minutes.

Remove the rabbit bones from the pan, crush them, then return them to the pan and reboil. Strain the preparation through a sauce strainer into another clean pan. Add thyme, check seasoning, add pepper, and add 50 g (1¾ oz) butter. Keep hot.

In a hot oven, 450°F (230°C), cook the rabbit as follows: the back (in fillets) for 5 minutes; the livers for 5 minutes; and the legs for 10 minutes.

Crush the remaining tomato halves and gently heat with the remaining butter and olive oil. Season with chives, tarragon, chervil, and the last garlic clove. Cut the rabbit legs and back lengthwise into thin slices and the livers into scallops and spread on a serving dish. Coat with the sauce and decorate with the spinach, tomato, and herb preparations. Serve hot.

Wine: *Fronsac or a cool Roussillon wine*   Serves: 6

La Devinière

61, boulevard Louis XIV, 59000 Lille
Tel: (20) 52-74-64
Proprietor/Chef: M. Waterlot

On this large boulevard, Louis XIV, near the Institute of Art, **La Devinière** brightens up this rather austere neighbourhood.

Just because M. Waterlot's last name is "Waterloo" spelled with a "t" at the end, it does not mean he is marked by defeat. Quite the contrary! His restaurant is a triumph of good food and service, and M. Waterlot is a victor among masters of fine dining. He prepares Stuffed Rabbit au Naturel and has it served to you by lovely waitresses.

Stuffed Rabbit

1 rabbit of 1.5 kg (3⅓ lb), emptied, liver reserved	1 bunch chopped parsley
400 g (¾ lb) pork throats, from butcher	2 carrots, chopped
	3 onions, chopped
200 ml (6 oz) Muscadet or Chinon Blanc wine	3 cloves garlic
100 ml (3 oz) champagne	125 g (¼ lb) lard
3 shallots	1 litre (2 pt) meat glaze or brown gravy
1 bouquet garni*	200 g (½ lb) fried gingerbread croutons
pinch of nutmeg	
1 egg	½ litre (1 pt) double cream (whipping cream)

Bone the rabbit, keeping the saddle* and the thighs together as one piece. Remove meat from the shoulders and front legs, mince with the pork throats and rabbit liver. Marinate the saddle and thighs overnight in the white wine and champagne with shallots, bouquet garni, and nutmeg. Mix the minced meats with egg and parsley and stuff the rabbit saddle with them. Line a casserole with carrots, onions, garlic, and the rabbit bones. Heat a pan, add lard, then brown the stuffed rabbit in the hot lard. When golden brown, add the rabbit, marinade, and ½ the meat glaze to the casserole. Simmer gently for 45 minutes. When the rabbit is cooked, remove it carefully. Reduce the cooking juices, add the croutons and cream, and mash well. Strain the sauce and keep it hot. Carve the rabbit into medallions, pour sauce over, and serve.

Serves: 6

Le Montillier

19, rue Notre-Dame-de-Lorette, 75009 Paris
Tel: 285-4606
Proprietor: Georges Montillier • Chef: M. Horey

Georges Montillier will greet you at the door of his restaurant with grace and savoir-faire, as though he has been in the business for years. Nevertheless, he hasn't. He was brought up in a family of restaurateurs, but he decided he would go into the theatre rather than follow the family tradition. After a stint "on the boards," he returned to the restaurant business to learn from his grandfather, a disciple of Escoffier, one of the first proponents of *grand cuisine.*

Today, he manages his restaurant with much success, frequently receiving visits from his friends in the theatre.

Traditional Rabbit with Mustard

1 rabbit of 1.2 kg (2½ lb)
160 ml (⅔ cup) peanut oil
butter, to sauté
7 - 8 tbsp French mustard
dry white wine, as needed
¼ litre (½ pt) double cream (whipping cream)
croutons, to garnish
1 bunch parsley, to garnish

Cut the rabbit into pieces; sauté pieces in oil and butter until golden. Take rabbit pieces out of the frying pan and put them in a slightly greased ovenproof pan. Cover them well with 4 - 5 tbsp of mustard, then put pan into the oven at 500°F (260°C) and roast. After 20 minutes, pour wine over the rabbit until it is half covered. Let cook 20 minutes more. Remove the rabbit and keep warm.

Add 3 tbsp mustard and the cream to the juices in the roasting pan. Stir and let simmer until it reaches the desired sauce consistency.

Cover the rabbit pieces with the sauce, top with croutons and parsley, and serve.

Serves: 4

Chiberta

3, rue Arsène-Houssaye, 75008 Paris
Tel: 563-7244
Proprietor: M. Richard • Chef: Jean-Michel Bedier

Wild Rabbit Fricassee with Ginger

1 young rabbit of 1.5 kg (3⅓ lb)	200 g (7 oz) pork rind
150 ml (½ cup) oil	few grains of coriander
3 onions	salt and pepper, to taste
2 shallots	1 piece root ginger, peeled and
50 g (1¾ oz) celery	cut julienne
350 ml (10½ oz) red wine,	50 g (1¾ oz) butter, and as needed
or as needed	1 pear, quartered
¼ litre (½ pt) water, and as needed	30 g (1 oz) chives
1 bouquet garni*	

Bone the rabbit, cut all the flesh (except the breasts) into strips, and crush the bones. In a pot, heat the oil, then sauté 1 onion, the shallots, and the celery (all chopped coarsely). Add 200 ml (6 oz) red wine and reduce to ½. Add the ¼ litre (½ pt) water, bouquet garni, pork rind, coriander, salt, and pepper. Cook slowly for ¾ hour, skimming the grease off continuously. Add water if necessary. (There should be 400 ml or 1½ cups left.) Strain the liquid. Sauté the ginger and 2 onions in butter until golden brown.

Poach the pear quarters in enough wine to cover them. Over high heat, sauté the rabbit pieces. Add 50 ml (1½ oz) red wine, then add the stock prepared above. Cook for 8 minutes, removing the breasts after 5 minutes, then add ginger. Let simmer for 2 minutes, add a small piece of butter, and check the seasoning.

To serve: Place the breasts, cut into fillets, on one side of the plate. Place the other rabbit parts with the onion sauce in the middle. Sprinkle all with chives and serve.

Serves: 4

At **Chiberta**, you will discover and experience a truly modern French ambiance. The decor is totally contemporary, as is the owner of Chiberta. M. Richard is young, sophisticated, and perfectly groomed, from his hair, to his grey flannel suit, to his fingernails. He opened in 1975 and hired a young chef — Jean-Michel Bedier. Together they are a perfect team.

Chiberta is energetic, youthful, and chic. The cuisine is *la nouvelle,* light and delicate. Jean-Michel prepares such treats as Supremes of Quail, Rabbit Terrine with Figs, Turbot with Sweet Pimentos, Wild Rabbit Fricassee with Ginger, and Rabbit with Sea Urchin Coral. M. Richard offers the perfect setting for the new Parisian lifestyle.

Château d'Isenbourg

68250 Rouffach
Tel: (89) 49-63-53
Proprietor: D. Dalibert • Chef: M. Truchetet

Wild Rabbit with Thyme and Mustard

4 pork cauls (the membrane that
  encloses the paunch) or use
  thin strips of salt pork
1 bouquet fresh thyme
4 rabbit thighs
4 rabbit kidneys
8 large potatoes
60 g (2 oz) butter
100 ml (3 oz) oil
salt and pepper, to taste
1 tbsp Dijon mustard
100 ml (3 oz) dry white wine
1 tbsp double cream
  (whipping cream)
1 tbsp chopped chives

Spread the cauls on a wooden board, sprinkle with thyme, and place one thigh and one kidney in each to form 4 small pouches. Cut the potatoes into cubes of 1 cm (2½ in). Dunk them in boiling water for a few minutes, then drain. In a large frying pan, heat the butter and oil. Season the rabbit pouches with salt and pepper, add to the frying pan and brown them and the potatoes on each side. After cooking, remove pouches and potatoes, spread mustard over the pouches and keep all warm in the oven.

To prepare the sauce: Add white wine to the pan just used and let the mixture reduce to the desired consistency. Add cream, pass through a fine strainer, and reseason if necessary.

Serve the thighs surrounded by potatoes, and serve the sauce separately in a sauceboat with the chopped chives.

Serves: 4

We find ourselves in the chateau valley once more, in the **Château d'Isenbourg**, which once belonged to M. Dacobert (back in 613). Surrounded by forests and flowers, it is a magnificent sight to behold. France is full of such treasures, where the ancient castles and the modern highways stand side by side. In a culture where past history is as important as current events, the respect for tradition will never cease. Here Chef Truchetet prepares dishes that respect that tradition. He cooks as an artist rather than a connoisseur, which explains the marvellous Hot Foie Gras Gâteau with Crayfish and the Wild Rabbit with Thyme and Mustard — both expertly prepared masterpieces.

Le Sully d'Auteuil

78, rue d'Auteuil, 75016 Paris
Tel: 651-7118
Proprietor/Chef: Michel Brunetière

Michel Brunetière has always aimed high. He learned with the best in prestigious Parisian establishments, George V and the Plaza, where he cooked for ambassadors and royalty. He has also organised receptions for popular people in show business, including Brigitte Bardot and Michèle Morgan. Today, he is owner and chef of his own restaurant, **Le Sully d'Auteuil**, located in the 16th *arrondissement* (district). It is decorated in elegance with luxurious accessories. The traditional cuisine is prepared delicately by this man who loves his work and who is respectful of tradition. The Sweetbrier Marmalade Pancake and the Calf's Head en Tortue (a Gothic recipe) are his tributes to the past.

Calf's Head in Tortue Sauce

2 calves' heads, 1.2 kg (2½ lb) each, simmered in white court bouillon*
   for 2 hours
broth made by poaching 2 whites of leeks in 100 ml (3 oz) boiling water
   for 9 minutes
100 ml (3 oz) vinegar
300 ml (9 oz) double cream (whipping cream)
10 gherkins
6 quenelles of puréed pike (or gefilte fish), sliced
50 shrimps, cooked and shelled
juice of 1 lemon
salt and pepper, to taste
3 hard-boiled eggs, chopped
1 tbsp each: chervil, chives, and parsley

Cut the calves' heads into small squares of 5 cm (2 in), then simmer them in the leek broth for 1½ hours. At the end of the cooking, add vinegar and cream and reduce to ½. Add gherkins, sliced quenelles, and 36 shrimps. Adjust the seasoning and add lemon juice.

Place all on a serving plate, garnish with the remaining shrimps, sprinkle with the crushed eggs and the herbs, and serve.

Wine: *Pouilly Blanc Fumé*
    Serves: 8

Le Petit Colombier

42, rue des Acacias, 75017 Paris
Tel: 380-2854
Proprietor/Chef: Bernard Fournier

M. Delouvier opened his restaurant, **Le Petit Colombier**, many years ago. From the beginning, everyone enjoyed this family inn, so quaintly situated in the open country. M. Delouvier insisted that the cuisine reflect the cuisine of his birthplace in central France, so he found himself a young chef (who later married his daughter) who could cook that way. Today, Bernard Fournier is in charge of Le Petit Colombier, and he runs the restaurant exactly as his father-in-law did. Le Petit Colombier has maintained the family tradition and good service.

The dishes are hearty and tasty and include Beef Fillet in Crust, Chicken in Burgundy Wine, Braised Knuckle of Ham with Choux Paste, and the marvellous, traditional Braised Calf's Liver, which is truly a masterpiece.

Braised Calf's Liver

1 kg (2¼ lb) calf's liver, in one piece	**24 very small onions**
salt and pepper, as needed	**125 g (¼ lb) butter**
3 branches thyme, without leaves	**6 medium white mushrooms,**
1 bay leaf, crushed	**quartered**
180 g (⅓ lb) lard in 1 thick strip	**150 g (5¼ oz) semi-salted bacon,**
2 tbsp vinegar	**cut into cubes**
90 ml (2¾ oz) water	**1 tsp sugar**

Season the liver well with salt and pepper and sprinkle with thyme and crushed bay leaf. Spread out the strip of lard. Place the calf's liver in the middle, fold the lard around it, and fasten with a string. Over high heat, in a pot with no added grease, sauté the wrapped liver 5 minutes on each side. Lower the heat and cook, uncovered, for 20 minutes. Near the end of the cooking time, add the vinegar and water; cook for 5 more minutes. Remove the calf's liver; keep it warm. Reduce the cooking liquid to half and reserve and keep warm.

To prepare the garnish: Cook the onions 10 - 12 minutes in water with ¾ of the butter. In a separate pan, sauté the cubes of bacon and the mushrooms in the remaining butter. Add the small onions and sprinkle all with the sugar. Caramelise this preparation slightly.

Remove the lard strip around the liver. Place the liver on a hot plate and surround with cubes of bacon, mushrooms, and the small onions. Pour the reserved, reduced liquid from the calf's liver on top and serve.

Suggestion: Serve this dish with sautéed courgettes (zucchini).

Serves: 6

Château de Marcay

Marcay, 37500 Chinon
Tel: (47) 93-03-47
Proprietor: M. Mollard • Chef: Daniel Dumesnil

Daniel Dumesnil, a gentleman chef of fine reputation and a prestigious background, has entered the country of Rabelais, the Chateau Valley of the Loire River. In 1972, he turned a 15th century fortress into a majestic restaurant-hotel-castle with fine cuisine.

Within the warm, wooden dining room, Daniel offers an interesting menu that includes Minced Salmon, Ragout of Hard-Boiled Eggs and Onions, Loire Mousseline with Leeks, Crayfish, Calf's Liver in Raspberry Vinegar, Chicken Fricassee in Cider Vinegar, and "Rabelaisian" Tournedos that are poetry. The platter of local cheeses is served with rye bread, and among the desserts, the Chocolate Cake with Orange Salad and the Lime Ice Soufflé are absolutely divine.

Calf's Liver in Raspberry Vinegar

4 slices of calf's liver
salt and pepper, to taste
125 g (¼ lb) butter
2 shallots, finely chopped
60 ml (2 oz) raspberry vinegar
100 ml (3 oz) veal stock*
50 g (1¾ oz) grapes, Smyrne preferred
150 g (5¼ oz) fresh raspberries

Season the slices of liver with salt and pepper, then cook the liver in butter for 5 minutes on each side. Put liver aside and keep warm. Sauté the shallots in the same pan the liver was cooked in. Pour in the raspberry vinegar and the veal stock, and let reduce slightly. Add the remaining butter.

Place the calf's liver slices on a hot serving platter and pour the sauce over the liver. Decorate the liver with grapes and raspberries.

Suggestion: Onion fondue may accompany this dish.

Wine: *Bourgueil or Chinon Rouge*   Serves: 4

Le Pouilly-Reuilly

68, rue André-Joineau, 93310 Le-Pré-Saint-Gervais
Tel: 845-1459
Proprietor/Chef: Jean Thibault

This inn was opened before World War II. It was a cheerful place where the proprietors, "Mom" and "Dad" Roussillon, cooked for their friends, and the Berri white wine was poured from the counter.

In 1965, Jean Thibault acquired the inn. He was wise not to change the joyous familiarity of this place, especially the rustic, tasty cooking. Here, you will always find Sautéed Chicken with Crayfish, Stuffed Slices of Veal, Veal Paupiettes "Berrichonnes" Style, Black Pudding or Broiled Pork Sausage, Leg of Duck with White Beans, and Calf's Feet with Vinaigrette Dressing. The wine cellar contains a great selection from Bordeaux. The greeting, cooking, and the wine haven't changed in all these years.

Stuffed Slices of Veal

6 scallops of veal
6 slices ham, chopped
6 cloves garlic
50 g (1¾ oz) butter
250 g (½ lb) shallots
4 fresh tomatoes
100 ml (3 oz) of cognac
2 tbsp tomato paste
1 tbsp flour
1 litre (2 pt) dry white wine
1 litre (2 pt) chicken stock*
salt and pepper, to taste
2 tbsp double cream (whipping cream)

Flatten and trim the scallops of veal. Cover them with a stuffing made by mixing the veal trimmings and the chopped slices of ham together. Fasten well so the stuffing will not come out. In a skillet, sauté the veal in garlic, butter, shallots, and tomatoes. Flame with cognac. Add the tomato paste, flour, white wine, chicken stock, salt, and pepper. Cook gently for 40-45 minutes. Just before serving, add the cream.

Wine: *Pinot Gris de Reuilly or Bordeaux Rouge*   Serves: 6

La Voile d'Or

06290 Port de Saint-Jean-Cap-Ferrat
Tel: (93) 01-13-13
Proprietors: M. and Mme. F. Lorenzi • Chef: Jean Crépin

On the waterfront of Saint-Jean-Cap-Ferrat is **La Voile d'Or**, a sumptuous hotel built in 1968 by M. Lorenzi. He and his wife have staffed their establishment with some of the most talented people available. Armand Melkonian is one of the best sommeliers in France, and the chef, Jean Crépin, came here in 1975 after working in Le Chapon Fin in Bordeaux, Drouant in Paris, La Poste in Avallon, and Barrière in Tours. You will appreciate the Crayfish and Asparagus Feuilleté, Veal Kidneys "Ali-Baba" Style, the Turbot with Pear Mousseline, the Red Mullet Fillet with Moelle Sauce, and the Pullet with Raspberry Vinegar and Onion Compote. The tasty desserts are prepared by the talented hands of Michel Joffre.

Veal Kidneys "Ali-Baba" Style

4 veal kidneys
salt and pepper, to taste
200 g (7 oz) strong Dijon mustard
80 g (2¾ oz) butter
zest* of 1 lemon
½ litre (1 pt) double cream (whipping cream)
10 peppercorns, crushed
few drops of champagne
1 tbsp butter

Remove the fat from the kidneys. Season kidneys with salt and pepper, cover them with mustard, then place them on a greased cooking sheet; bake for 10 minutes at 350°F (175°C).

In a saucepan, bring the lemon zest, cream, and crushed peppercorns to a boil. After a few minutes, add the kidneys and cook for 10 minutes. Drain the kidneys and slice them. Add the juice from the kidneys to the saucepan, then add a few drops of champagne. With a whisk, add 1 tbsp butter. The sauce should be creamy and light. Adjust the seasoning, then strain the sauce through a fine strainer.

Arrange the kidneys on a serving plate and cover them with the sauce.

Suggestion: Accompany with rice pilaff.

Serves: 4

Le Ski d'Or

73320, Lac de Tignes
Tel: (79) 06-51-60
Proprietor: Jean-C. Bréchu • Chef: Yves Sauret

Le Ski d'Or merits its nickname, "The Golden Fork," because here the cuisine is rich in perfection. The Veal Kidney "en Chemise," the Saddle of Lamb, and the Cassoulet of Pickled Duck meet the requirements of the most demanding gourmets.

Your dinner here will certainly delight you, and the view overlooking the snow-covered mountains might just take your breath away.

Veal Kidneys "en Chemise"

2 veal kidneys
salt and pepper, to taste
few leaves fresh sorrel
2 slices of fresh goose liver

Clean the kidneys well, remove the skins, and season with salt and pepper. Place the kidneys on a sheet of aluminum foil surrounded with sorrel. Place the fresh goose liver on top. Fold the aluminum foil over all to form an envelope. Bake in the oven for 10 minutes at 475°F (250°C), then remove the aluminum foil. Slice the kidneys and place them on a serving dish.

Suggestion: Serve with sautéed potatoes or crepes with garlic seasoning.

Wine: *Volnay-Clos des Chènes*

Serves: 2

Restaurant Napoléon

38, avenue de Friedland, 75008 Paris
Tel: 227-9950
Proprietor/Chef: Guy-Pierre Baumann

Veal Knuckle

1.6 kg (3½ lb) knuckle of veal, cut in 8 slices
flour, as needed
50 g (1¾ oz) lard
1 onion
2 sprigs parsley
1 sprig thyme
1 bay leaf
1 clove
1 tbsp capers
salt and pepper, to taste
300 ml (9 oz) veal or chicken bouillon

Dust the slices of veal with flour, then sauté in a skillet with lard. Spread the veal in a terrine.

Peel the onion, wash the parsley, and put these ingredients in the terrine along with the thyme, bay leaf, clove, capers, salt, and pepper. Add veal or chicken bouillon and bring to a boil. Place the terrine in the oven for 3 hours at 350°F (175°C). Serve it very hot.

Serves: 4

They call Guy-Pierre "the Napoléon of Choucroute (sauerkraut)" because **Restaurant Napoléon** serves the best there is anywhere. Although it is served many ways here, I recommend Choucroute with Oysters above the others.

Guy-Pierre owns other establishments, but this particular one is particularly elegant — almost imperial in style and decor. Here he prepares dishes only a master chef could prepare, such as a remarkable savoury *foie gras* and classics such as Tournedos à la Moelle and Veal Sweetbreads with Spinach. His wine cellar is equally fine.

Restaurant Napoléon is but two steps from the Place de l'Étoile where Napoleon himself is honoured; this restaurant, too, deserves its honours.

Auberge du Père Bise

Lac d'Annecy, 74290 Talloires
Tel: (50) 60-72-01
Proprietor/Chef: François Bise

Veal Knuckles "Savoyarde"

4 potatoes, julienne
200 g (7 oz) butter
6 tomatoes
olive oil, as needed
2 cloves garlic
2 veal knuckles, cut into 4 cm
(1½ in) sections
flour, as needed
salt and pepper, to taste

2 shallots, chopped
4 carrots, julienne
16 small onions
4 turnips, julienne and blanched
1 stalk celery, chopped
1 bouquet garni*
100 ml (3 oz) white wine
veal stock* (optional)

Sauté the potatoes in foaming butter and reserve on a plate. Quarter 1 tomato and reserve. Peel, seed, and chop 5 tomatoes; cook in a little olive oil with some garlic, and reserve on a plate. Roll the pieces of veal knuckle in flour, season with salt and pepper, and brown them in butter in a large pan. Add any bones and trimmings, plus the shallots, carrots, onions, turnips, celery, bouquet garni, and the reserved quartered tomato. Add wine and water or veal stock, cover the pan, and simmer for 35 minutes, adding additional liquid as it reduces. Remove the vegetables as they cook and keep warm.

Arrange the veal and the vegetables on a plate with the reserved potatoes and chopped tomatoes. Reduce the cooking liquid in the pan to sauce consistency, correct the seasoning, and serve this sauce with the dish.

Wine: *Château Figeac Bordeaux*

Serves: 4

François Bise succeeded his father in the tradition of warm welcomes and good food, which has made his father's good reputation a lasting reputation for the family.

A dinner at **Auberge du Père Bise** is a return to nature, a feast for your palate. Everything is fresh and natural. The fish from the lakes (such as char, a kind of salmon) and alpine streams, the Savoy gratins (such as shrimp tails or simple potatoes), the warm Pâté in Sauce Poivrade (pepper sauce), the Veal Knuckles, and the Saddle of Lamb roasted over wood are all marvellous. The Beaufort, Reblochon, and Tomme are all exceptional Savoy cheeses. The wine cellar is divine. Do try the Roussette de Seyssel, a regional wine; it is an excellent choice.

Auberge du Grand Saint-Pierre

R.N. 2, "Les Haies à Charmes," Dourlers, 59440 Avesnes-sur-Helpe
Tel: (27) 61-17-58
Proprietor/Chef: Jeanne Drouin

In 1955, M. and Mme. Drouin assumed ownership of the Saint-Pierre, a 200-year-old hotel. Saint-Pierre soon became quite a success and quickly outgrew its walls, so the Drouins built the **Auberge du Grand Saint-Pierre**. This beautiful structure was built acording to the same plan as the first restaurant. Later, the Drouins' daughter took over her parents' establishment, and today, Jeanne cooks with as much imagination as her mother. The cuisine has a definite feminine touch. Jeanne's dishes are delicate treats served in plentiful portions. The Pork Chops "Avensoise," Cèpes Fricassee, Veal Sweetbreads, and Chicken with Morel Mushrooms and Cream are some of Jeanne's best dishes.

Veal Sweetbreads à la Jeanne Drouin

4 veal sweetbreads
flour, as needed
butter, as needed
1 sliced shallot
125 g (¼ lb) white mushrooms, sliced
rum, to flame
100 ml (3 oz) Macvin d'Arbois (white wine)
2 tbsp stewed tomatoes
salt and pepper, as needed
juice of 1 lemon
1 tbsp double cream (whipping cream)
fine herbs, to garnish

Dust the sweetbreads well in flour, then cook them gently in a pan with butter, sliced shallot, and sliced mushrooms, until golden brown. Let all ingredients cook 5 more minutes, then flame with rum. Add the Macvin d'Arbois, stewed tomatoes, salt, pepper, and lemon juice. Continue to cook gently.

Add the cream and let the sauce reduce until it is rich and creamy. Sprinkle some fine herbs over all and serve.

Wine: *A white Arbois wine*   Serves: 4

Le Cagnard

Rue Pontis-Long, 06800 Hauts-de-Cagnes
Tel: (93) 20-73-22
Proprietor: Félix Barel • Chef: Yves Johany

During the day, every angle of **Le Cagnard** is illuminated by the sun. This bastion of fine cuisine stands out prominently in the sunshine in this ravishing medieval town of Hauts-de-Cagnes. Modigliani, Renoir, Soutine, and Saint-Exupéry all came here to enjoy the peace and quiet of this tranquil little town.

Félix Barel and his chef have harmoniously blended their original cuisine with many old regional recipes, therefore Le Cagnard offers a light and delicate cuisine that combines originality, modernity, and tradition in the South of France. A fine example is the excellent Veal Sweetbreads and Duck Liver Pie.

Veal Sweetbreads and Duck Liver Pie

2 veal sweetbreads, 400 g (14 oz) each
salt and pepper, to taste
50 g (1¾ oz) butter
2 chicken breasts
50 ml (1½ oz) champagne
30 g (1 oz) truffle juice
200 ml (6 oz) double cream (whipping cream)
800 g (1¾ lb) puff pastry dough*
160 g (5½ oz) fresh duck (or chicken) liver, sliced
1 egg

Pare the sweetbreads and slice into average slices. Season with salt and pepper. In a pan with butter, cook the sweetbreads 3 minutes on each side. Put them on a plate in the refrigerator.

In the same pan, cook the 2 chicken breasts for 2 minutes on each side, then remove them from the pan and save for another recipe. Add champagne, truffle juice, and the cream to the same pan. Reduce over high heat to a rich creamy consistency. Pass the sauce through a fine strainer and keep warm.

Roll out 8 layers of puff pastry dough, 12 cm (5 in) in diameter and 2 mm (¹⁄₁₆ in) thick. Place 4 of the layers on a moistened cooking sheet, but let 1 cm (½ in) hang over the edge. Spread the sweetbreads and the duck liver onto the dough and cover with the remaining 4 layers. Pinch the edges together, tightly seal, brush with egg, and let cook in the oven for 25 minutes at 425°F (220°C). When done, cut the pie into slices and serve with the sauce on the side.

Suggestion: Accompany with a green leaf salad with vinaigrette dressing.*

Wine: *A red Bandol or white Domaine Tempier*   Serves: 2

Bourrier

1, place Parmentier, 92200 Neuilly-sur-Seine
Tel: 624-1119
Proprietor/Chef: Yves Bourrier

In 1929, after years at Lasserre and the Plaza, Yves Bourrier decided to work for himself. He opened his restaurant in Neuilly, where the gourmands are plentiful and sometimes hard to please.

Yves devised a unique formula for his restaurant; he kept it as a small bistro where you may dine for a fixed price. **Bourrier** has no waiters or waitresses; the members of the kitchen staff serve their own preparations. Here the chef is also the culinary advisor, cook, and waiter. He will describe to you the "Fernand Pont" Langoustines, the "Dombes" Ragoût, The Chicken from Bresse with Vinegar, and the Veal Sweetbreads Rennet. There is also a plentiful supply of Saint-Joseph and Côtes du Rhône wines.

Veal Sweetbreads Rennet

125 g (¼ lb) butter
2 shallots, finely chopped
1 sprig thyme
1 pinch nutmeg
salt and pepper, to taste
400 g (14 oz) raw calf's liver, finely ground in a food processor
2 egg yolks
2 sweetbreads of veal, blanched
1 tsp rennet
12 fresh spinach leaves, blanched
400 ml (12 oz) Madeira wine
100 ml (3 oz) veal stock*

Place ½ the butter and the finely chopped shallots, thyme, nutmeg, salt, pepper, liver, egg yolks, and spinach into a pan and mix together to make the stuffing. Cut the sweetbreads into 8 thin slices. Place ¼ tsp rennet and ¼ of the stuffing between 2 slices of sweetbreads. Wrap in 3 leaves of spinach. Do the same with the next 6 sweetbread slices.

Braise the 4 pouches with the Madeira wine and veal stock for 5–7 minutes. Swirl in the remaining butter to make the sauce creamy, then serve.

Serves: 4

El Chiquito

126, avenue Paul-Doumer, 92500 Rueil
Tel: 751-0053
Proprietor: Edith Besson • Chef: Serge Bioux

M. Besson, better known as El Chiquito, established a restaurant in luxurious style at Rueil-Malmaison. Edith Besson, M. Besson's widow, discovered Serge Bioux, a chef of great talent. Edith, loving everything that comes from the sea, wanted a quality seafood menu with a sense of style. Serge proposed that they blend seafood with classicism; Edith agreed.

El Chiquito may be the only restaurant in the city that offers Lobster Thermidore prepared the original, classical way (using a hundred-year-old recipe) and a true Tournedos Rossini. You may prefer, however, Leg of Lamb with Pastry or Veal Sweetbreads with Crayfish; both are excellent choices.

Veal Sweetbreads with Crayfish

600 g (1⅓ lb) veal sweetbreads
½ tsp vinegar
28 crayfish (or large shrimps)
3 tbsp olive oil
50 g (1¾ lb) butter
salt and pepper, to taste
2 chopped shallots
2 tbsp white wine
2 tbsp double cream (whipping cream)
¼ litre (1 cup) sauce Américaine*
1 tsp chopped parsley

Poach the sweetbreads for 10 minutes in a pot of boiling water containing vinegar. Peel the sweetbreads carefully and cut them into 3 cm (1¼ in) squares.

Sauté the crayfish in very hot olive oil, then separate the tails from the heads and carefully remove the tails from the shells. Keep the crayfish tails warm.

In a skillet, heat the butter. Add the sweetbreads, salt, and pepper, and sauté them for 5 minutes without browning. After 5 minutes, add the shallots and cook for 1–2 minutes, then add the white wine. Remove the sweetbreads from the skillet and keep warm. Add the cream and the sauce Américaine to the skillet. Simmer until mixture is very rich. At the last moment of cooking, put the sweetbreads and the crayfish tails back into the pan and boil briefly, just enough to warm the crayfish. Sprinkle with parsley and serve.

Wine: *Sancerre or Pouilly Fumé*

Serves: 4

Chez Maître Paul

12, rue Monsieur-le-Prince, 75006 Paris
Tel: 354-7459
Proprietor/Chef: A. Gaugain

This small, very Parisian restaurant was created in 1945 by Paul Maître. In 1962, M. Gaugain acquired it and continues to run it in the style of the original owner. His Fillets of Sole, Veal Sweetbreads with Morels and Wine, Foie Gras of Veal in Paille Wine, Chicken in Yellow Wine from Arbois, and the exceptional cheeses are all testaments to a true gourmet's restaurant. M. Gaugain even imports his tasty sausage and morels from the Jura region.

At **Chez Maître Paul**, you won't find luxurious comfort or extra fancy decor, but, rather, you will find a warm welcome from Mme. Gaugain and a comfortable, cosy atmosphere where you are among friends.

Veal Sweetbreads with Morels and Wine

100 g (¼ lb) dried morel mushrooms	1 bouquet garni*
350 ml (10½ oz) white Jura wine	pepper, as needed
3 veal sweetbreads	100 ml (3 oz) brandy, Jura preferred
2 tbsp peanut oil	1 litre (2 pt) veal or chicken stock*
40 g (1½ oz) butter	coarse salt, to taste
3 carrots, sliced	½ litre (1 pt) double cream
1 large onion, sliced	(whipping cream)
1 garlic clove, crushed	150 ml (5 oz) yellow wine

Soak the morels for 2 - 3 hours in cold water. Add 150 ml (5 oz) white wine and simmer 2 hours. Drain. Reserve morels and cooking liquid. Soak the sweetbreads in several changes of cold water. Blanch in fresh water. Drain and trim. Put oil and ½ the butter in a sauté pan. Add carrots, onion, garlic, bouquet garni, and pinch of pepper. Heat for 5 minutes. Add sweetbreads and cook gently 2 - 3 minutes per side. Heat the brandy in a covered pan for 1 minute; light it and pour over the sweetbreads. Add remaining white wine and boil 5 minutes. Add enough stock and reserved morel liquid to cover the ingredients. Bring slowly to the simmering point; add salt and pepper to taste, and cover. After 15 minutes, check sweetbreads (they're done when juice runs clear). Remove, drain, and cool them.

Finish cooking the vegetables. Strain the cooking liquid. Add cream and reduce to a creamy, shiny consistency. Correct the seasoning. Slice the cold sweetbreads and sauté on both sides in a pan with the remaining hot butter. Sauté the morels in a saucepan. Deglaze with yellow wine and add morels to the sauce. Nap* the sweetbreads with sauce and serve.

Wine: *Wines from Jura*   Serves: 4

Jacques Cagna

14, rue des Grands-Augustins, 75006 Paris
Tel: 326-4939
Proprietor/Chef: Jacques Cagna

Jacques Cagna is a man with a young spirit and 25 years of experience. For the past six years, he has been on the Left Bank in a surprisingly intimate pub. Under the varnished beams are Dutch tile floors, antique chandeliers, and beautifully set tables with flowers placed by Annie, Jacques's sister.

Annie will greet you and seat you as Jacques prepares the fabulous Fricassee of Squirrel with Croutons, Veal Sweetbreads with Oysters and Truffles, Sliced Fillet of Veal with Ginger, Squab with Small Onions, Confits with Hot Sliced Apples, and Cinnamon Ice. One of the most sumptuous treats is Wild Duck with Lemon and Orange Zest in Burgundy Wine Sauce. The wine cellar is also rich in choice and flavour.

Veal Sweetbreads with Oysters and Truffles

600 g (1⅓ lb) veal sweetbreads
80 g (2¾ oz) butter
2 sliced shallots
½ litre (1 pt) of white wine
12 oysters
250 ml (8 oz) truffle juice
3 tbsp double cream (whipping cream)
salt and pepper, as needed
truffles, cut julienne, to garnish

Blanch, cool, and peel the sweetbreads. Keep the cooking liquid. In a saucepan, heat 10 g (⅓ oz) butter, then add the shallots and simmer briefly. Add the sweetbreads and wet all with the white wine. Cover and cook in the oven for 15 minutes at 400°F (205°C).

Open the oysters and add their liquid to the pan with the sweetbread liquid. Add the juice from the truffles and reduce to ¾. Add cream and let simmer for 3 - 4 minutes. Add the remaining butter, salt, and pepper. Stir until the sauce is smooth; do not boil sauce. Add the oysters to warm them in the sauce; they will poach on contact.

Slice the sweetbreads and cover with sauce. Surround sweetbreads with oysters and cover with julienne truffles.

Wine: *Meursault or Puligny Montrachet*   Serves: 4

La Closerie des Lilas

171, boulevard du Montparnasse, 75006 Paris
Tel: 326-7050
Proprietor: Jacqueline Milan • Chef: Yves Rivoal

Veal with Mussels

800 g (1¾ lb) fillet of veal (tenderloin)
50 g (1¾ oz) butter
100 ml (3 oz) dry wine
2 shallots
100 ml (3 oz) double cream (whipping cream)
curry, to taste
2 kg (4½ lb) cooked mussels, cooking liquid reserved
2 sliced apples, fried
2 slices pineapple
125 g (¼ lb) raisins

Slice the veal into 8 thick slices of about 100 g (3½ oz) each. Sauté the veal in a skillet in butter for 2-3 minutes per side, then take out the veal and keep warm. Pour ½ the wine into the skillet, then simmer the shallots in the wine. Add the cream and curry and reduce to sauce consistency. To finish the sauce, add the water from the cooked mussels.

Garnish the veal with fried apples, sliced pineapple, raisins, and the cooked mussels with shells removed.

Wine: *Gamay de Tourrain*   Serves: 4

La Closerie des Lilas is only a moment away from Montparnasse, and Montparnasse is in the centre of the city. At the bar of La Closerie, we are reminded of the poets (Paul Fort, Verlaine, Moréas), artists (Renoir, Modigliani, Toulouse-Lautrec), and writers (André Gide, Appolinaire, Oscar Wilde, and Ernest Hemingway) who frequented this spot.

Since 1953, Jacqueline Milan (now assisted by her son, Jean-Pierre) has brought back the magic La Closerie once had. It is a beautiful place with a bar on the terrace and a restaurant-gallery in the covered garden on the ground floor. The ambiance of those earlier wonderful years is still felt. La Closerie is one of the oldest and most artistic cafes in Paris.

La Grand Veneur

6, rue Pierre Demours, 75017 Paris
Tel: 574-6158
Proprietor/Chef: M. Dattas

Venison Chops with Pepper Sauce

60 ml (¼ cup) oil
60 ml (¼ cup) wine vinegar
120 ml (½ cup) dry red wine
salt, pepper, coriander, rosemary, and other seasonings, to taste
1.2 kg (2½ lb) venison chops
butter and olive oil, to sauté
70 ml (2 oz) champagne
20 g (¾ oz) pepper
Poivrade sauce* (pepper sauce), prepared in advance

Mix the first 3 ingredients together and season to taste. Marinate the venison chops for 3 days in this mixture. Turn it over twice a day.

Sauté the chops for 5-6 minutes per side in butter and oil. Deglaze the pan with champagne. Add the Poivrade sauce, season with pepper and salt, and let reduce to sauce consistency. Strain the sauce over the chops.

Suggestion: Serve the venison chops covered with sauce and garnished with puréed chestnuts.*

Wine: *A red Burgundy*   Serves: 4

M. Dattas is a man of adventure and obvious success. His restaurant almost looks like a museum honouring great game hunters. The walls are covered with his prize heads, and the decor is very rich in colour and atmosphere. He definitely has a unique restaurant with a special ambiance.

Don't be alarmed by any of the decorations. M. Dattas offers well prepared dishes, specialising in game, and a wine cellar full of Saint-Hubert.

Chez Frédante

7, rue des Glacis, 20000 Ajaccio
Tel: (95) 21-31-85
Proprietor/Chef: Antoine Villa

Corsica — island of love and eternal beauty. The most beautiful city on this exquisite island is, of course, Ajaccio. This ancient city, with its 16th century homes, flourishes as a tourist retreat. In 1977, Antoine Villa purchased an old house and transformed it into a lovely restaurant. **Chez Frédante** has three stories, a huge reception room, a foyer, and two beautifully decorated dining rooms.

Antoine prepares all his dishes with local products. The fine Fricassee of Langoustines with Wine, the Roast Kid, Blackbird and Wild Mushroom Casserole, and Mussels and Basil in Dough are all followed by an excellent platter of local cheeses.

Blackbird and Wild Mushroom Casserole

1 onion
2 shallots
50 g (1¾ oz) butter, and as needed
150 g (5¼ oz) wild boleteus mushrooms, chopped
12 blackbirds, livers removed and reserved
4 chicken livers
salt and pepper, to taste
80 g (2¾ oz) sharp cheese, Romano or Parmesan
1 tsp fine herbs
3 leaves sage
1 tbsp *eau-de-vie* (brandy)
6 unpeeled garlic cloves
2 branches wild thyme
½ bay leaf

To prepare the stuffing: Finely dice the onions and shallots. Sauté them in butter over medium heat until they begin to colour. Add the chopped mushrooms. Stir over high heat and reserve.

Colour the livers of the blackbirds and the 4 chicken livers in a pan of sizzling butter. (They must be very underdone.) Mix them with the onions and shallots, then add the salt, pepper, cheese, fine herbs, sage, and brandy. Purée the stuffing in a blender.

Stuff and sew the birds. Season with salt and pepper. Brown them in a sauté pan. Add the garlic, wild thyme, and bay leaf. Cover the pan and cook in a very hot oven, 475°F (250°C), for 18 minutes, then serve.

Suggestion: This recipe can be used for any other game bird of this size.

Wine: *Vin Rouge de Patrimonio*   Serves: 12

La Bonne Auberge

Route Nationale 7, 06600 Antibes
Tel: (93) 33-36-65
Proprietor/Chef: Jo Rostang

La Bonne Auberge was established some 30 years ago. It is luxurious, attractive, and beautifully decorated. Ten years ago, Jo Rostang took it over and now manages it with great pleasure. You see, the cuisine at La Bonne Auberge is a combination of expertise and fantasy.

The menu offers so much that sometimes it is difficult to make a choice. This is also true of the wine cellar, which contains a vast selection of fine wines. The dinners here are unforgettable, with such offerings as Sliced Capon Fillet with Courgettes (Zucchini) and Strawberry Vinegar, Capon with Kale, Duckling with Roast Pears and Turnips, and the cheese platter with fresh cheeses from Isère (where Jo originally came from).

Capon Fillet with Courgettes (Zucchini)

1 fillet of capon (breast) of 1.5 kg (3⅓ lb)
400 g (14 oz) long courgettes (zucchini)
125 g (¼ lb) butter
6 cloves garlic
salt and pepper, to taste
100 ml (3 oz) strawberry vinegar
chopped parsley, to garnish

Cut the fillets of capon into 70 g (2½ oz) strips. Peel and slice the courgettes in 4 medium slices. In a pan, melt ½ the butter, then add 4 garlic cloves, crushed but not peeled. Once the butter is golden brown, add the courgettes and sauté until golden in colour. Season with salt and pepper.

Place the capon fillets in another pan with the remaining butter and garlic and sauté them for 2 minutes on each side. Remove the capon and keep warm. Discard ½ the grease from the pan. Wet the pan with strawberry vinegar and reduce to ⅓. Add the butter from the courgettes.

To serve: Place the capon slices on a bed of courgettes and surround with the vinegar mixture. Top with chopped parsley and serve.

Serves: 4

Le Chêne Vert

35, boulevard Ledru-Rollin, 03500 Saint-Pourçain-sur-Sioule
Tel: (70) 45-40-65
Proprietor: Jean Giraudin • Chef: Jean-Guy Siret

Cheese-Flavoured Chicken

1 chicken of 1.6 kg (3½ lb)	60 g (2 oz) flour
chicken stock,* as needed	60 g (2 oz) butter
2 carrots, sliced	2 egg yolks
2 onions, sliced	200 ml (6 oz) double cream
1 leek, sliced	(whipping cream)
1 bouquet garni*	80 g (2¾ oz) grated Gruyère or
1 stalk celery, chopped	Swiss cheese
1 clove	50 g (1¾ oz) grated Fourme d'Ambert
crushed peppercorns and salt,	cheese (a hard, strong cheese
to taste	from the Limagne, also called
100 ml (3 oz) white wine	Cantal cheese)
¼ litre (½ pt) milk	

Poach the chicken in enough chicken stock to cover it and add carrots, onions, leek, bouquet garni, celery, clove, peppercorns, salt, and white wine. Gently whisk milk, flour, and butter into this mixture to make it velvety. Let it simmer for a few minutes, then add egg yolks and cream; stir well.

Cut the chicken in quarters. Pass the velvety liquid through a sieve or fine strainer, then pour it over the chicken. Sprinkle the chicken with Gruyère and Fourme d'Ambert. Bake in the oven at 325°F (160°C) until cheese turns slightly golden. Serve immediately.

Serves: 4

Saint-Pourçain-sur-Sioule is another one of the many small towns in France where it seems time has passed it by. **Le Chêne Vert** is the only large and fine restaurant in this town. Jean Giraudin took over an old, rundown establishment a few years ago and totally transformed it. He redecorated and beautified it, and even included a flowered terrace. Jean runs Le Chêne Vert with the assistance of his family.

The restaurant contains two dining rooms where you will feast on regional delicacies such as Cheese-Flavoured Chicken, Veal Sweetbreads Terrine, Fillet of Anglerfish Poached in Red Wine, Special Soft-Boiled Eggs, and Veal Liver with Apples and Cider. You will also discover the best wines from the region are available here.

Lou Marquès

Hôtel Jules César, Boulevard de Lices, 13000 Arles
Tel: (90) 96-49-76
Proprietor: M. Albagnac • Chef: Roland Petrini

Chicken "Arles" Style

1 chicken of 1.4 - 1.5 kg (3 - 3⅓ lb)
100 ml (3 oz) olive oil
80 g (2¾ oz) butter
4 cloves garlic, chopped
2 large onions, finely chopped
salt and pepper, to taste
1 tbsp mixed herbs (thyme, savory, marjoram)
200 ml (6 oz) white wine
2 kg (4½ lb) tomatoes, seeded and crushed
2 tbsp tomato paste
½ litre (1 pt) clear chicken broth or bouillon
parsley, to garnish

Cut the chicken into pieces. Sauté them in olive oil and butter until brown. Remove the chicken and keep warm. Brown the onions and garlic in the same pot. Return the chicken to the pot and season with salt and pepper. Add the mixed herbs. Wet with the wine and add tomatoes, tomato paste, and chicken broth. Let stew on low heat for 2 hours.

Degrease the pan. Remove the chicken pieces. Reduce the cooking liquid to sauce consistency and correct the seasoning. Bone the chicken.

Place the chicken on a plate, cover with sauce, sprinkle with parsley, and serve.

Wine: *Château Simone Rouge*

Serves: 4

Your visit to **Lou Marquès** will be a memorable one. Under the soft, warm sunshine in Provence, the cuisine of Roland Petrini is light and deliciously provincial. Dining at Lou Marquès could become a regular outing for you because to come here once is never enough; I've learned that from experience.

Roland prepares sumptuous traditional dishes, and the wines are from local vines. Lou Marquès is really a very popular place for the locals as well as for the tourists. The Chicken "Arles" Style must be tried if you're interested in a fine example of the regional cuisine.

Le Restaurant d'Olympe

8, rue Nicolas-Charlet, 75015 Paris
Tel: 734-8606 and 783-4976
Proprietors: M. and Mme. Nahmias • Chef: Dominique Nahmias

Mme. Dominique Nahmias is one of the youngest, most congenial, and most gifted of today's fashionable chefs. And fashion is such that her establishment has become a sort of Mecca for gourmand snobbery. Brushing aside the somewhat overpowering Parisians who come here, take the time to admire the varnished panels stripped from the last Orient Express and the coach suspension springs. While you wait for your dinner, sit down and chat over a few glasses of wine, which Albert Nahmias selects most admirably — it will put you in good stead for food that really is worth waiting for: Crayfish with Garlic, Chicken Cooked in Beer with Leeks, Raw Sea Bream, Smoked Duck Soup, or Raviole with Broccoli Sauce, and truly inspired desserts.

Chicken Cooked in Beer with Leeks

1 chicken of 1.6 kg (3½ lb)
4 tbsp butter
3 shallots
⅓ litre (¾ pt) dark beer
1 bay leaf
1 sprig thyme
salt and pepper, to taste
1 bunch leeks, white parts only
2 litres (½ gal) salted water
100 ml (3 oz) chicken stock*
300 ml (9 oz) double cream (whipping cream)
1 bunch chives, chopped

Quarter the chicken; chop the liver and gizzard and brown them in butter in a frying pan. Add the shallots, chicken parts, and brown without overcooking. Pour the beer over the chicken. Add bay leaf, thyme, salt, and pepper, then cover and let simmer for 20 minutes. (The wings will cook sooner than the legs; remove them when done and keep warm.) Wash the whites of the leeks thoroughly, then cook them in boiling salted water for about 12 minutes. Strain, then put into an ovenproof pan with the chicken stock, salt, pepper, and 120 ml (4 oz) cream. Bring to a boil, then keep warm.

Remove the skin from the cooked chicken pieces and put the wings back into the frying pan. Add the remaining cream and bring to a boil. Let boil for about 3-4 minutes to thicken the sauce. Check the seasoning.

Serve the chicken pieces coated with the sauce on a warm serving dish. Sprinkle with chopped chives and place the leeks on top.

Wine: *Chablis*   Serves: 4

Le Cheval Blanc

2, place du 6-Juin, 14500 Vire
Tel: (31) 68-00-21
Proprietor: Mme. Delaunay • Chef: Jean-Paul Delaunay

Normandy, the northern part of France, is known for its small towns, warm people, hearty food, and most especially, Mont Saint-Michel — that staunch, Gothic style, feudal castle, which still attracts tourists from every corner of the world. Another attraction to this area is **Le Cheval Blanc**, where you will be greeted with a warm smile from Mme. Delaunay. Lel Cheval Blanc is a comfortable family restaurant-hotel. The rooms are modern and the service is prompt.

Jean-Paul serves excellent dinners prepared with finesse and care. His menu offers Fillet of Sole with Apples, Normandy Black Pudding, Roast Duck Flamed with Calvados, and Chicken "Father Chauvel" Style, among others. Jean's menu is fabulous, as is his selection of wines.

Chicken "Father Chauvel" Style

1 chicken of 1 kg (2¼ lb)
salt and pepper, to taste
butter, to sauté
port wine and cognac, to flame
100 ml (3 oz) double cream (whipping cream)
4 crepes,* prepared
chestnut purée,* as needed

Cut the chicken in 4 parts and season with salt and pepper. In a pan with a little butter, sauté the chicken for 20 minutes. When almost cooked, flame with port and cognac. Take the chicken out of the pan, add cream to the pan, and reduce to sauce consistency.

Stuff 4 small crepes with chestnut purée. Place a piece of chicken on each crepe, then fold each crepe in half. Cover with the sauce and serve.

Suggestion: Serve with fresh vegetables such as spring peas, spinach, tomatoes, and turnips and young fried potatoes.

Serves: 4

La Tour Rose

16, rue du Boeuf, 69005 Lyon
Tel: (7) 837-2590
Proprietor/Chef: Philippe Chavent

Chicken Fricassee with Bell Pepper Sauce

3 soft bell peppers
125 g (¼ lb) butter
1 chicken of 1.8 kg (4 lb)
salt and pepper, to taste
4 cloves garlic
1 litre (2 pt) dry white wine
300 ml (9 oz) double cream (whipping cream)

Remove the seeds from the bell peppers and cut off the stems. Put the peppers in the oven for 3-4 minutes at 350°F (175°C). Take the peppers out of the oven, peel them, and slice them. In a pan with some butter, quickly sauté the pepper slices without colouring them. Let cool. Chop the peppers very finely.

Cut the chicken into pieces; season with salt and pepper. In a pot with the remaining butter and the unpeeled garlic clove, sauté the pieces of chicken until golden. Cover and bake in the oven for 4-5 minutes at 350°F (175°C). Take the chicken out of the oven, remove from the pot, and keep warm. Skim the grease from the pot. Add the white wine and reduce the preparation to ⅔. Add the chopped bell peppers and the cream. Let reduce to ⅓. Put the chicken pieces back into the preparation, adjust the seasoning, and serve hot.

Serves: 4

La Mère Blanc

01540 Vonnas
Tel: (74) 50-00-01
Proprietor/Chef: Georges Blanc

It was in 1872 that the Blancs established themselves here at the edge of Veyle, and soon afterwards "Mother" Blanc became famous to the point where Curnonsky declared her the "first lady chef of France." Her Sautéed Chicken from Bresse and her Small Potato Crepes brought her this glory. Georges Blanc, her grandson, took over the restaurant in 1968 and has continued to please even the most critical gourmets.

This old auberge, on the road to the Côte d'Azur, is a sumptuous inn that has been made feminine and elegant by Mme. Jacqueline Blanc. The decor is flowered, the furniture is a bit antique, and the wine cellar contains 600 bottles of the best names.

Visiting **La Tour Rose** is like taking a tour of historical buildings. This structure is a beautiful example of Renaissance architecture, the most important style in France. It was built of lovely, pink stone and is situated in Old Lyon. There are two dining rooms: one is decorated in Louis XIII style and the other dates from 1625. This is a restaurant in a city known for its cuisine, and the food *must* be good. Philippe Chavent's cuisine is impeccable. He presents specialities such as Gâteau of Goose Liver with Crayfish Sauce, John Dory with Oysters and Marjoram, and Chicken Fricassee with Bell Pepper Sauce, all wonderful. The wine cellar contains a large selection of wines dating from 1900 to 1968.

Chicken Fricassee with Vinegar

1 chicken of 1.6 - 1.8 kg (3½ - 4 lb)
150 g (5¼ oz) butter
salt and pepper, to taste
3 carrots, in large dice
5 small onions, or 1 large onion, quartered
3 cloves garlic
2 sprigs fresh tarragon
100 ml (3 oz) tarragon wine vinegar
200 ml (6 oz) clear broth
2 tsp flour
2 tbsp tomato purée
500 ml (2 cups) double cream (whipping cream)
1 cup tomato, concasse*
1 tsp chopped tarragon
250 g (½ lb) creole rice, cooked

Cut the chicken into 8 pieces and brown in a heavy pan with some butter. Season with salt and pepper. Add carrots, onions, garlic, and whole tarragon. Cover the pan and cook in the oven at 425°F (220°C). After it is half-cooked (about 15 minutes), begin to periodically add splashes of vinegar to the pan so the flavour penetrates the chicken. When cooking is complete (another 15 minutes), remove the chicken and keep warm. Remove exess fat from pan. Caramelise the juices and deglaze with the remaining vinegar and the clear broth. Reduce to sauce consistency. Mix the flour and tomato purée in a cup. Pour into the sauce and stir well. Add cream and tomato concasse. Correct the seasoning. Pour the sauce over the chicken, garnish with chopped tarragon, and serve with the rice.

Serves: 4

L'Auberge Bressane

166, boulevard de Brou, 01000 Bourg-en-Bresse
Tel: (74) 22-22-68
Proprietor/Chef: Jean-Pierre Vullin

The most famous chicken is the chicken from Bresse. It is the softest and the tastiest kind of chicken there is. **L'Auberge Bressane** serves some of the finest preparations of this fowl.

Nevertheless, Jean-Pierre Vullin knows that people eat more than just chicken, therefore, he also offers a vast selection of successful meat and vegetable dishes, but, be sure to try the chicken; it is a very special treat, especially in this restaurant.

Chicken in Tarragon Cream

1 chicken of 1.5 - 1.8 kg (3½ - 4 lb), with giblets reserved
1 bouquet of fresh tarragon
1 litre (2 pt) chicken bouillon
125 g (¼ lb) butter
salt and pepper, to taste
½ litre (1 pt) cream
1 tbsp flour

Stuff the chicken with the tarragon (reserving some for decoration). Boil the chicken in the bouillon with the giblets and ½ the butter, salt, and pepper for 45 minutes. Remove chicken and giblets and keep warm.

To prepare the sauce: Simmer the cooking liquid, then add cream. Gently mix the remaining butter and flour together, then blend into the sauce to thicken it.

Cover the chicken with the sauce, decorate with remaining tarragon, and serve.
Suggestion: Serve with creole rice.

Serves: 4

Oustau de Baumanière

Les Beaux-de-Provence, 13520 Maussane
Tel: (90) 97-33-07
Proprietor/Chef: Raymond Thullier

Oustau de Baumanière is a luxurious, patrician hotel with personalised rooms surrounding a swimming pool. The dining rooms have high, wood-beamed ceilings and fresh, beautiful flowers. Raymond Thullier says that his "cuisine and wine are secrets," however, it is possible to visit his kitchen where you can watch him. Raymond has many culinary secrets, as you will discover, especially when you taste his Red Mullet Mousseline, Lobster Soufflé, Sole with Morel Mushrooms, Veal Sweetbreads, Chicken with Anchovies, and Leg of Mutton in Crust. The desserts are sumptuous, and you also have a choice of 35,000 Burgundies, Bordeaux, and Château Lafite-Rothchild wines. Enjoy!

Chicken with Anchovies

2 chicken livers
60 g (2 oz) lard
chopped chervil and chives, to taste
6 anchovy fillets, finely chopped
1 chicken, quartered
strips of pork fat, as needed
50 g (1¾ oz) butter
100 ml (3 oz) wine
100 ml (3 oz) vermouth

To prepare the stuffing: Finely chop the liver and lard, mix together, and add chervil, chives, and 3 chopped anchovy fillets. Put this stuffing under the legs, wings, and breast flap skin of the chicken. Wrap all in a thin layer of pork fat.

Bake the chicken for 40 minutes in the oven at 400°F (205°C). Baste often with butter. Remove chicken and degrease the pan. Make a light sauce in the pan by combining white wine and vermouth with the cooking juices. Let reduce to sauce consistency. Add butter, stir, and keep warm. Before serving, add 3 finely chopped anchovy fillets to this sauce.

Serves: 4

La Poularde chez Lucullus

9, rue Gustave-Deloye, 06000 Nice
Tel: (93) 85-22-90
Proprietor/Chef: Marcel Normand

In Nice, finding a good restaurant is never a problem; they are all excellent. **La Poularde** is one of them, and it is a classic among classics. La Poularde has been pleasing regular customers for years, and because it is the most Parisian of all the restaurants in Nice, Parisians on vacation who dine here can feel they are never too far from home.

The Suprême de Sole "Lucullus" and the Turbot Poached in Hollandaise Sauce, as well as the Country Chicken and Châteaubriand Béarnaise, satisfy all who come here.

Country Chicken

1 fat pullet or chicken of 1.8 kg (4 lb)
flour, to dust
2 tbsp peanut oil
150 g (5¼ oz) butter, and as needed
500 g (1 lb) new potatoes
200 g (7 oz) mushrooms, cut in pieces
salt and pepper, to taste
2 sprigs parsley, crushed

Cut the pullet into 8 pieces. Flour them lightly.

In a thick, copper skillet, melt oil and butter (but keep butter from browning). Place pieces of pullet in the skillet and sauté all the pieces until lightly coloured (about 10 minutes). Add the new potatoes. Simmer them with the pieces of pullet. (Make sure there is still butter in the pan.) After 10 minutes, add the mushrooms. Season with salt and pepper. Let simmer for another 7-8 minutes. Just before serving, sprinkle with crushed parsley.

Wine: *Rosé de Provence or Bandol Rouge*

Serves: 4

La Chèvre d'Or

06360 Eze-Village
Tel: (93) 41-12-12
Proprietor: Bruno Ingold • Chef: Elie Mazot

In 1952, Eze-Village, a thousand-year-old lookout that dominates the Mediterranean between Nice and Monte Carlo, saw its chateau ruins restored and transformed into a wonderful restaurant called **La Chèvre d'Or**. In 1976, Bruno Ingold acquired the restaurant. He is now assisted by Elie Mazot, a chef who comes from the Ritz. Together they have created an intimate ambiance with soft background music and excellent service.

For your dining pleasure, try the Scampi Soup, Raw Salmon Salad, Perch with Sea Urchin Cream, Lobster Fricassee with Courgettes (Zucchini), Grilled Veal Sweetbreads, Rich Chicken Pot-au-Feu, or Fillet of Beef with Mustard Seeds; all are accompanied by excellent wines from Jean-Pierre Buffo's cellar.

Rich Chicken Pot-au-Feu

1 chicken of 1.5 kg (3 lb)
1 veal knuckle
court bouillon,* as needed
24 carrots and turnips,
   cut in oval shapes
24 small onions
4 leeks
1 tsp each: chopped shallots,
   parsley, crushed black peppercorns

50 g (1¾ oz) sliced mushrooms
200 ml (6 oz) white wine
¼ litre (1 cup) veal stock*
125 g (¼ lb) butter
6 beef tournedos,* 60 g (2 oz) each
6 slices raw goose liver

Simmer the chicken and the veal knuckle for 1 hour in enough court bouillon to cover them both. Remove the knuckle and cut it into 6 slices. Remove the chicken, remove its bones, and slice the chicken meat. Keep knuckle and chicken warm.

Cook the vegetables *al dente** in the same court bouillon; remove and keep warm. Reserve the court bouillon.

To prepare the sauce: Sweat* the shallots, parsley, tarragon, peppercorns, and mushrooms in the wine. Add the veal stock and reduce by ½. Strain. Gradually whisk in the butter, piece by piece. Correct the seasoning and keep hot.

Poach the tournedos in the reserved court bouillon for 3 minutes.

Cook the goose liver quickly in a pan with very little oil.

Pour a little sauce onto each plate. Arrange a selection of meats and vegetables on top. Serve the remaining sauce separately.

Serves: 6

Restaurant Le Paris

9, rue de l'Hôtel-de-Ville, 39600 Arbois
Tel: (84) 66-05-67
Proprietor/Chef: André Jeunet

There is an expression derived from an old proverb concerning the wine of Arbois that says, "The more you drink, the straighter you walk." André Jeunet is the master of **Restaurant Le Paris**, and with his son's assistance in the kitchen, he prepares many authentic regional dishes to complement the superb wine of the region. The dining room here has a rustic decor, with walls decorated with trophies and diplomas signifying many culinary achievements.

André acquired his talent for cooking from his mother, who for years devoted herself to gourmet cooking. André is proud of his excellent dishes from Provence, especially the Smoked Sausage and the Rooster in Wine with Morel Mushrooms.

Rooster in Wine with Morel Mushrooms

1 rooster of 1.5 kg (3⅓ lb)
salt and pepper, to taste
50 g (1¾ oz) flour
200 g (7 oz) butter
200 ml (6 oz) Arbois or Château Chalon wine
200 g (7 oz) morel mushrooms
½ litre (1 pt) double cream (whipping cream)

Quarter the rooster. Season the pieces with salt and pepper, coat lightly with flour, and brown in butter in a sauté pan. Put the pieces of rooster in a covered pot, and let cook over medium heat for 20 minutes without colouring the meat.

Take pot off heat and deglaze with the wine. Add the morel mushrooms and cream. Adjust the seasoning. Let cook, uncovered, over low heat until rooster is done (check drumsticks for pinkness) and sauce is reduced.

Suggestion: Serve the rooster pieces napped* with sauce on a bed of rice.

Wine: *A yellow Arbois wine*   Serves: 4

La Vieille Maison

5, rue au Lait, 28000 Chartres
Tel: (37) 34-10-67
Proprietor/Chef: Roger Bernard

If you are hungry and thirsty, you need to find **La Vieille Maison**. It is located in the old quarter of Chartres on a tiny, narrow street. If you try, you will stumble upon this little restaurant where the reward for your effort is waiting.

Roger serves a fine Terrine of Langoustine Tails, Chicken with Cider and Turnips, Veal Sweetbreads and Noodles with Foie Gras, followed by a delicious Tangerine Soufflé. You will leave relaxed, satisfied, and rewarded by this truly fine gastonomic experience.

Sliced Chicken with Cider and Turnips

2 breasts of chicken, skinned and boned
1 bottle cider
1 kg (2¼ lb) turnips, cut in oval shapes
1 tbsp sugar
1 tbsp fresh goose liver fat
salt and pepper, to taste
125 g (¼ lb) butter
2 tbsp double cream (whipping cream)
120 g (¼ lb) goose liver, cubed

Marinate the chicken breasts in ¼ litre (1 cup) cider for 1 hour.

To glaze the turnips: Place turnips in a frying pan with sugar, goose liver fat, and ¼ litre (1 cup) cider. Let cook, but watch carefully; turnips should remain firm.

Drain and reserve the marinade from the chicken. Dry the chicken breasts, then season with salt and pepper. Brown in an ovenproof skillet with butter, but just long enough to stiffen them. Put the skillet in the oven at 400°F (205°C) for 10 minutes. Remove the breasts and slice thinly. Deglaze the skillet with the reserved marinade and the remaining cider. Reduce to sauce consistency. Add cream. When the sauce is at its peak, add goose liver cubes and mix everything in the skillet together well.

Arrange the slices of breast on a plate with the turnips. Pour the sauce over the slices and serve hot.

Wine: *Pauillac*   Serves: 2

La Colombe d'Or

06570 Saint-Paul-de-Vence
Tel: (93) 32-80-02
Proprietor: Francis Roux • Chef: Serge Oblette

If anything can put you in the right mood for dining and really stimulate your appetite, **La Colombe d'Or** will. The decor here is very impressive, especially all the mirrors and Picassos, the terrace, and the pool. This is a very special restaurant that attracts very special people — gourmets. Whether they be in Paris or Provence, travelling to La Colombe d'Or is never a problem for these people because the food here is fabulous.

When you're not busy trying to photograph Simone Signoret and Yves Montand, find the time to stop in and enjoy the beauty of this provincial restaurant and its great food.

Small Chicken Sausages

120 ml (½ cup) veal stock*
125 g (¼ lb) butter
60 ml (¼ cup) Madeira wine
60 g (2 oz) julienne truffles
salt and pepper, to taste
250 g (½ lb) chicken meat
2 egg whites
nutmeg, to taste
¼ litre (1 cup) thick double cream (whipping cream)
1 chicken of 1 kg (2¼ lb)
caul (or salt pork), cut in long, thin strips, as needed
bread crumbs, as needed
clarified butter, as needed

To prepare the sauce: Reduce the veal stock by ½; add butter, Madeira wine, truffles, salt, and pepper.

To prepare the mousse: Finely grind the chicken meat and pass through a fine strainer. Slowly add the egg whites, salt, pepper, and nutmeg. Put all on ice, then add cream.

Take the legs and wings off the chicken. Remove the bones from the carcass and mix the chicken meat with the mousse. Divide the mixture into 125 g (¼ lb) portions. Roll each portion in a strip of caul to enclose it. Cover these "sausages" with bread crumbs and cook in clarified butter until hot and golden brown (about 8 - 10 minutes).

To serve: Spread the "sausages" on a platter and serve the sauce separately.

Serves: 2

Le Muniche

27, rue de Buci, 75006 Paris
Tel: 633-6209
Proprietors: The Layrac Brothers • Chef: Christian Tourault

Here at **Le Muniche**, the Layrac brothers possess quite a gold mine. This restaurant, which is always cheerful and busy, is located in the most active part of town — Saint-Germain, a neighbourhood known for its old buildings and its artists colony. At Le Muniche, specialities from Auvergne take priority.

The Layrac brothers are very proud of their success here, so they have decided to open a boutique and sell their products packaged to take home. The house *foies gras, petits salés, confits,* and *cochonnailles* are truly special treats, as are the Stuffed Chicken and the desserts.

Stuffed Chicken

1 chicken of 1.8 kg (4 lb)
200 g (7 oz) bread, cut in pieces
70 ml (2 oz) milk
200 g (7 oz) cooked ham
parsley, to taste
tarragon, to taste
3 cloves garlic
3 shallots, chopped
1 pinch salt
1 pinch pepper
1 pinch nutmeg
3 litres (¾ gal) water
400 g (14 oz) carrots
300 g (10½ oz) turnips
2 medium-sized onions
3 cloves
2 pinches coarse salt

To prepare the chicken: Remove the giblets. Reserve the heart, liver, and gizzards. Clean the inside of the chicken.

Mix the next 10 ingredients together with the reserved heart, liver, and gizzard to make a stuffing. Fill the chicken with the stuffing and fasten the end with string or skewers. Simmer the stuffed chicken in the water with all the remaining ingredients for 2 hours. Take out the vegetables as they are cooked and keep warm. Once the chicken is cooked, serve it hot with the vegetables on the side.

Wine: *Gamay de Tourine*

Serves: 6

À Sousceyrac

35, rue Faidherbe, 75011 Paris
Tel: 371-6530
Proprietor: Gabriel Asfaux • Chef: Patrick Asfaux

Stuffed Chicken Rolls

1 chicken of 1.8 kg (4 lb)	1 egg yolk
1 carrot	1 tsp starch, dissolved in water
1 onion	20 g (¾ oz) chopped truffles
1 stick celery	120 g (4 oz) goose liver
1 bouquet garni*	roux, made from 125 g (¼ lb) butter
2 litres (2 qt) cold water	and 125 g (¼ lb) flour, blended
salt and pepper, to taste	100 ml (3 oz) port wine
8 large white mushrooms	200 ml (6 oz) double cream
butter, as needed	(whipping cream)
lemon juice, to taste	4 slices toast

Bone the chicken breast and flatten the flesh to obtain 4 scallops.

To prepare the chicken stock: Put the carcass and the next 6 ingredients in the water, bring to a boil, reduce heat, and simmer 1½ - 2 hours or until reduced by half.

To prepare the stuffing: Cook mushrooms in butter for 3 minutes. Season with salt, pepper, and lemon juice. Blend in egg yolk and starch. Add chopped truffles and let cool. Spread the stuffing on each scallop of chicken. Divide the goose liver among them. Roll each piece of chicken like a cigar. Wrap each separately in aluminum foil and place in an ovenproof casserole. Cook in an oven for 40 minutes at 350-400°F (180-200°C). Remove chicken from oven, let stand 5 minutes, then remove aluminum foil.

To prepare the sauce: Mix the roux and reduced stock in a saucepan and let cook 10 minutes. At the last minute, add port, cream, and lemon juice (seasoning should taste strong).

To serve: Place each chicken roll on toast on a plate and cover with sauce. Serve warm.

Wine: *An old Cahors or Bordeaux*   Serves: 4

Sousceyrac was the home of Pierre Benoît, the writer, whose novel *Au Déjeuner de Sousceyrac* was set in this restaurant. In 1923, the Asfaux family started this restaurant. Two sons continued the business; one disappeared, Gabriel stayed. He now manages the restaurant, and his son, Patrick, manages the cuisine. The restaurant features old-fashioned decor and offers a fine regional cuisine, enhanced by Patrick, especially the recipes for truffles and the cassoulets. (This region fascinates and attracts people from all over the world — people such as Laurence Olivier and Prince Ali Khan.) The entire menu is abundant with truly exquisite food. I highly recommend the Stuffed Chicken Rolls.

Château-Pétrus was once a grand castle belonging to a very distinguished gentleman from Pomerol. Today, Jacques Douté runs **Les Trois Toques** with his wife. Jacques transformed the old castle into a modern and lively restaurant-hotel. Jacques prepares his favourite foods served with his favourite wines: *cuisine Bordelaise* with Bordeaux wines. Les Trois Toques expresses harmony and gentleness; the gardens are ravishing, the rooms impeccable, and the dining room is a blend of simplicity with elegance. Les Trois Toques serves such specialities as Pigs Feet with Green Sauce, Vegetable Terrine, and Duck Breast with St. Émilion Wine — all are delicious.

Les Trois Toques

Hôtel Loubat, 32 rue Crinzy, 33500 Libourne
Tel: (56) 51-17-58
Proprietors: M. and Mme. Jacques Douté • Chef: Guy Degoul

Duck Breast in St. Émilion Wine

1 duck breast, skinned and boned
salt and pepper, to taste
1 pinch shallots, chopped
30 ml (1 oz) cognac
200 ml (6 oz) St. Émilion wine
2 tbsp veal stock*
1 tbsp double cream (whipping cream), and as needed
½ tsp butter, and as needed

Season the duck breast with salt and pepper. Sauté it over high heat on each side, but keep the meat rare. Remove the grease and add shallots. Flame with cognac. Add wine. Remove the breast and slice it.

Flame the wine. Let the mixture reduce. Add the veal stock, 1 tbsp cream, and ½ tsp butter. Let reduce until sauce is very smooth and rich-looking. Add a touch more of cream and butter. Correct the seasoning.

Strain the sauce, then pour it over the slices of duck breast, and serve.

Serves: 1

Relais du Val d'Orbieu

11200 Ornaisons-Lézignas-Corbières
Tel: (68) 27-10-27
Proprietor: Maricha Sanitas • Chef: Bernard Martin

What was once a trite and unattractive motel-bar-restaurant in Corbières has now become, by the grace of Mme. Sanitas, a picturesque motel-bar-restaurant, situated on the border of Orbieu. Its rustic Louis XIII decor, all in warm colours, gives you a soothing feeling. The bar is very intimate, the rooms have all been individually decorated, and there is a large pool in the yard.

Preparing meals for this unique place is Bernard Martin, who successfully blends tradition and fantasy. You should try his Anglerfish with Meaux Mustard, Turbot Fricassee with Seaweed, Duck Breasts with Lettuce, Eel Stew, Scallops with Tomato Sauce, Calamari Soup, and Sole with Cucumbers. Everything at **Relais du Val d'Orbieu** is fresh and prepared superbly.

Duck Breasts with Lettuce

4 hearts of lettuce
50 g (1¾ oz) butter
4 carrots, sliced
6 shallots, thinly sliced
2 thin leeks
50 ml (2 oz) sherry wine vinegar
4 limes, thinly sliced
8 tbsp aspic (or gelatine)
salt and pepper, to taste
4 duck breasts, skinned and boned

Steam the hearts of lettuce to soften them; reserve and keep warm.

In a separate pan with butter, sauté the carrots, shallots, and leeks. Deglaze with ½ the vinegar. Add the sliced limes and cook for a few moments. Wet the preparation with the aspic and the remaining vinegar; season with salt and pepper. Roast the breasts for 20-30 minutes at 375°F (190°C). Keep them juicy. Cut the breasts into thin slices.

To serve: Place the slices of duck breasts on a hot plate. Pour the lime preparation around them and place the steamed lettuce on the same plate.

Wine: *Châteauneuf du Pape or Aloxe Courton*   Serves: 4

L'Échaudé Saint-Germain

21, rue de l'Échaudé, 76005 Paris
Tel: 354-7902
Proprietors: S.A.R.L. L'Aubracienne, Messrs. Layrac • Chef: Jean-Paul Chossat

Saint-Germain is well-known for being a very unique neighbourhood in Paris. It is the place where movie stars, painters, writers, and very wealthy people meet. The streets are very narrow, and the buildings are very old. This is also the perfect place for lovers because of its charming atmosphere.

Jean-Paul Chossat is the imaginative and creative chef at **L'Échaudé Saint-Germain**. He blends in with the crowd here very well because he, too, is talented — in the kitchen. Jean-Paul offers Black Pudding Stew, Small Vegetables in Coquilles, and another fine classic dish, Breast of Duck with Meaux Mustard.

L'Échaudé is a good place to satisfy your appetite and warm your heart.

Duck Breasts with Meaux Mustard

1 duck breast with its fat
salt and pepper, to taste
100 ml (3 oz) cognac
500 ml (1 pt) double cream (whipping cream)
½ tsp Meaux mustard

Split the duck breast and put in a frying pan. Season with salt and pepper and sauté for 2 minutes on each side. Remove the breasts and put them in an ovenproof pan. Loosely cover pan with foil and place in the oven at 475°F (250°C) for 15 minutes.

To prepare the sauce: Reduce the juices in the frying pan to ½, then flame with cognac. Mix this flamed and reduced mixture with the cream and mustard. Adjust the seasoning. Serve the duck breasts covered with this sauce.

Serves: 2

La Tour du Roy

02140 Vervins
Tel: (23) 98-00-11
Proprietor/Chef: Annie Desvignes

Annie Desvignes is the daughter of a prominent lady chef, however, Annie did not stick to her mother's recipes; she wanted to learn the more complex cuisine of the great chefs. She began her trade with Claude Peyrot (of Vivarois) and the great Raymond Oliver.

La Tour du Roy is situated in an old manor, the same one where Henry IV was recognized as King of France in 1598. The furnishings in this manor are also from that era. Annie has established a restaurant that specialises in regional cuisine. The *flamiche* (cheese tart), Rabbit with Cider, and Duck Breasts with Fruit Sauce are fine examples. Annie is also very proud that she is one of the most celebrated members of the Association of Women Restaurateurs and Chefs.

Duck Breasts with Fruit Sauce

4 duck breasts, skinless and boneless
salt and pepper, to taste
1 bay leaf
1 sprig thyme
hazelnut oil, as needed
butter, to sauté
Grand Marnier, to flame
sugar syrup,* to taste
100 ml (3 oz) sherry wine vinegar
2 tbsp chives, chopped
2 tsp garlic, crushed
½ litre (1 cup) chicken stock*
½ bottle Cherry Marnier (or any cherry liqueur)
juice of 4 oranges
juice of 4 lemons
2 tsp redcurrant jelly

Marinate the breasts of duck for 24 hours in a marinade made of salt, pepper, bay leaf, thyme, and enough hazelnut oil to cover. Remove the breasts and sauté in butter for 5 minutes. Flame with Grand Marnier. Remove the breasts and cut them into 6 thin slices each.

To prepare the sauce: Mix together the remaining ingredients and let simmer in a saucepan for 20 minutes to reduce it.

Add the slices of duck breasts to the sauce, long enough to heat them, and serve.

Serves: 4

L'Espérance

17, rue René-Couard, 58150 Pouilly-sur-Loire
Tel: (86) 39-10-68
Proprietor/Chef: Jacques Raveau

Some of the most beautiful vineyards of France are in the Loire Valley. From these vines come the Sauvignon and Chasselas wines. These are the wines that Jacques Raveau serves in his restaurant. This gentleman has 35 years of experience as a chef and, without a doubt, in pleasing gourmets.

The Loire region is a historic area in France, and its people don't take well to change. In this land of earthy, simple folks, Jacques Raveau offers precisely what the people want. Saupiquet (ham in sweet and sour sauce) is a regional speciality; the Chicken in White Wine, Chicken Sautéed with Morels, Duck in Red Wine, Pike with Beurre Blanc, Squirrel Pie, and Eggs Poached in Wine are all superb.

L'Espérance is not chic or sophisticated; it is down-to-earth and relaxed.

Duck in Red Wine

2 wings and 2 breasts of duck
salt and pepper, to taste
butter, as needed
1 tsp chopped shallots
100 ml (3 oz) Armagnac
100 ml (3 oz) Pinot rouge or Sancerre red wine

Season the wings and breasts of duck with salt and pepper. In a skillet with butter, brown the breasts and wings, but keep the meat pink. Once cooked, remove the pieces to a serving platter.

Skim the grease from the skillet, add the shallots and sweat* them in the juices. Add Amagnac and wine and let reduce to ½ the original amount. Add ½ tsp of butter, adjust the seasonings, and cover the duck parts with the sauce. Serve.

Wine: *Clos du Roy or Bue en Sancerre*

Serves: 2

Château de Castel-Novel

19240 Varetz
Tel: (55) 85-00-01
Proprietor: Albert Parveaux • Chef: Jean-Pierre Faucher

Duck in Walnut Wine

2 ducks, 1.4 kg (3 lb) each, cut up
300 ml (9 oz) red wine from Cahors
salt and pepper, to taste
500 ml (1 pt) walnut liqueur*
300 ml (9 oz) wine vinegar
30 g (1 oz) walnuts
chopped chervil, to garnish

Remove the wings and thighs from the ducks. Remove the bones from the breasts while leaving the cartilage on to preserve the skins when cooking. Cook the breasts in the oven at 300°F (150°C) for 1 hour. Prepare 500 ml (2 pt) of duck stock* with the bones from the carcasses, red wine, and water. Salt and pepper the thighs and wings, and fry them in butter for 2 minutes. Add to the pot with the breasts cooking in oven. Because the wings cook first, take them out once they are pink.

To prepare the sauce: Add the walnut liqueur to the duck stock and adjust the seasoning. Heat, and when it starts to boil, add the vinegar and walnuts. Let it reduce to the desired sauce consistency.

Remove the cartilage from the breasts, slice the breasts thinly, and arrange them in the centre of a serving plate. Place the thighs (cut in 2) and the wings on the plate, cover with sauce, sprinkle with chervil, and serve.

Wine: *Cahors de Côteaux*

Serves: 8

Castles in France are still very much alive. For many generations, families have carried on their proud heritage by working and living in the family chateau. **Château de Castel-Novel** is one such castle; it is located in the lush forest in the Périgord region. Five centuries of history have filled its walls. Many famous people have resided in this castle, including Henri de Jouvenel, the well-known journalist and politician, and his famous wife, Colette.

Presently, Albert Parveaux runs this fine castle and offers a menu fit for a king. It features Truffle Tart, Fresh Smoked Salmon, Duck in Walnut Wine, Anglerfish Soup with Saffron, and a wide choice of fabulous cheeses and fancy pastries.

La Ligne

30, rue Jean-Mermoz, 75008 Paris
Tel: 225-5265
Proprietor/Chef: Jean Speyer

Duck Leg with Peaches

1 large duck leg, drumstick and thigh attached
200 g (7 oz) lard
salt and pepper, to taste
1 bouquet garni*
60 ml (2 oz) white rum
4 canned peaches with syrup
50 ml (1¾ oz) chicken aspic (gelatine)
2 onions, sautéed in butter
2 carrots, sautéed in butter
1 stalk celery, sautéed in butter
½ tsp butter

Remove the bones from the thigh. Fold over drumstick and tie with string so it looks like a round boneless ham. Sauté over medium heat to release its fat. Brown the duck in the lard, then add salt, pepper, and the bouquet garni. Pour in the rum and flame. Let cool. Remove duck from pan and place in a casserole. Pour on the peach syrup, then add the chicken aspic, sautéed onions, carrots, and celery. Simmer on the stove for 20 minutes. Remove the duck and keep warm.

To prepare the sauce: Mix the first preparation (lard, rum, etc.) and the second (peach syrup, aspic, sautéed vegetables, etc.) together and reduce to sauce consistency. Adjust seasoning, then swirl in ½ tsp butter.

To serve: Take the string off the duck. Place the duck in the centre of a serving plate, spread the peaches around the duck, cover duck with the sauce, and serve.

Serves: 1

La Ligne was once an old, run-down bistro in a beautiful neighbourhood. It still is in a beautiful neighbourhood, only Jean Speyer has given the bistro a facelift. He had the entire place rebuilt from top to bottom. Today, La Ligne is a beautiful restaurant with a fabulous menu. Nicole, his wife, will greet you and graciously seat you. Prepare yourself to choose from a great variety of fine dishes.

Jean has a great talent for preparing food as pleasing to the eye as to the tastebuds. Try the Lobster Salad au Pamplemousse with Avocado Purée, Goose Leg with Asparagus Tips, Veal Kidney with Anchovies, Duck Legs with Peaches, and of course, the rich, yet delicate, desserts. They are all beautifully served as well as delicious.

L'Hôtel de Paris et de la Poste

97, rue de la République, 89103 Sens
Tel: (86) 65-17-43
Proprietor/Chef: Charles Godard

L'Hôtel de Paris et de la Poste is almost 100 years old, and for a long time it was one of the great stop-offs on the road from Paris to the Riviera, at the crossroads of Burgundy and Champagne. Some have called this place the gateway to the sun for food lovers, but all good things come to an end, and the Paris et Poste went into hibernation. Charles Godard has been at the helm for a year now and has revived it.

His menu is truly fine; Black Pudding à la Sens with Apple is to be found along with Smoked Salmon in Cider Vinegar, Snails "Burgundy" Style, the famous Duck à la Gaston Godard, Miniature Lamb Cuts in Orange Marinade, Tart Tatin, Sirloin Fried with Carrots and Bacon, and Quail Pâté with Mushrooms. The gateway is open once again.

Duckling à la Gaston Godard

1 duckling of 2 - 2.5 kg (4½ - 5½ lb), with gizzard, liver, neck, wings, etc., removed and reserved
50 g (1¾ oz) butter
2 large onions, coarsely chopped
2 carrots, coarsely chopped
4 shallots, coarsely chopped
flour, as needed
1 bottle Côte de Beaune Burgundy
½ litre (1 pt) duck or chicken stock,* with all fat skimmed off
salt and freshly ground pepper, to taste
1 bouquet garni*
2 large cloves garlic, crushed
200 ml (6 oz) sherry
2 generous tbsp double cream (whipping cream)

To prepare the sauce: Dice the meat from the duckling wings and the other trimmings (except the liver) in large pieces, then brown them in butter in a skillet. Add the chopped onions, carrots, and shallots. Sprinkle 2 large pinches of flour on top and heat until it colours a little. Pour in the wine and the stock and reduce. Add salt, pepper, bouquet garni, and garlic. Simmer for 3 hours.

Oven roast the duckling for 1 hour at 350°F (175°C), then season with salt and pepper. Cut the bird up, remove the meat from the carcass, cover, and keep hot. Grind the carcass and put it into a pan. Add sherry and sweat* for 15 minutes over low heat. Pour the mixture into the simmering wine sauce and cook for another 15 minutes. Strain the sauce, squeezing all juice out of the vegetables with a spatula. Return the sauce to the heat and bring it quickly to a boil. Complete the sauce by adding freshly sieved duckling liver and the cream. Do not boil. Check the seasoning and serve sauce poured over the duckling.

Wine: *Burgundy Côte de Beaune*

Serves: 4

Au Caneton

32, rue Grande, 14290 Orbec
Tel: (31) 32-73-32
Proprietor/Chef: Joseph Ruaux

Orbec is a very old, small town in French Normandy. All the houses are constructed of wood (which is a sign of antiquity) and are adorned with flowers throughout the year. **Au Caneton**, which is housed in one of these old houses, is a superb restaurant that also offers impeccable service.

Joseph Ruaux is a champion of regional cuisine. He created his famous Duckling with Apples in 1948, and since, it has become his trademark. If you should order his fine duckling for dinner, may I suggest you accompany it with a good Bordeaux from the wine cellar, which is stocked with 40,000 bottles.

Duckling with Apples

1 duckling of 1.2 kg (2½ lb)
100 ml (3 oz) oil
100 ml (3 oz) Calvados
2 onions, sliced
2 carrots, sliced
2 whites of leeks, sliced
1 bouquet garni*
salt and pepper, to taste
½ litre (1 pt) chicken stock*
100 ml (3 oz) Muscadet wine
6 tart apples, sliced
50 g (1¾ oz) butter
200 ml (6 oz) double cream (whipping cream)
3 egg yolks

Truss the duckling with string, then sauté it slowly in a pan with oil for ½ hour. Flame with Calvados, then add onions, carrots, leeks, bouquet garni, salt, and pepper. Wet with chicken stock and Muscadet and let simmer for 35 minutes.

Sauté the apples in butter.

Remove the duckling from its pan and keep warm. Remove the grease from the pan and reduce the remaining cooking stock to sauce consistency. Add cream and egg yolks, and heat gently until mixture thickens. Reseason if needed.

On a hot serving plate, place the duckling on the sautéed apple slices, cover with the sauce, and serve.

Wine: *Bordeaux*

Serves: 4

La Tour d'Argent

15, quai de la Tournelle, 75005 Paris
Tel: 354-2331
Proprietor/Chef: Claude Terrail

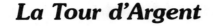

Duckling with Chinese Pepper

2 ducklings, 2 kg (4½ lb) each
cognac, to taste
4 tbsp Chinese pepper (or black peppercorns)
1½ litre (3 pt) Poivrade sauce*
2 tbsp double cream (whipping cream)
salt and pepper, to taste
1 Golden Delicious apple, diced
butter, to sauté

Halve the ducklings and roast them in the oven at 400°F (205°C) for 1 hour. Reduce the cognac with the Chinese pepper in a saucepan until nearly dry. Add the Poivrade sauce and cook for 10 minutes. Strain sauce and add cream. Simmer until the desired sauce consistency is reached. Check the seasoning. Sauté the apple in butter. Place duckling halves on 4 plates, nap* with sauce, surround with sautéed apples, and serve.

Suggestion: Garnish each dish with cranberries and sliced pistachios, and serve with rice or Parisian potatoes.

Serves: 4

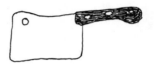

What can one say about **La Tour d'Argent** that has not been said a hundred times already? Since 1582, this restaurant has defied time; it is still grandiose, beautiful, and spectacular. There is much history here: from the forks of Charles V and the heron pâté of Henry IV to the *chocolat* of the Marquis de Sévigné. One is reminded of all the famous people (royalty, show business, government, etc.) who have dined here. To them, La Tour d'Argent is an incontestable best seller.

This is a restaurant of luxury and the best of cuisine. It could be said that any duckling cooked at La Tour d'Argent is as much a masterpiece of cuisine as is Notre-Dame of architecture and a Rembrandt of painting. Today the complete success of this jewel is owed to Claude Terrail.

Pharamond

24, rue de la Grande-Truanderie, 75001 Paris
Tel: 233-0672 and 236-5129
Proprietor: Susanne Hyvonnet • Chef: Alain Hyvonnet

Duckling with Green Peppercorns

1 duckling of 1.7 kg (3¾ lb)
125 g (¼ lb) butter, and as needed
salt and pepper, to taste
100 ml (3 oz) duck (or chicken) stock*
20 g (¾ oz) green peppercorns

Divide the duckling in half; remove all the bones except those in the thighs and wings. In a covered pan with butter, sauté the duckling over medium heat for 8-10 minutes. Remove the wings and continue to cook the duckling for another 8-10 minutes per side. Season with salt and pepper. Add the duck stock and cook for an additional 2 minutes. Remove the duckling and keep warm.

Reduce the cooking stock until it becomes smooth and of sauce consistency. Pass the sauce through a fine strainer, whisk in 1 tbsp butter, and add the green peppercorns at the last moment. Nap* the pieces of duckling with the sauce and serve.

Serves: 2

In 1932, this old house in Les Halles, the famous marketplace in Paris, was called La Petite Normande. Today it is called **Pharamond**, which to Parisians is synonymous with gourmet delicacies.

Alain Hyvonnet kept all the original decor, the beautiful ceramic decorations in the dining room, the mirrors, and the grand circular staircase. Not only is this restaurant truly gorgeous inside, but the cuisine is delicious, especially the Grilled Pork Sausage, Duckling with Green Peppercorns, Lamb Kidney with Roquefort Cheese, and the Grilled Steak accompanied by Apple Soufflé that is a tradition here. You will also discover the famous cider from the Auge Valley.

Mancini

Rue des Messageries, 17100 Saintes
Tel: (46) 93-06-61
Proprietor/Chef: Robert Baty

In 1978, Paris celebrated the anniversary of Marie Baty, the lady chef who brought 60 years of success to **Mancini**. Today, her son Robert manages Mancini with as much success as his mother did. Marie's grandson is also in the business; he began to oversee the cuisine at Mancini after acquiring much experience in Switzerland and London.

Mancini is a calm and comfortable hotel located in the heart of prestigious Cognac. The cuisine here is classic and elegant: the Escalope Viennoise, the Fillet of Beef in Brioche with Madeira Sauce, and the Duckling with Peaches are all excellent choices.

Duckling with Peaches

1 duckling of 1.3 kg (3 lb)
4 fresh peaches
500 ml (1 pt) veal stock*
500 g (1 lb) sugar
200 ml (6 oz) vinegar
½ litre (1 pt) aspic (or gelatine)
lemon juice, to taste

Roast the duckling in the oven for 25-30 minutes at 400°F (205°C). Poach the peaches in the veal stock; peel, slice, then glaze them under a salamander or broiler.

Caramelise the sugar in a saucepan, add vinegar, and let boil for 1 minute. Mix the aspic with the caramel and vinegar. Adjust the taste with lemon juice.

To serve: Place the duckling on a serving platter. Place the peaches around the duckling. Pass the sauce through a very fine strainer, pour it over the duckling, and serve.

Serves: 2

Restaurant Marc Annibal de Coconnas

2, bis, place des Vosges, 75004 Paris
Tel: 278-5816
Proprietors: Claude Terrail, Geneviève Gorge • Chef: Richard Piganiol

Class and elegance is not only in the limelight of Paris. We can find it as far away as the Vosges. Here at the **Coconnas**, we have the pleasure of wining and dining at the hands of Richard Piganiol, a master of cuisine.

The quality of his dinners is greater than the variety, however you will never be deprived of the finest gourmet treats such as the Pickled Duck or Veal Paupiettes with Vegetable Crepes.

You may be far away from the sophisticated city life, but dining is equally as fine here at the Vosges, at the Restaurant Marc Annibal de Coconnas.

Pickled Duck

1.5 kg (3⅓ lb) carrots
500 g (1 lb) turnips
4 leeks, white parts only
1 whole stalk celery
4 potatoes, peeled
2 litres (½ gal) water
200 g (7 oz) coarse salt
thyme, bay leaf, and parsley (leaves and stems), to taste
1 duck of 2-2.5 kg (4½-5½ lb), quartered
cloves, salt, and peppercorns, to taste
¼ litre (1 cup) veal stock*
100 ml (3 oz) Madeira wine
½ litre (1 pt) double cream (whipping cream)

Cook the carrots, turnips, leeks, celery, and potatoes in water and set aside. Place the salt, thyme, bay leaf, and parsley stems into 2 litres (½ gal) water and bring to a boil. Dunk the duck into the water, take the pot off the heat, and let duck marinate in it for 8-9 hours. Take out the duck and drain well. Put the duck in an ovenproof casserole along with the cooked vegetables and cloves, parsley leaves, salt, and peppercorns. Bake at 400°F (205°C) until the skin begins to loosen from the backbone.

To prepare the sauce: Reduce the veal stock to ½. Reduce the cream to ½ and add the Madeira wine. Mix the cream and Madeira mixture with the veal stock. Adjust the seasoning, and keep very warm.

Serve the duck and vegetables with the sauce.

Serves: 4

La Corbeille

154, rue Montmartre, 75002 Paris
Tel: 261-3087
Proprietor: Mme. Viot • Chef: Christian Viot

Pickled Duck with Broth

1 duck of 1.7 kg (3¾ lb)
300 g (10½ oz) coarse salt
salt, to taste
1 bouquet garni*
1 onion stuck with 4 cloves
750 g (1½ lb) carrots, chopped
300 g (10½ oz) turnips
4 leeks
2 stalks celery
peppercorns, to taste

Halve the duck then put in a terrine with the salt for 24 hours. When time has elapsed, wash the duck halves thoroughly with cold water, then put them in a large pot with 3 litres (2½ qt) cold water and the remaining ingredients. Bring to a boil, skim off the fat, then cover and cook slowly in the oven at 350°F (175°C) for 3 hours.

Remove the duck and vegetables to a serving platter and serve the broth separately.

Serves: 2

La Corbeille is a small restaurant situated in the famous artists quarter of Paris. However, its clientele is not made up of artists, but rather of businessmen, lawyers, and stockbrokers. During the first 40 years of its existence, La Corbeille catered to the snobs. The cuisine was also snobbish until Christian Viot took over and changed everything.

Today, La Corbeille serves famous speciality dishes (especially those from Bordeaux) and excellent Saint Émilion wines accompany your dinner. Christian has done wonders to this old place to make it enjoyable for anyone to eat here.

Hostellerie du Château

02130 Fère-en-Tardenois
Tel: (29) 82-21-13
Proprietor: Girard Blot • Chef: Robert Parguel

Sliced Duck Breasts in Blackcurrant Vinegar

1 duck of 2 kg (4½ lb)
salt and pepper, to taste
100 ml (3 oz) veal or chicken stock*
½ tbsp blackcurrant vinegar
2 tbsp blackcurrants
50 g (1¾ oz) butter

Remove giblets from the duck. Take off the legs. Reserve. Salt and pepper the inside of the duck. Place the legs and giblets in an ovenproof pan with the body of the duck. Place pan in the oven at 400°F (205°C) for 20 minutes. Take the pan from the oven, remove the duck, and heat pan on the stove on high heat until the maximum juice is released from the giblets and legs. Deglaze the pan with veal or chicken stock and reduce until sauce is thick and rich. Add vinegar and currants. Let cook for 2 - 3 minutes. Whisk in butter. Adjust seasoning and strain sauce through a very fine strainer.

Skin the duck breasts and cut the meat into thin slices. Place slices on a hot plate, pour vinegar sauce over, and serve.

Serves: 4

The **Hostellerie du Château** is not only a grandiose castle, it is also a very prestigious restaurant. Here, inside these noble walls, you will discover a gourmet's delight. The menu offers fine foods prepared to perfection and served with impeccable finesse.

The Crayfish Terrine with Champagne, Coq au Cumières, Duck Breasts in Blackcurrant Vinegar, and Venison Noisettes are dishes that have made Hostellerie du Château a gourmand's paradise.

Relais de l'Armagnac

32110 Luppé-Violles
Tel: (62) 09-04-54
Proprietor/Chef: Roger Duffour

Strips of Duck in Vinegar and Oil

500 g (1 lb) duck, breast meat only
1 tbsp shallots, finely chopped
5 grains green peppercorns
salt and pepper, to taste
100 ml (3 oz) peanut oil
30 ml (1 oz) wine vinegar

Cut the breast meat into strips, lengthwise. Flatten these strips with a large kitchen knife. On a plate, spread the raw duck breast strips, one next to the other. Sprinkle the chopped shallots, green peppercorns, salt, pepper, oil, and vinegar on top. Serve.

Serves: 2

Roger Duffour made a trip around France and Europe before settling at the **Relais de l'Armagnac**.

Roger, so happy in his rustic restaurant with his copper cookware, has blended all the beauty and goodness of his homeland into his cooking. His personal collection of Armagnacs and his excellent cuisine are examples of all the fine things this country has to offer.

Roger has captured *La Belle France* in his restaurant and his cuisine, as he said he would. This is evident in his casseroles, his wonderful *foies gras,* his beef, his duck, and his chicken.

La Belle Epoque

10, rue de Pas, 59000 Lille
Tel: (20) 54-51-28
Proprietor: Paul Aubursin • Chef: Christian Leroy

Strips of Duckling Breast with Strawberries

1 duckling breast of 500 g (1 lb)
butter or oil, to sauté
250 ml (1 cup) wine vinegar
200 g (7 oz) strawberries, puréed
250 ml (1 cup) veal stock*
1 pinch sugar
salt and pepper, to taste
50 g (1¾ oz) fresh butter
crushed strawberries, to garnish

Sauté the duckling breast to the bloody point in a frying pan with butter or oil (about 8 minutes), then set aside.

Add the vinegar to cool the frying pan, then add the strawberry purée. Pour in the veal stock, then add sugar, salt, and pepper. Let cook gently for 3-4 minutes, then mix the sauce in a blender and add the butter. Very thinly slice the duckling breast. Strain the sauce (it must be without particles) and serve over the duckling breast. Place some crushed strawberries on top to garnish.

Suggestion: Serve with mushroom flan.

Serves: 2

Lille is another culinary capital of France. People in the restaurant business all know this. **La Belle Epoque** is a special restaurant in this special city.

Paul Aubursin and his young chef, Christian Leroy, offer a menu that is nothing short of astonishing in their pretty dining room. Scallops with Mangos, Sautéed Turbot with Cucumbers, and Strips of Duckling Breast with Strawberries are only a few of the many specialities.

Even the cover of the menu is enchanting.

Le Moulin de Mougins

L'Étoile d'or (Concorde Lafayette Hotel)

Le Trianon

Aux Deux Taureaux

206, avenue Jean-Jaurès, 75019 Paris
Tel: 607-3931
Proprietor: Roberte Tollet-Pelissou • Chef: Georges Pelissou

Stuffed Duck Necks

4 ducks
20 g (¾ oz) salt
5 g (pinch) pepper
125 ml (1 cup) juniper berries
125 ml (1 cup) Burgundy wine
3 cloves
2 sprigs parsley
10 thyme flowers
2 shallots, chopped
4 garlic cloves, chopped
1 kg (2¼ lb) pork throat, from butcher
50 g (1¾ oz) flour
4 eggs

Cut the ducks into sections. Remove and reserve the carcass bones, the giblets, and the necks.

To prepare the stuffing: Grate the livers, hearts, lobes of gizzards, and all the fat together and marinate for 24 hours in a mixture of salt, pepper, juniper berries, Burgundy, cloves, parsley, thyme, shallots, and garlic.

Using the carcasses, make a stock* in which to poach the duck necks.

In a blender, mix the marinated stuffing mixture with the flour and eggs. Stuff the duck necks with the mixture.

Tie the ends of each neck with string, wrap in aluminum foil, and poach in the duck stock for 1 hour at medium heat, then for ½ hour at low heat. Let cool in the pot. Skim the grease from the liquid in the pot, strain it, and refrigerate it to make an aspic to serve with the necks.

Serves: 4

Roberte Tollet is the daughter of a restaurateur. Since childhood, she has been surrounded by people in the restaurant business. She also happened to fall in love with a chef, which enabled her to stay in the environment she likes best. In 1975, Roberte and her husband established themselves in Paris, in a neighbourhood frequented by connoisseurs of fine food.

Aux Deux Taureaux has a beautiful mahogany bar and burgundy velvet decorations. The interor is very rich and plush. Everyone who dines here is pleased with the fine selection of wines and dinners from which to choose. The Omelette Soufflée au Roquefort, Pork Sausage "A.A.A.A.A." Style, Beef Short Ribs with Shallots, and Stuffed Duck Necks are very good examples of their gourmet cuisine.

Napoléon Chaix

46, rue Balard, 75015 Paris
Tel: 554-0900 and 554-0960
Proprietor: Jocelyne Pousse • Chef: Gérard Magnan

Traditional Duck

1 duck of 2 kg (4½ lb)
salt and pepper, to taste
200 ml (6 oz) cognac
1 litre (2 pt) water
2 shallots, sliced
2 pinches chopped chervil
250 g (½ lb) fresh lard, cubed
salt and pepper, to taste
4 sprigs thyme

125 g (¼ lb) pork rind
1 calf's foot or veal knuckle
250 g (½ lb) lean bacon
125 g (¼ lb) butter
4 onions, chopped
garlic, to taste
4 carrots, chopped
chicken stock* or bouillon, as needed

Cut the duck into 4 pieces and season. Marinate the duck for 2 hours in ⅔ of the cognac, ⅔ of the white wine, the shallots, and 1 pinch of chervil.

Season the lard cubes with salt, pepper, thyme, remaining chervil, remaining cognac, and wine. Let stew for 1 hour. Meanwhile, in a saucepan with cold water, cook the pork rind and the calf's foot. Bring to a boil and boil for 5 minutes. Rinse and cool the calf's foot and pork rind with cold water, then cut them into small pieces.

Drain the marinade from the duck and reserve it. On a kitchen paper (paper towel), dry the pieces of duck, then sauté them in a pan with butter for 5 minutes. Place the pork rind and calf's foot pieces, bacon, onions, garlic, carrots, and the duck into an ovenproof pot. Add the marinade, lard mixture, and enough stock so the liquid comes up 1 cm (2½ in) higher than the duck. Bake in the oven for 1½ - 2 hours at 390°F (200°C). Serve.

Serves: 4

Jocelyne Pousse, this charming and gentle woman, is owner and hostess of **Napoléon Chaix** and the wife of the well-known comedian, professor, and businessman, Albert Simonin. Albert had Napoléon Chaix constructed in 1976, and he adorned the place with flowers and original oil paintings.

Preparing the excellent food in this restaurant is Gérard Magnan, who gained 14 years of experience by working at Maxim's. He can prepare such marvels as Red and White Cabbage with Confit of Duck, Traditional Duck, Haddock Choucroute, admirable fresh pâtés, fine sorbets (sherbets), and desserts. The wine list is exceptional, and the liqueurs are of the finest quality.

Hostellerie du Bas-Bréau

22, rue Grande, 77000 Barbizon
Tel: (6) 066-4005
Proprietor/Chef: Jean-Pierre Fava

Wild Duck with Champagne Vinegar Sauce

4 wild ducks
salt and pepper, to taste
170 g (6 oz) butter
40 ml (1¼ oz) champagne vinegar
2 shallots, chopped
300 ml (9 oz) double cream (whipping cream)
2 tbsp gelatine

Season the ducks with salt and pepper, then roast them for about 1 hour with 50 g (1¾ oz) butter in the oven at 350°F (175°C).

To prepare the sauce: Reduce the vinegar and shallots in a pan to sauce consistency. Add the cream and gelatine. Simmer for 10 minutes. Whisk in the remaining butter, bit by bit. Adjust the seasoning.

Suggestion: Cut the ducks in half, nap* with the sauce, and serve with fresh green noodles.

Wine: *Côtes de Beaune or Côtes de Nuits*   Serves: 8

For artists, Barbizon is the charming home of Impressionist painters. For the nature-minded, it is a refuge in a beautiful forest. For gourmands, this is the location of the **Hostellerie du Bas-Bréau**, a grand restaurant that has been managed by the Fava family for three generations. Here, everything is luxurious and elegant. You eat in a large dining room, decorated in the classic style, around a fireplace or on the terrace in good weather. Jean-Pierre Fava serves the finest cuisine: Salmon Gâteau, Scallops with Red Peppercorns, Sliced Veal Liver with Lime, Lamb with Curry and Mangos, Beef Ribs with White Mustard, Wild Duck with Champagne Vinegar Sauce, and Hot Chocolate Soufflé, among others.

Le Bellecour

22, rue Surcouf, 75007 Paris
Tel: 551-4693 and 555-6838
Proprietor: Gérard Goutagny • Chef: Christian Theule

Wild Duck with Pears

1 wild duck of 700 g (1½ lb), plucked and drawn
salt and pepper, to taste
1½ tbsp butter
⅓ litre (1½ cups) Demerara (brown) sugar
⅓ litre (1½ cups) red wine
1 cinnamon stick
pinch of coriander
6 white peppercorns
zest* of 1 orange
zest* of 1 lemon
1 pear
4 tbsp duck (or chicken) stock*

Season the duck with salt and pepper, and roast until medium done (about 20 minutes) at 450°F (230°C). Let the duck rest for 15 minutes.

Mix the butter, sugar, and 6 tbsp water together and bring to a boil. Cover and cook for 3 minutes. Add ½ the wine, the cinnamon, coriander, peppercorns, orange zest, and lemon zest, and bring mixture to a boil. Poach the pear in this for 15 minutes. Halve, core, and slice the pear.

Remove the breasts from the duck. Remove and bone the legs. Keep the bones and chop the carcass. Slice the breast meat into scallops.

Deglaze the duck's cooking pan with the remaining wine. Add the chopped carcass and the duck stock. Simmer for 3 minutes, then season with salt and pepper and strain the sauce.

Arrange the scallops of duck breasts on a serving dish, cover with the strained sauce, and garnish with the pear slices.

Wine: *Red Burgundy*   Serves: 2

It could be said that the Place Bellecour of Paris is the Place de la Concorde of Lyon. Since 1973, Gérard Goutagny has prospered with his specialities from Lyon.

Gérard also manages this elegant restaurant and its refined kitchen. Christian Theule will offer you the finest dishes from Lyon, such as Hot Salami, Pike Quenelles, and Poultry in Vinegar. Other specialities are Wild Duck with Pears, Avocado with Roquefort Cheese, and Langoustine Ragout. The cheeses and the wines are of the highest quality.

Service is under the direction of Jean-Louis, a good fellow whose disposition measures up to the cuisine and helps make your dining even more enjoyable.

L'Auberge de Maître Corbeau

15, rue Maurice-Elet, 27530 Ezy-sur-Eure
Tel: (37) 64-73-29 and 64-74-96
Proprietors: Paul Giral, Michel Guillet • Chef: Guy Vallée

Guinea Chicks Braised with Young Leeks

1 tsp olive oil
2 guinea chicks, 800 g (1¾ lb) each, cleaned and cut in half
salt and pepper, to taste
1.5 kg (3⅓ lb) young leeks, white parts only
250 ml (1 cup) chicken stock*

In a pan, heat the olive oil. Season the guinea chicks with salt and pepper and sauté them for 5 minutes on each side in the hot oil. Remove the guinea chicks. Put the leeks, chicken stock, and the sautéed chicks into a covered pot and cook for 15 minutes on low heat. Remove the guinea chicks and keep warm on serving plate.

Over high heat, reduce the chicken stock to ½ its original amount with the leeks still in the pot. Reseason if necessary.

To serve: Place the leeks around the guinea chicks on a serving plate, nap* the chicks with sauce, and serve very hot.

Serves: 4

When you enter **L'Auberge de Maître Corbeau**, you will not be surrounded by huge bouquets of flowers or plush, elegant furniture, however you will receive a warm greeting from Messrs. Giral and Guillet and, from the kitchen, you will be served fine dinners prepared by Guy Vallée.

L'Auberge de Maître Corbeau is one of the culinary treasures on Maurice-Elet, and the Braised Guinea Chick and Poached Eggs with Mussels are only two of the fine offerings available here.

Château-Hôtel de Nieuil

16270 Nieuil (Charente)
Tel: (45) 71-36-38
Proprietor/Chef: Luce Bodinaud-Fougerat

Raspberry Flavoured Guinea Fowl Fillets

2 guinea fowl
1 tbsp goose fat
1 tbsp raspberry vinegar
250 ml (½ pt) guinea fowl (or chicken) stock*
250 ml (½ pt) double cream (whipping cream)
1 tbsp raspberries
salt and pepper, to taste

Fillet the 4 breasts from the guinea fowl. Grease a pan with the goose fat and sauté the fillets for a few minutes until pink and soft. Reserve and keep them warm.

Skim the grease from the pan, add the raspberry vinegar, guinea fowl stock, and cream. Reduce to sauce consistency. Add raspberries, salt, and pepper and mix together well.

Serve the breast fillets sliced and covered with the sauce.

Wine: *A light Bordeaux*

Serves: 8

Charente is a historic land where the French and English fought many brutal battles. It was English property at one time, until Louis XV took it back. This castle was the property of a royal family until this century.

In 1937, Luce Bodinaud-Fougerat turned it into a hotel-restaurant. Luce mastered her trade with some of the finest chefs in France, one being Girardet, the culinary advisor for all the Hiltons in Europe.

In this magnificent castle, you may sleep peacefully and dine admirably. Everything in the **Château-Hôtel de Nieuil** respects tradition and exemplifies perfection.

Le Cabouillet

5, quai de l'Oise, 95290 L'Isle-Adam
Tel: (3) 469-0090
Proprietor: Mme. Gandilhon-Moreau • Chef: Arnaud Bisseti

Chicken and Duck with Mushrooms and Marsala Sauce

1 chicken of 3.5 kg (2¾ lb)
1 duck of 1.5 kg (3⅓ lb)
1 tbsp butter
1 tbsp lard
4 shallots, chopped
salt and cracked pepper, to taste
100 ml (3 oz) cognac
500 ml (6 oz) Marsala wine
3 tbsp tomato paste
250 g (½ lb) chopped white mushrooms, partially cooked and juice reserved
1 sliced truffle
½ litre (1 pt) double cream (whipping cream) (optional)

In a pot, cook the duck and chicken in the butter and lard until brown. Sprinkle with shallots, salt, and pepper. Pour in cognac and Marsala. Add the tomato paste and the juice of partially cooked mushrooms. Let cook for 40 minutes on medium heat, then remove the birds, cut them into serving pieces, and keep warm.

Reduce the juices left in the pan, then add the chopped mushrooms, sliced truffle, and cream (if desired). Check the seasoning.

Arrange the pieces of chicken and duck on a serving plate, cover with sauce, and serve.

Serves: 8

The Oise area, on the outskirts of Paris, is still very much like the old days. It has kept its Gothic Renaissance appearance. The cathedrals and the arched bridges still stand after all these decades. Today, **Le Cabouillet** is the neighbourhood restaurant.

Mme. Moreau has run this small inn ever since she took over from her mother. She still serves the celebrated Cabouillade (chicken and duck with mushrooms and Marsala wine sauce), plus Fish Stew, Chicken in Wine, Scallops in Lime Sauce, Turbot Braised in Wine, and a fine Crab Terrine.

Le Paris

52, bis, rue Esquernoise, 59000 Lille
Tel: (20) 55-29-41
Proprietor/Chef: Martin Loic

Potjesvleesch

1 chicken
1 duck
1 rabbit
100 ml (3 oz) oil
2 calf's feet
2 medium onions, chopped
10 shallots, chopped
1 clove garlic, chopped
2 sliced lemons
400 ml (3 cups) dry white wine
200 ml (6 oz) Madeira wine
200 ml (6 oz) court bouillon*
salt and pepper, to taste
1 thin sheet gelatine, if necessary
1 bouquet fine herbs, finely chopped

Cut the chicken, duck, and rabbit into medium-sized pieces. Sauté the pieces in oil for 10 minutes. Add the calf's feet, onions, shallots, garlic, and slices of lemon. Once the ingredients are coloured, cover and let cook gently for 10 minutes. Add the white wine and Madeira. Bring to a boil and add court bouillon. Season with salt and pepper. Let simmer for about ½ hour. While cooking, skim off grease. If necessary, add gelatine to thicken the liquid. At the end of cooking, add the herbs. Serve hot.

Serves: 12

A city that truly deserves to be proclaimed the capital of beauty is Lille, capital of Flanders. Lille — where the ancient and the new melt in perfect harmony and the songs of Jacques Brel come to life.

Martin Loic managed to find a few old Flemish recipes, and it is no wonder that **Le Paris** is such a success; the dishes Martin prepares (such as Potjesvleesch) can be found nowhere except at Le Paris.

Relais Louis XIII

1, rue du Pont-de-Lodi, 75006 Paris
Tel: 326-7596
Proprietor: Jean Poindessault • Chef: Manuel Martinez

As Naomi Barry so rightly wrote about this restaurant, "One dinner here has made me fall in love with Paris all over again." I couldn't agree with her more. Jean Poindessault has a gem in Paris — **Relais Louis XIII**. The building in which the restaurant is housed was once an ancient Augustine convent, and it was here that Louis XIII learned of the plot to assassinate his father, Henry IV.

This restaurant is rich in history and decor. The three dining rooms are filled with 16th century paintings, wood beams, columns, exquisite crystal and silver, damask linens — all creating a remarkable effect. The cuisine is sumptuous. The wine list is exceptional, and the maître sommelier, Jean Chauche, will be happy to advise you in your choice.

Pheasant with Fresh Noodles

1 pheasant of 1.4 kg (3 lb), prepared for cooking
salt and pepper, to taste
60 g (2 oz) butter
4 cloves garlic
80 ml (2½ oz) honey vinegar
250 ml (1 cup) dry white wine
40 ml (1¼ oz) cognac
2 tbsp mustard
2 tomatoes, concasse*
100 ml (3 oz) double cream (whipping cream)
1 tsp chervil

Joint the pheasant into 4 pieces. Season with salt and pepper. Heat a heavy saucepan with ½ the butter, then brown the joints in it. Remove the pheasant pieces. Add honey vinegar to the cooking juices and stir vigorously with a wooden spoon to dissolve the caramelised juices. Allow to reduce by ¾.

Whisk the white wine, cognac, mustard, and tomatoes together in a bowl. Pour this mixture into a saucepan and let reduce for 5 minutes over low heat. Add cream and remaining butter, stirring vigorously to obtain a smooth sauce. Strain the sauce into a sauceboat.

Place the pheasant on a serving dish and garnish with the chervil.

Suggestion: Serve the pheasant pieces with the sauce and fresh pasta.

Wine: *St. Émilion, 1970*   Serves: 4

Restaurant Saint-James

Place Camille-Hostein, 33360 Boulliac
Tel: (56) 20-52-19
Proprietor/Chef: Jean-Marie Amat

Jean-Marie Amat is one hundred percent Bordelais — his personality, his hard working attitude, and his cooking. He created **Restaurant Saint-James** in 1970, and in 1981 he moved it to the suburb of his proud city.

Jean's culinary abilities are exceptional and his menu is eclectic. The Duck Bouillon with Raviolis, Gingered Breast of Chicken Salad, Duck Stuffed with Sole, and Grilled Spiced Pigeons are superb demonstrations of his talent.

To accompany all this, Jean has a huge selection of excellent regional wines.

Grilled Spiced Pigeons

4 pigeons, 400 g (14 oz) each
salt, as needed
800 g (1¾ lb) white onions
pepper, to taste
1 tbsp cumin
¼ tsp cinnamon
⅛ tsp sugar

Remove the bones from the pigeons. Salt the thighs and wings. Place the pieces of the pigeons on a baking sheet.

Slice the onions thinly, salt them lightly, and cook them in a skillet over low heat until all the juice from the onions is gone. Adjust the seasoning with salt and pepper.

Broil the pigeons for about 20 minutes or until pink, turning once. Dust the pigeons with cumin, cinnamon, and sugar.

Suggestion: Serve the pigeons with the onions and a mixed salad topped with sautéed pigeon livers.

Wine: *Côtes de Fronsac*   Serves: 4

Duc d'Enghien

3, avenue de Ceinture, 95880 Enghien-Les-Bains
Tel: 989-9595
Proprietor: Société Casino d'Enghien • Chef: Alain Passard

Dining at **Duc d'Enghien** must, without a doubt, stir a feeling of nostalgia. This restaurant has the flair and charm of the days of Napoleon III when theatre, opera, gambling, and parlours were the great fashion. They still are the fashion because François Minoret assures it. He will greet you most hospitably as he welcomes you to this small wonderland designed by Jacques Mariller to be like a theatre. Alain Passard, a worthy student of *Chef Conseiller* Michel Kéréver, will prepare extravagant dishes for you from superb hors d'oeuvres to sumptuous desserts. The Pigeon Wings with Goose Liver and Truffles in Cabbage, Sole with Saffron, Fennel Flan, and Salmon Scallops with Fresh Asparagus are simply marvellous. If you have a sweet tooth, you will love the Gratin of Oranges.

Pigeon Wings with Goose Liver and Truffles in Cabbage

1 large green cabbage
1 pigeon of 400 g (14 oz)
salt and pepper, to taste
40 g (1½ oz) butter
1 tbsp oil
2 slices fresh goose liver, 125 g (¼ lb) each
40 g (1½ oz) fresh truffle, sliced

Blanch the cabbage leaves. Cool, spread on kitchen paper (paper towel), and let dry. Remove the pigeon wings; season with salt and pepper. Sauté them over very high heat in butter and oil until golden. Set aside. In a pan, heat the 2 slices of goose liver, seasoned with salt and pepper, to a golden colour.

Place 1 slice goose liver, 1 slice truffle, and 1 pigeon wing in the centre of 2 - 3 cabbage leaves. Fold the leaves up to make a small pouch. Do the same for the other wing. Steam cook for 4 - 5 minutes then serve.

Serves: 1

Le Crillon

10, place de la Concorde, 75008 Paris
Tel: 296-1081
Proprietor: Jean Taittinger • Chef: Jean-Paul Bonin

Paris is the city of lights and incomparable fascination, filled with endless beauty and sights to see. Is there anything more capturing than the view from the Champs Élysées over to the Place Concorde at night? When all the lights are lit and illuminating the magnificent landmarks, **Le Crillon** must be considered among those landmarks. Beautiful, prestigious, and first class, Le Crillon is the place where the privileged pamper themselves.

Jean-Paul Bonin will spoil you with such delicacies as Perch Fillet with Broccoli Cream Sauce, Watercress Salad with Foie Blond, and Squab in Mushroom Sauce. Philippe Roche created, in Le Crillon, a most fabulous and chic restaurant. For those who like to wine and dine as kings, this is the place to visit.

Squab in Mushroom Sauce

4 squabs, prepared for cooking
salt and pepper, to taste
50 g (1¾ oz) butter
2 shallots, chopped
300 ml (9 oz) white wine
1 pinch coarsely ground pepper
300 ml (9 oz) pigeon or chicken stock*
1 bunch spring onions (scallions)
800 g (1¾ lb) sliced mushrooms

Cut open the squabs, then season them with salt and pepper. Quickly sear the squabs in very hot butter in a frying pan (about 2 minutes per side). Remove squabs from pan, place on a roasting pan, and keep warm.

Add shallots and wine to the fat in the pan and reduce until almost all the liquid is evaporated. Add the ground pepper and stock and cook gently for 10 minutes. Strain the stock.

Pour the strained stock over the squabs and roast them in the oven at 350°F (175°C) for 45 - 60 minutes or until squabs are tender. During the last ½ hour of cooking, add the onions and sliced mushrooms. Serve warm.

Serves: 4

Le Chapon Fin

5, rue Montesquieu, 33000 Bordeaux
Tel: (56) 44-76-01
Proprietor: M. Labatuit • Chef: Jean Ramet

Squab "Madame Raymonde"

6 squabs
oil, to sauté
400 g (14 oz) cèpe mushrooms sautéed in mirepoix* and butter
60 g (2 oz) green beans
60 g (2 oz) truffles
60 g (2 oz) asparagus
salt and pepper, to taste
brandy and vermouth, to taste
300 g (10 oz) butter

Remove the bones from the squabs. Remove the livers; sauté and chop them. Mix the mushrooms, beans, truffles, and asparagus together to make a stuffing. Season with salt and pepper. Stuff the squabs and roast at 350°F (175°C) for 45-60 minutes. Remove the birds from the pan. Mix the brandy and vermouth with the cooking juices, reduce, then thicken with butter. Check the seasoning.

Suggestion: Serve the squabs and sauce with a garnish of carrots and asparagus tips.

Serves: 6

Le Chapon Fin is Bordeaux's answer to both Maxim's and Mecca; everyone who loves good food is attracted here. The decor is unique — a sort of flowered cave that blooms all year, and the cuisine is exemplary.

With Jean Ramet, Le Chapon Fin has found a new soul. He used to be with Les Troisgros and Lasserre. Here he combines classicism and imagination to produce the very finest of dishes. From Braised Bass in Medoc Wine and squab prepared as a tribute to Raymonde (Mme. Ramet) to Escalope de Foie Gras in Raspberry Vinegar and Fresh Fish with Chanterelle Mushrooms, every dish is an opportunity to blend the pleasures of tasting food and one of the great wines from the cellar.

La Caravelle

14, place Duclos, 22100 Dinan
Tel: (96) 39-00-11
Proprietor/Chef: Jean-Claude Marmion

Squab Supreme with Cabbage

4 small squabs
salt and pepper, as needed
chicken fat, as needed
80 g (2¾ oz) semi-salted lard, cut in bits
4 small young cabbages
1 head lettuce
100 ml (3 oz) wine vinegar
300 ml (9 oz) walnut oil

Pluck the squabs and remove the giblets. Take off the thighs, salt them, and keep them in enough chicken fat to cover them. Two hours before serving, roast all giblets, meat, and bones (except the thighs and the 2 fillets adjoining each breastbone) at 400°F (205°C). Reserve the juices.

Sauté the lard in a pan until crisp. Reserve the crisp pieces. Put the cabbages in the reserved juice in a pot and be sure they are well saturated. Let the cabbages cook on medium heat for 15 minutes.

Season the breast fillets and roast them in the oven at 450°F (230°C). Keep them rose coloured (8-10 minutes after they get plump). Reseason if necessary. Fry the thighs separately. Season the lettuce with salt, pepper, and wine vinegar mixed with walnut oil.

On one side of each serving plate, place the fried thighs on top of the seasoned lettuce. On the other side of each plate, place the small bits of crisp lard on the cooked cabbage. In the centres, place the squab fillets. Cover everything with the reserved juices from the roasting of the bones and the cabbage and serve hot.

Wine: *St. Émilion Pomerol*

Serves: 4

Standing in the heart of Dinan is **La Caravelle**. One reason La Caravelle is very special is because of its unique appearance; its roof is supported by rustic columns, there is a granite chimney (Brittany is very famous for its pink granite), and inside, the walls are covered with suede and tapestries. This restaurant seats only 30 and the dining is very elegant.

Jean-Claude has been here for the past 12 years, and his motto has never changed — "Cuisine is love and sacrifice. It should seduce and not astound the gourmet." Testimonies to this philosophy are his Warm Oysters with Shallots, Lobster Salad with Artichoke Hearts, Baby Rabbit with Beets, and Squab Supreme with Cabbage. There is a marvellous assortment of crepes and soufflés for dessert, as well.

Les Santons

Route Nationale, 83360 Grimaud-Village
Tel: (94) 43-21-02
Proprietor/Chef: Claude Girard

Grimaud, a village perched high above the Mediterranean, is the real Provence — that of the typically Provençal Christmas crib wood carvings (this restaurant's name in English). Claude Girard learned the ABC's of cooking at the "classics": Lapérouse, Maxim's, and George V. When he opened here in 1963, he knew exactly what he wanted: namely to create a warm and intimate environment while remaining very Provençal, an establishment with all the comforts, a place where locally caught fish, locally raised pigeons, and Sisteron lamb take the honours. You should come along between the ruined feudal castle and the Roman church, under the arcades of the old houses, at any time of the year.

Squab with Honey

1 squab, prepared for cooking
salt and pepper, to taste
400 g (14 oz) melted butter
125 g (¼ lb) peeled small onions
200 g (7 oz) small peeled potatoes
125 g (¼ lb) cèpes or girolles mushrooms
1 tbsp honey
1 tbsp red wine vinegar
¼ litre (1 cup) clear chicken broth

Season the squab with salt and pepper, then baste with ¼ of the butter. Place the onions around the squab and roast in the oven at 400°F (205°C) for 20 minutes. Turn and baste frequently.

Cook the potatoes in a separate pan with another ¼ of the butter. When they are half-cooked, add the mushrooms and cover the pan. Keep on low heat.

Remove the cooked squab from the oven (it should be a little pink) and put it and the onions onto a serving dish and keep warm.

Remove the excess fat from the pan in which the squab was cooked, deglaze it with honey, heat on the stove until honey is caramelised, then add vinegar and broth and reduce to a syrup-like consistency. Add the remaining butter in small pieces, swirling continually, to finish the sauce.

Place the potatoes and mushrooms on the serving dish with the squab and the onions, nap* with a little sauce, and serve the rest of the sauce separately.

Wine: *A young Bandol red wine or a light claret*

Serves: 2

Chavant

38320 Bresson/Eybens
Tel: (76) 25-25-38 and 25-15-14
Proprietor: Emile Chavant • Chef: Jean-Pierre Chavant

In the heart of the country, five kilometres from Grenoble, you will discover **Chavant**. Chavant has been a family enterprise ever since granddaddy Chavant created it in 1925. Chavant is the perfect refuge, tranquil and comfortable, and far away from everything else.

Emile Chavant is a man of experience with a fine background. He has worked in some of the largest and most famous restaurants in France. Today, Emile manages his restaurant with the help of his son and two daughters. This is a fine establishment with a very special touch. There are treasures in the wine cellar; the collection of Armagnac is outstanding.

Quail "Emile Chavant" Style

1 plump quail
salt and pepper, to taste
stuffing made from chopped quail livers and forcemeat
2 slices of truffle
1 tsp fresh goose liver
1 artichoke heart
1 tsp butter
1 handful morel mushrooms
50 ml (1½ oz) Madeira wine

Remove all bones from the quail except the head and feet bones, then season the quail. Spread a thin layer of stuffing mixed with the truffle slices and goose liver inside the quail, then sew the quail back together. In a pan, cook the quail over low heat for 15 minutes until it is golden brown. Remove quail from pan.

Sauté the artichoke heart in butter in the same pan for a few minutes; take out the artichoke. Still in the same pan, add morel mushrooms and Madeira wine. Return quail to pan. Let cook gently 3-5 minutes, uncovered. Season to taste.

To serve: Place the artichoke heart on a serving plate, put the quail over it, top with morel mushrooms, and serve hot.

Serves: 1

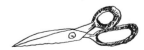

Auberge des Templiers

Les Bézards-Boimorans, 45290 Nogent-Vernisson
Tel: (38) 31-80-01
Proprietors: Jacques and Philippe Depée • Chef: Jean-Pierre Rigollet

Woodcock and Chestnut Soufflé

700 g (1½ lb) chestnuts
6 eggs, separated
70 g (2½ oz) butter, and as needed
salt and pepper, to taste
pinch of cayenne pepper
2 woodcocks, cut in pieces,
   intestines chopped and reserved

30 g (1 oz) carrots
30 g (1 oz) onions
15 g (½ oz) celery
30 ml (1 oz) cognac
400 ml (12 oz) demi-glace
   (light brown stock)
1 bouquet garni*

Peel the chestnuts and steam them. Purée them in a blender. Add 6 egg yolks, 50 g (1¾ oz) butter, salt, pepper, and cayenne pepper to the chestnuts.

Brown the legs of the woodcocks in butter, bone them and reserve the bones. Dice the meat and mix the meat into the chestnut mixture. Brown the woodcock breasts in butter, let them get cold, then cut them into scallops. (Reserve bones.) Fill a buttered soufflé mould with alternate layers of the puréed chestnut mixture and the scallops of woodcock breast, starting and finishing with the purée. Bake at 350°F (175°C) for 18 - 20 minutes.

To prepare the sauce: Finely slice the vegetables and sweat* them in butter with the bones of the woodcocks. Add the chopped intestines after a few minutes, then flame with cognac. Moisten with demi-glace, add the bouquet garni. Simmer gently for 1½ hours, skimming fat and scum from the surface. (If the sauce reduces too quickly, partially cover the pan.) Strain the sauce, place in a clean saucepan, and reduce to 200 ml (6 oz). Adjust the seasoning and serve the sauce separately with the soufflé.

Serves: 4

This is a triumph of quality over time. **Auberge des Templiers** has been around for centuries. It was destroyed in 1314, rebuilt, and used as a *relais de poste* (an inn and stopping place for travellers) in the 19th century. It fell into ruins again until 1945 when M. and Mme. Depée took over the establishment, reconstructed it, and made it one of the nicest inns on Nationale 7.

Jacques and Philippe Depée, sons of the Depées, are wine connoisseurs as well as the present owners of this family enterprise. They hired the talented chef, Jean-Pierre Rigollet. You must taste his Squirrel Feuilleté with Cream Sauce, his Turnip Salad with Foie Gras, his Woodcock and Chestnut Soufflé, and his "Walter Scott" Duck. The white cheese is local, and the desserts are quite good.

Chez Sam

87, Route Nationale, 78760 Pontchartrain
Tel: 489-0205
Proprietor: Sam Letrone • Chefs: Sam Letrone, Pierre Poirier

Anglerfish Piccata in Pepper Cream

500 g (1 lb) fillets of anglerfish (monkfish or cod)
salt and pepper, to taste
bread crumbs, as needed
50 g (1¾ oz) Parmesan cheese
butter, to sauté
3 green peppers, scalded
1 dash Escoffier sauce, purchased
2 hearts of artichokes

Cut the anglerfish into 8 scallops, season with salt and pepper, and cover in bread crumbs. Roll the pieces in Parmesan cheese and gently brown in butter for 3 - 5 minutes.

Remove the pips from the peppers, then purée the pulp in a blender. Cook and thicken the peppers in butter, season with salt and pepper, and add a dash of Escoffier sauce. Place 2 anglerfish scallops on each plate and pour some pepper cream sauce around them. Serve with artichoke hearts cut into long, thin slices and the remaining sauce separately.

Serves: 4

Sam Letrone has been a showoff for over 25 years. This is not meant to be derogatory. On the contrary, this troubadour juggles music, short stories, and dishes (cooked of course) all the same delicious way. He has travelled the world over, with his musical gags in his suitcase and chef's hat on his head, training his cocks, thereby doubly deserving his name *maître coq*.

Here he is back home, assisted by a great young chef, Pierre Poirier. They are right when they say on their menu, "Cooking is a great art which evolves down the ages, but which would fall heavily to earth if ever it forgot its roots." Their Anglerfish Piccata in Pepper Cream displays their respect for their heritage.

Le Petit Coq aux Champs

La Pommeray, Champigny, 27500 Pont-Audemer
Tel: (32) 41-04-19 and 41-04-30
Proprietor/Chef: Patrick Pommier

Francis Pommier has been cooking since he was seven. Because he used to run a restaurant in Paris called Le Petit Coq, and because one day he heard the call of nature, he created **Le Petit Coq aux Champs**. That was in 1973. The name is most appropriate. The structure is a Normandy thatched cottage from the last century set in a village on the edge of a forest just a few minutes away from Pont Audemer, the Venice of Normandy. Francis Pommier's son, Patrick, serves light, very regional food; for example duckling is served in cider, veal sweetbreads in cream of mustard, and the anglerfish in simple glazed onions. The food is not very salty (which is wisdom, indeed) and is cooked with very little fat (which is even better). It is all very tasty.

Anglerfish Steak with Glazed Onions

200 g (7 oz) butter
50 small white onions
100 ml (3 oz) consommé
pinch of salt
15 g (½ oz) sugar
2 anglerfish (monkfish or cod), 1.4 kg (3 lb) each
salt and pepper, to taste
60 ml (2 oz) Calvados
500 ml (1 pt) cream
2 egg yolks
1 bunch fresh chives, cut very finely

To prepare the onions: Melt ½ the butter in a thick frying pan, add the onions, consommé, salt, and sugar. Cover with a lid and let cook gently for 7-10 minutes. Reduce the cooking stock until thick and roll the onions in the reduced stock to glaze them. Set aside.

Fillet the anglerfish and season them. Cook the fillets in a thick frying pan with the remaining butter, turning and browning each side. Flame the fillets with Calvados, add cream and the glazed onions, and finish cooking until fillets flake easily with a fork. Remove pan from heat, check the seasoning, then stir in the egg yolks to the sauce. Sprinkle the fish with cut chives and serve.

Wine: *A very dry white Burgundy, Meursault Blanc*   Serves: 4

Le Petit Nice

Corniche Kennedy, 13007 Marseilles
Tel: (91) 52-14-39
Proprietors: Jean-Paul and Albertine Passédat • Chef: Jean-Paul Passédat

Lodged between two hills and facing the islands is a modern Marseillais hotel exemplifying the Côte d'Azure style. This hotel is a small oasis, well situated, that is run by the talented Jean-Paul Passédat, who is also the chef. From his kitchen, he offers hearty Scallop Cassolettes "Frédéric Mistral" Style, Bouillabaisse Pudding, Fish Soup with Mussels, Sea Bream Fillet with Olive Oil, Anglerfish with Saffron and Garlic, Beef Fillet with Capers and Braised Onions, Sliced Veal Kidneys with Sauce, and Duck Livers with Baby Artichoke Fricassee.

There is a fine wine cellar. The dining room has a panoramic view of the sea, which captures all the beauty of the expansive coastline.

Anglerfish with Saffron and Garlic

1 medium-sized potato
5 cloves garlic
50 ml (1½ oz) olive oil, and as needed to soak
2 slices bread
1.2 kg (2½ lb) anglerfish (monkfish or cod) in fillets
90 g (3 oz) butter
salt and pepper, to taste
50 ml (1½ oz) dry white wine
3 g (pinch of) saffron
100 ml (3 oz) fish stock*
3 tsp double cream (whipping cream)

Cook the potato in its skin. Peel it and mash it to a purée with 3 cloves garlic, using a mortar and pestle. Gradually blend in 50 ml (1½ oz) olive oil. Soak the sliced bread in olive oil. Grill to a golden colour in a hot oven or broiler, then rub with 2 cloves garlic. Cut the fish fillets into a total of 12 medallions. Melt butter in a sauté pan. Colour the fish, seasoned with salt and pepper. Add white wine to deglaze. Add saffron and fish stock. Cover the pan and braise for 5 minutes in the oven at 350°F (175°C). Remove the fish and keep hot. Add the potato mixture and cream to the pan. Reduce this sauce by ½; strain. Correct the seasoning. Place 3 slices of bread on each plate, cover with a portion of fish, cover with strained sauce, and serve.

Serves: 4

Julius

6, boulevard Camélinat, 92230 Gennevilliers
Tel: 798-7732
Proprietor/Chef: Julius

Sliced Anglerfish with Leeks

200 g (7 oz) butter
500 g (1 lb) sliced leeks
50 ml (1½ oz) peanut oil
600 g (21 oz) fillet of anglerfish (monkfish or cod)
salt and pepper, to taste
200 ml (6 oz) double cream (whipping cream)
100 ml (3 oz) white wine
50 ml (1½ oz) fish fumet*

Melt ¼ of the butter in a thick frying pan, then add leeks. Pour the oil and another ¼ of the butter into another frying pan. When hot, add the fish fillets, season with salt and pepper, then put into a hot, 425°F (220°C), oven and cook for 10 minutes.

After 10 minutes, when the leeks have become completely soft, add cream and let boil for a moment, then add salt and pepper.

Remove the fat from the frying pan used for the fish fillets and deglaze with white wine. Add the fumet, reduce by ½, thicken with the remaining butter, and season to taste.

Place the leeks in the middle of a serving dish, put the fillets around the edge, coat them with sauce, and serve.

Wine: *Sancerre White*   Serves: 4

In this restaurant, class and gastronomy are one and the same. Outside you are struck by the brightness of the restaurant, and inside the glimmering lights seem to bring the best out of such fine dishes as Young Turbot with Prawn Sauce, Sliced Anglerfish with Leeks, and Succulent Duck in Peppers.

Even though **Julius** is a suburban establishment, it attracts top quality clientele from just about everywhere. These customers come as connoisseurs, to appreciate all the tricks of the trade from the chef.

Le Moulin de Mougins

Quartier Notre-Dame-de-Vie, 06250 Mougins
Tel: (93) 75-78-24
Proprietor: Roger Vergé • Chef: Serge Chollet

Supremes of Bass in Lettuce

1 sea bass of 1.5 kg (3⅓ lb),
cleaned and filleted
salt and pepper, to taste
2 tbsp flour
70 g (2½ oz) butter
oil, as needed
2 heads Boston or Bibb lettuce
1 tbsp shallots, finely chopped
50 ml (1½ oz) dry white wine
50 ml (1½ oz) white vermouth
50 ml (1½ oz) double cream
(whipping cream)
1 egg yolk

Cut each fillet in half, season with salt and pepper, and sprinkle with flour. Heat 10 g (⅓ oz) butter with a drop of oil in a frying pan. Sauté the fillets for 1 minute on each side over high heat. Set aside.

Scald the outer leaves of the lettuce by blanching them in 2 litres (1 qt) boiling water. Remove immediately. Place in cold water then drain. Repeat this with the hearts, but let them cook for 5 minutes. Cut the hearts in half, vertically, and flatten them slightly.

Butter a gratin dish and sprinkle the chopped shallots in it. Wrap the fish fillets in the lettuce leaves and arrange on top of the lettuce hearts. Place on top of shallots. Pour the white wine and vermouth over and bake for 12 minutes at 350°F (175°C). Drain the fish and lettuce and arrange on a serving dish with the fish on top. Reserve the cooking liquid.

Reduce the cooking liquid to 2 generous spoonfuls. Mix the cream and egg yolk in a bowl, then add to the reduced cooking liquid. Bring just to the boiling point, whisking constantly. Remove from heat and whisk in the remaining butter in small pieces. Correct the seasoning. Cover the fillets with sauce and serve.

Wine: *A white wine*   Serves: 4

Mougins was a small provincial town until Roger Vergé arrived. He came from the Côte d'Azure bringing his talent and his wife. He, then, came upon an old mill and, with the help of his lovely Denise, remodelled it. Today, **Le Moulin de Mougins** is a restaurant of fine quality.

Roger Vergé is a man with many references, since he has worked in many famous restaurants throughout the world. After his years of experience, he wrote a book about his life in the kitchen called *Ma Cuisine de Soleil*, which was well received. The thoughts I have about Roger's restaurant are warm and delicious. The Poultry with Mussels "Improvisé," Supremes of Bass in Lettuce, and Denise's warm hospitality always leave me with a lovely memory of this beautiful place.

Le Petit Trianon

1, boulevard Général de Gaulle, 06290 Saint-Jean-Cap-Ferrat
Tel: (93) 01-31-68
Proprietor/Chef: Jean-Luc Brouchet

Brill à la Vallée d'Auge

1 brill (or any white fish) of 1.2 kg (2¾ lb)
4 shallots
100 ml (3 oz) white wine
100 ml (3 oz) water, and as needed
3 apples
juice of ¼ lemon
200 g (7 oz) butter
¼ litre (1 cup) double cream (whipping cream)
2 tsp Dijon mustard
salt and pepper, to taste

Bake the brill with the shallots, white wine, and 100 ml (3 oz) water at 350°F (175°C) until fish flakes easily with a fork (about 30 minutes). Baste regularly. Peel the apples, cut into slices, and soak in water with lemon juice. When the brill is cooked, remove the dark skin and place on a buttered serving dish. To the stock from the brill, add cream and reduce to a thin sauce consistency. Add mustard and thicken with butter. Check the seasoning.

Strain the apples and sauté them in butter on high heat. Add the apples to the sauce and coat the brill; glaze quickly under a grill and serve.

Wine: *Sancerre white*   Serves: 4

From high up on the ledge of the cliffs, your eyes hit upon one of the most fairytale-like scenes of the Riviera: the peninsula of Saint-Jean-Cap-Ferrat, which is hemmed in by Nice and Monaco. Do drive down. Leave Nationale 7 (the main road) and discover this famous port, the ramparts of the citadel, the arched streets, the chapel of Picasso, the boats lazily at anchor, and the shady flower-decked gardens of **Le Petite Trianon**.

As lively as ever after 35 years at the ovens, Jean-Luc Brouchet will greet you with a Lobster Provençale, Brill à la Vallée d'Auge, Norway Lobster with Herbs, or a Young Guinea Fowl with Thyme. This is one of those charming spots that you will never forget.

Le Croquant

28, rue Jean Maridor, 75015 Paris
Tel: 558-5083
Proprietor/Chef: Hervé Rumen

Fricassee of Eels with Fine Herbs

1.2 kg (2¾ lb) eels
15 g (½ oz) butter
40 g (1½ oz) shallots, chopped
100 ml (3 oz) St. Nicholas de Bourgueil red wine (light red wine from the Loire region)
8 g (¼ oz) salt
2 g (pinch of) pepper
1 g (small pinch of) sugar
fresh tarragon leaves, chives, and chervil, as needed

Skin the eels, starting from the head, then remove the fillets from the whole length of the fish. Cut them into slices of 10 cm (4 in) in length. Fry the slices in a little butter for about 2 minutes. When hot, remove the secondary skin with a vegetable knife.

Remove the fat from the pan. Sweat* the shallots in the pan, then add wine and reduce slightly. Season with salt, pepper, and sugar. Serve the eels on a plate sprinkled with fine herbs.

Suggestion: Serve with spinach or white beet (Swiss chard) leaves.

Wine: *St. Nicholas de Bourgueil, young and slightly chilled*   Serves: 4

This little restaurant, very much out of the way, rustic, and quite charming, is presently in the hands of Hervé Rumen, who hails from Brittany. He has quite wisely kept the country style dishes from the region, but has added a few fish dishes from his native Brittany. He is a young chef who has proved his worth — notably with Christian Constant, one of the best restaurateurs in Paris.

Here, everything is small (except the helpings), pleasant, and calm. The little wines, purchased directly from the growers, as well as the listed great vintages, go very nicely with the cuisine of this Parisian style **Croquant**. You will be truly won over by the Fricassee of Eels with Fine Herbs.

Le Haut Tournebride

Busset, 03270 Saint-Yorre
Tel: (70) 41-26-87
Proprietor/Chef: Simone Lemaire

Haddock in Pastry

150 g (5¼ oz) puff pastry dough*
150 g (5¼ oz) butter
400 g (14 oz) chopped onions
salt and pepper, to taste
300 g (10½ oz) double cream (whipping cream)
400 g (14 oz) haddock desalted in ½ litre (1 pt) milk for 5 hours
1 large handful sorrel or spinach
1 egg yolk

Roll out 6 very thin strips of dough until almost transparent, about 20 cm (8 in) long and 10 cm (4 in) across. Place on a baking tray and prick with a fork. Bake the dough in the oven at 400°F (205°C) for 8 minutes. Gently cook the onions in ⅓ of the butter to get a thick sauce. Thicken with 50 g (1¾ oz) cream. Season with salt and pepper and keep hot.

Brown the haddock in ½ the remaining butter on low heat, then add 75 g (2½ oz) cream. Mix well, then season with pepper. Divide the onion sauce into thirds. Place the layers of pastry on top of each other with the onions and haddock in between each layer. Finish with a layer of pastry. Bake for 3 minutes at 400°F (205°C).

To prepare sabayon with sorrel (or spinach): Add the sorrel and the remaining cream to the remaining butter, which should be soft and frothy. Boil thoroughly to thicken, then remove from heat and, very carefully, add the egg yolk. Season with salt and pepper; do not boil again.

Serve the haddock coated with sorrel sabayon on very hot plates.

Serves: 2

Busset-en-Nourbonnais, the royal cradle of the Bourbons, has the additional privilege of playing host to Simone Lemaire, the President of the Association of Women Restaurateurs and Chefs. In this pretty, little, 18th century, nobly provincial restaurant, Simone Lemaire cooks "as the bird sings," as Curnonsky put it — light cooking but with respect to the Bourbon land and to the region of her own origins, Normandy.

In good weather, the service is outside in a park atmosphere; otherwise, it is in a beautiful room dressed with old style furniture. Warm Puff Pastry "Copains" Style with Cheese from Ambert, Shellfish Sausages in Cream of Spinach, Haddock in Pastry, Streak with Nuts, Mint Ice Cream Coated with Hot Chocolate — all appear on the menu.

Le Clodenis

57, rue Caulaincourt, 75018 Paris
Tel: 606-2026
Proprietor/Chef: Denys Gentes

Fillets of John Dory* with Tomato and Onion Purées

1 kg (2¼ lb) fresh tomatoes
1 kg (2¼ lb) spring onions (scallions)
salt and pepper, to taste
10 g (pinch of) raw, peeled, and finely grated ginger
6 porgy or John Dory fillets, 200 g (7 oz) each
200 g (7 oz) seaweed

Separately, blanch the tomatoes and onions, then peel the tomatoes. Drain each well and (separately) purée each in a food processor or blender. Pass each purée through a fine sieve. Season both with salt and pepper. Season the tomatoes with ginger as well.

Fill the bottom of a steamer with salted water. Place the fillets in the basket on a bed of seaweed. Heat the water and cook for 5 minutes from the moment the water contained in the lower section starts to boil. Serve the fillets with the tomato and onion purées.

Wine: *A dry white wine*

Serves: 6

Denys Gentes, chef and owner, has given this pleasant little bistro at the foot of Montmartre the name of **Le Clodenis** (which loosely translates to "Denys's own"). The decor, refined yet innocently pretty, suggests a quality restaurant. So does the menu and excellent cuisine.

The menu states that the pâtissier, Claude Lesage, is involved in the preparation of dishes selected according to the seasons and the daily markets. The food is prepared with the authority of a master who has no wish whatsoever to exclude imagination from traditional recipes. In season, the game dishes are very good, and the fish is very properly steam cooked. There are very creamy sauces, and there is a most honourable wine cellar, too.

Le Vaccarès

Place du Forum, 13200 Arles
Tel: (90) 96-06-17
Proprietor/Chef: Bernard Dumas

Arles, an old Roman town, is one of the most famous artistic towns in France, with its "Alley of the Tombs," its arenas, and its antique theatre. There is also a firmly rooted tradition for good eating here, and just a stone's throw from the Camargue, with the forum just before you, is a menu of the greatest distinction and depth that is signed: Bernard Dumas. Bernard is still tender of age, but has worked with masters in Nîmes and elsewhere. He has also met up with André Guillot, from whom he acquired quintessence — the art of preparing light flaky pastries and a deep respect for this homeland cooking, which includes dishes such as Salty Cod (pounded in oil, garlic, and cream and cooked in batter), John Dory "Arlatan," Bouffado "Sailor" Style, and Blanquette of Pike Perch.

John Dory* "Arles" Style

2 - 3 ripe tomatoes
1 porgy or John Dory of 1.6 kg (3½ lb)
100 ml (3 oz) very good olive oil
300 ml (9 oz) water or fish fumet*
100 ml (3 oz) white wine
salt and pepper, as needed
100 g (3½ oz) butter
2 sprigs basil

Blanch the tomatoes in boiling water for 30 seconds, then soak them in cold water. Remove the skins, cut in half, then remove the pips by squeezing them.

Draw, clean, and bone the fish. Cut the 2 fillets into round knobs. Place the fish in an ovenproof dish with olive oil. Dice the tomatoes and spread over the fish. Moisten with water or fumet, white wine, and oil. Add a little salt and pepper and bake at 350°F (175°C) for 7-8 minutes. Watch the cooking carefully and baste regularly. Remove the fish pieces and keep hot.

Pour the fish and tomato stock into a thick-bottomed frying pan and reduce on high heat until 200-300 ml (6-9 oz) of syrupy liquid are left. Still on high heat, add the butter and whisk. Add basil and check the seasoning. Serve the fish on a long serving platter coated with hot sauce.

Suggestion: Serve with rice.

Wine: *White, a young Châteauneuf du Pape*   Serves: 4

À L'Huîtrière

3, rue des Chats-Bossus, 59000 Lille
Tel: (20) 55-43-41
Proprietor: Jean Proye • Chef: François Fouassier

This restaurant is as a restaurant should be. Bourgeois, should I say? All the more so since Jean Proye also runs a fish market with turn-of-the-century decor that goes very nicely with his seafood restaurant.

Despite a few classical dishes of good meat and poultry, here the sea takes the top spot — from a wide choice of oysters to a salad of warm cod to sea bream, sole, anglerfish (with turnips and little onions), John Dory, and others.

Chef François Fouassier does not, however, forget the Flemish classics (such as Waterzoöi, eel, and Beef in Caramel) or the pleasures to be had from dishes dating from the Middle Ages (such as Tongues of Cod).

There is a very good wine cellar and there is a salon upstairs.

John Dory* "Champvallon" Style

125 g (¼ lb) butter
4 large or 8 medium-sized potatoes
4 large tomatoes
1 porgy or John Dory of about 2 kg (4½ lb)
4 cloves garlic
2 sprigs thyme
2 bay leaves
salt and pepper, to taste
1 pinch saffron
3 tbsp fish fumet*

Generously butter a large, ovenproof dish. In the bottom of the dish, place ½ the potatoes (finely sliced), ½ the onions (peeled and melted in butter, but not browned), and ½ the tomatoes (pipped and cut into slices).

Put the fish on the bed of vegetables along with the garlic, thyme, bay leaves, salt, pepper, and saffron. Cover the fish with the remaining potatoes, tomatoes, and onions (with potatoes on top). Moisten with fumet, cover with aluminum foil, and cook in the oven for 30 minutes at 350-400°F (180-220°C). Five minutes before the dish is cooked, remove the foil and let the potatoes brown slightly. Serve in the cooking dish.

Wine: *Pouilly-Fuissé, Hermitage Blanc*   Serves: 4

Violon d'Ingres

22, place Jean-Epinat, 03200 Vichy
Tel: (70) 98-97-70
Proprietor/Chef: Jacques Muller

John Dory* Fillets with Pickled Lemon

1 kg (2¼ lb) lemons
4 handfuls granular salt
2 porgy or John Dory, 600 g (1⅓ lb) each
60 g (2 oz) butter, and as needed
1 chopped shallot
salt and pepper, to taste
200 ml (6 oz) champagne
300 g (10½ oz) double cream (whipping cream)
1 kg (2¼ lb) spinach
50 g (1¾ oz) truffles
lemon peel, to garnish

Quarter the lemons and place in a jar. Add the salt, cover with water, and leave to stew and pickle for *at least 2 months*.

Trim and remove the 4 fillets from the fish. Butter a thick frying pan and add the shallot. Lay the fillets in the pan, add salt and pepper, pour on the champagne, and cover with aluminum foil. Cook quickly on high heat for 25 seconds. Remove the fillets, place them on a dish, and *immediately* recover them with foil so the cooking continues for 5-6 minutes in the pan.

Bring the stock in the pan to a boil, reduce by ½, add cream and pickled lemon, and let cook for 4-5 minutes. Thicken with butter and remove from heat. Put the fillets back into the pan and warm gently for 2 minutes.

To serve: Place a ring of spinach around the outside of each plate, put the fish in the middle, and coat with sauce. Place the truffles and trimmed lemon peel on top.

Wine: *Champagne*   Serves: 4

Le Bec Rouge

12, avenue Saint Charles, Monte Carlo
Tel: (93) 30-74-91
Proprietor: Roger-Claude Roux • Chefs: Roger-Claude Roux, Christian Lerat

Gratin of Langoustines

2 langoustines, 1 kg (2¼ lb) each
50 g (1¾ oz) finely chopped tarragon
200 g (7 oz) finely chopped shallots
50 ml (1½ oz) cognac
300 g (10½ oz) softened butter
250 g (½ lb) white mushrooms
juice of 1 lemon
1 litre (2 pt) double cream (whipping cream)
salt and cayenne pepper, to taste

Cut the langoustines in half and cook in a thick frying pan gently to release all the juices. Add tarragon and shallots, flame with cognac, then cut off tails and cut tails into disc shapes. Chop up the shells and claws and add to the butter. Strain the mixture through a sieve. Fry the mushrooms with the lemon juice on high heat, then strain. Heat the cream, add the langoustine purée, and season to taste. Let reduce until thick. Add the langoustine tail discs and let reduce again.

Suggestion: Place on a dish with duchess potatoes or a small bed of rice. Sprinkle the langoustines with a little Parmesan cheese and cook *au gratin* (brown) under a grill and serve.

Wine: *Puligny Montracher, 1978*   Serves: 4

Vichy, the city of cures and mineral water for overworked livers, is also Vichy, the city of gourmands — thanks mainly to this son and grandson of chefs who, in 1974, at the age of 36, transformed a bistro into a regal restaurant where his charming and somewhat shy wife is an incomparable hostess. This is a small, flower-filled, and colourful restaurant that respects both the classicism of the culinary arts and the "deviations" of folklore. The menu, with its definite penchant for fish, is one continuous surprise from Salmon Flan in White Butter to Scallop Salad to John Dory Fillets with Pickled Lemon. When the desserts come along, even the flagging appetite perks up. The cures and remedies in Vichy are not just hot springs and mineral water!

The symbols of Monaco are roulette tables, Rolls Royces, and Grand Prix racing rather than cooking, except for **Le Bec Rouge**.

It comes as no surprise, then, that Roger-Claude Roux caters to high society and that Prince Rainier is a local customer here and a fan of the delicate blinis (soft, salted pastries, vaguely similar to muffins, that are made in a minute), the Gratin of Langoustines, and the sensational array of cheeses. And in the summer, the musicians lead the celebrations right through until sunrise.

Jean Lenoir was born in 1934 in Auvillers-les-Forges, a small village in the Ardennes Mountains. After learning the family cooking secrets from his mother, he entered a hotel school in Belgium. Upon his return to the family nest, he created his own hotel. This was in 1955. Recently, Jean celebrated his 25th anniversary as a chef.

Assisted by his sister, Ginette, Jean offers a nice menu with original creations. "Cooking is an art and all art is patience," says Jean.

Try the "Egyptian Homecoming" Lobster, Arden Thrush Mousse, "Czar" Boiled Eggs, Scallops in Bouzy, Veal Kidneys in Mint, Venison with Grapes, Hot Fish Pâté with Sorrel, Duckling with Cherries, and Quail with Lime — you won't be disappointed.

Hostellerie Lenoir

Auvillers-les-Forges, 08260 Maubert-Fontaine
Tel: (24) 36-30-11
Proprietor/Chef: Jean Lenoir

"Egyptian Homecoming" Lobster

4 small lobsters, 400 g (¾ lb) each
100 g (3½ oz) butter
50 ml (1½ oz) mandarin liqueur
1 shallot, chopped
100 ml (3 oz) Muscadet wine
2 medium-sized oranges, cut in half and squeezed, juice and half-skins reserved
salt and cayenne pepper, to taste
2 tomatoes, peeled, seeded, and chopped
1 clove garlic
1 sabayon, made by mixing 2 egg yolks and 100 ml (3 oz) double cream (whipping cream) together and heating gently
60 g (2 oz) creole rice, cooked
tangerine or orange segments, as needed

Plunge the lobsters into boiling water for 1 minute. Remove and cut each in half down the middle.

To prepare coral butter: Extract the creamy parts and the coral. Mash these with ⅛ of the butter and ⅛ of the mandarin liqueur.

To prepare sauce: Colour the shallot in a sauté pan. Add lobster halves and broken-off claws. Cover and stew for 5 minutes. Flame with remaining liqueur. Add Muscadet and orange juice. Season with salt and cayenne pepper. Add tomatoes and garlic. Cook for 5 minutes. Remove lobster pieces; extract all meat and keep warm. Rapidly reduce cooking liquid. Add coral butter and bring to a boil once. Whisk in remaining butter and sabayon, away from heat. Purée in a blender.

Fill the orange halves with rice and lobster claws. Heat orange segments in a little sauce and fill the lobster heads with them. Arrange the lobster tails, filled with their meat, on the dish. Cover with a little sauce and serve the rest on the side.

Wine: *Côte Beaune or St. Émilion red*   Serves: 4

La Cotriade

Port de Piégu Pléneuf, 22370 Val-André
Tel: (96) 72-20-26
Proprietor/Chef: Jean-Jacques Le Saout

The name of this restaurant is the name given to bouillabaisse "Breton" style, and what other name could you choose when you set up shop in Port de Piégu, a little seaside resort in the Côtes du Nord district, at the foot of the ruins of a castle called the "Bien Assis"?

Jean-Jacques Le Saout, who opened this restaurant, is indeed Breton through and through. He will never disappoint you with the quality of his produce or, especially, anything that comes from "his" sea. The vast bay gives a good view of the open sea where the delicious lobsters in his Cotriade come from. To taste the bouillabaisse at **La Cotriade** is to taste the true flavour of Brittany.

Grilled Lobster "Cotriade" Style

4 live lobsters, 500 g (1 lb) each
salt and pepper, to taste
pinch of paprika
2 sprigs basil, chopped
2 sprigs tarragon, chopped
250 g (½ lb) butter
1 dash Pernod liqueur
juice of ½ lemon
200 ml (6 oz) double cream (whipping cream)

Stun the lobsters and cut them in half lengthwise. Remove the intestines and coral and keep in a cool place. Flatten the lobsters slightly, then add salt, pepper, and a sprinkling of paprika, basil, and tarragon. Brush each half-lobster with ½ the butter, then cook in the oven at 475°F (250°C) for 12 minutes.

Mix the coral with the remaining butter (half-melted) and Pernod and use to coat the lobster cases. Glaze the coated lobsters under a hot grill, then remove and set aside.

Strain the remaining stock through a conical sauce strainer, add the lemon juice, reduce, and add cream. Serve the sauce with the warm lobster.

Wine: *Muscadet or Pouilly Fumé*   Serves: 4

La Table des Cordeliers

32100 Condom
Tel: (62) 28-03-68
Proprietor: Maïté Sandrini • Chef: Jacques Pastor

The late and beloved René Sandrini purchased and patiently restored this 14th century chapel in the heart of the Armagnac and turned it into a small hotel with a fine dining room. Maïté Sandrini, ably seconded by her chef, Jacques Pastor, has kept the flag flying. This gourmand's stop-off, with its few very comfortable rooms, has become one of the great places to visit in Gascony.

In the large, stone vaulted room, you will find regional, classic dishes such as Foie Gras, Confit of Duck, Crayfsh Salad with Oysters, Macaronnade (fresh pasta, lamb sweetmeats, and mushrooms), and Lobster Gâteau with Celeriac; the thought of even the simplest dish here makes my mouth water.

Lobster Gâteau with Celeriac

1 lobster, female preferred
1 egg white
1 litre (2 pt) sweet cream
1 tbsp grey shallots
200 ml (6 oz) dry vermouth
1 kg (2¼ lb) celeriac steeped in olive oil
juice of 1 lemon
butter, as needed

To prepare the mousse: Purée the lobster meat, egg white, and ½ the cream. Prepare a sauce by combining and heating the lobster shells, shallots, vermouth, and the remaining cream. Cook the celeriac in water and lemon juice until tender.

Put the mousse into 6 buttered ramekins and bake in the oven at 425-450°F (220-230°C) for about ½ hour. Serve the mousse coated with the sauce and celeriac.

Suggestion: Serve with rice pilaff.

Wine: *Meursault Cuvée Paul Bouchard*   Serves: 6

Rôtisserie de la Boule d'Or

25, rue du Maréchal Foch, 78000 Versailles
Tel: 950-2297
Proprietor: Claude Saillard • Chef: Pascal Delpierre

In 1968, Claude Saillard, the grandson and son of innkeepers and restaurateurs, settled here in Versailles. Hailing from the Franche-Comté region, he named his establishment Auberge Comtoise and chose the name **Boule d'Or** for his rôtisserie. It is a room with old, wooden beams and walls bedecked with tapestries, heavy curtains, and original 17th century paintings. Assisted by the young Pascal Delpierre, Claude offers two kinds of cooking. One is very much of France-Comté origin and the other consists of very old recipes — recipes of Taillevent (1373), of Massialot (1691), of Marin (1739), of Vincent La Chapelle (1733), and other great masters — recipes that have almost been forgotten but which are so singularly "modern-proof" that the so-called *la nouvelle cuisine* cannot even compare.

Lobster in Puff Pastry "Grand Century" Style

1 lobster of 1.5 kg (3⅓ lb), of which 400 g (14 oz) is meat
⅓ litre (1½ cups) choux paste*
100 ml (3 oz) sauce Américaine* (made from lobster shells)
100 ml (3 oz) court bouillon*
500 g (1 lb) puff pastry dough*
100 g (3½ oz) butter rubbed in an equal amount of flour (beurre manié)

Place lobster in enough cold, salted water to cover it. Bring to a boil, reduce heat, and let simmer for 15 minutes. Drain and shell it. Mix the choux paste, the sauce Américaine, and the lobster meat together. Butter a sheet of greaseproof (wax) paper, place the mixture on the paper, close, roll, and tie it up with string to form a quenelle. Poach in the court bouillon, then let cool.

Remove the paper and wrap the quenelle in the puff pastry dough. Bake in the oven for 10 minutes at 400°F (205°C), then for 40 minutes at 320°F (160°C). Thicken the sauce with *beurre manié* (butter rubbed in flour) and serve in a sauce dish.

Serves: 6

Le Mériadeck

5, rue Robert-Lateulade, 33000 Bordeaux
Tel: (56) 90-92-37
Proprietor: Frantel • Chef: Eric Deblonde

Le Mériadeck, just a few minutes away from the Gothic cathedral of Saint André, has become one of the *grands crus* (great vintages) among Bordeaux restaurants with the help of Eric Deblonde.

The Pink Raddish Soup with Goose Fat is astonishing, and the same is true of the Scallop of Salmon in Lentils, Lobster Poached in Wine and Vegetables, and the Young Chicken Stew. All are accompanied by the best bottles of claret.

This is a top quality restaurant.

Lobster Poached in Wine with Vegetables

3 live lobsters, 450 g (1 lb) each
3 litres (3 qt) hot fish fumet*
½ bottle champagne
3 carrots, julienne
1 bulb of fennel, julienne
3 turnips, julienne
1 stick celery, julienne
500 g (1 lb) green beans, julienne
3 egg yolks
200 ml (6 oz) double cream (whipping cream)
salt and pepper, to taste

Put the lobsters into the hot fumet, add champagne, and bring to a boil. Reduce heat and simmer for 15 minutes. When cooked, shell and place each half-lobster onto an ovenproof serving plate.

Cook the vegetables in the stock left from the lobsters until they are crisp. Place alongside the lobster halves. Mix the egg yolks, cream, and the stock from the lobsters and vegetables together and cook on medium heat until thick. Check the seasoning.

Serve the lobsters and vegetables hot and coated with this very light sauce.

Wine: *Champagne or Graves*

Serves: 6

Francis Robin

1, boulevard Georges Clémenceau, 13000 Salon de Provence
Tel: (90) 56-06-53
Proprietor/Chef: Francis Robin

There's one name that engraves a select place for itself in the annals of great gastronomy — namely Francis Robin in Salon de Provence. With enthusiasm and professionalism, he serves great cooking without all the trimmings. The chic simplicity of his restaurant is also reflected in his menu, which is rich, but not over-powering. Top quality products reach your table only after having been prepared properly.

Here, at the gates of the Camargue, do not hesitate to treat yourself to the Escalope of Veal Sweetmeats with Grapes and Pink Peppercorns, the Young Rabbit with Tarragon, or the Lobster Stew. Everything will be perfect.

Lobster Stew

5 shallots
2 onions
6 tbsp olive oil
1 lobster of 2.5 - 3 kg (5½ - 6½ lb), cut in pieces
120 ml (4 oz) Armagnac
1 litre (2 pt) Banyuls (sweet liqueur wine)
1 tsp butter
1 tsp flour
seasoning, to taste
1 tbsp each: parsley, chervil, and chives

Peel and chop the shallots and onions, then brown them very gently in some olive oil in a thick frying pan.

In another similar pan, brown the lobster in the remaining oil, flame with Armagnac, then add the Banyuls. Mix the 2 preparations together and let cook gently for 15 minutes. Remove the lobster pieces and keep hot.

Rub the butter in the flour *(beurre manié)* and mix with the lobster entrails to thicken the sauce. Check the seasoning. Place the pieces of lobster on a hot dish, coat with sauce, sprinkle herbs over, and serve immediately.

Wine: *Château Simone White or Gigondas Rosé*   Serves: 6

La Caravelle

International Airport, Tarbes-Ossun-Lourdes, 65290 Juillan
Tel: Tarbes (62) 96-27-13
Proprietor/Chef: Emile Rouzaud

La Caravelle is a charming restaurant with a marvellous view of the Pyrenees, and the contrast between the snow-covered slopes and the soft atmosphere of the restaurant, with its English style bar and indoor garden with green plants, aquarium, and exotic birds, is delightful. The chef, Emile Rouzaud, is a man of great experience and a real professional. Emile has been cooking traditional, albeit somewhat lighter, food here since 1958, when the restaurant opened. A fine example is his Eggs "Caravelle" Style which is the recipe of Louis Rouzaud, his father, and dates from the beginning of the century. Don't forget to ask him for his goose *foie gras* cooked whole à *la paysanne* or his Lobster with Cream. They are simply marvellous!

Lobster with Cream

court bouillon,* enough to cover lobster
1 lobster of 800 g (1¾ lb)
1 litre (2 pt) mussels
2 chopped shallots
300 ml (9 oz) dry white wine
200 ml (6 oz) milk
150 g (5¼ oz) tomato concasse*

Boil the court bouillon in a saucepan. Put the lobster in the pan and cook for 8 minutes. Remove the lobster from the pan, sever the claws, and cook the claws for another 5 minutes.

Place mussels, chopped shallots, white wine, milk, and tomatoes in a stainless steel thick frying pan and cook on high heat until mussels open. Remove the shells and set mussels and their cooking stock aside.

Split the lobster lengthwise; scoop out the coral; remove the shell from the tail, the cases, and the claws; let all simmer for a few minutes in the stock from the mussels. Serve the lobster surrounded by the mussels and the sauce, which will be brightly coloured from the coral.

Wine: *Pacherencq du Vic Bilh*   Serves: 2

Chez Max

19, rue de Castellane, 75008 Paris
Tel: 265-3381
Proprietor/Chef: M. Clessienne

This establishment was founded after the last war by Max Maupuy, the former head fish cook at the Ritz, who hailed from Vouvray sur Loire and was the creator of many famous original dishes. His successor, M. Clessienne, has kept up this top quality menu, and **Chez Max** is still a great little place to go to — "Great food in a small house," as the gourmet Francis Amunatequi put it.

The wine cellar no longer harbours the extraordinary bottles of Vouvray 1921, now collectors items, and so the debate goes on: What do you drink with the Cardinal des Mers du Jardin d'Allah (Lobster with Oranges)? Curnonsky suggested a sweet Anjou, others proposed champagne or even a Champigny red wine. Why not come to Chez Max and decide for yourself?

Lobster with Oranges

1 lobster of 1 - 1.2 kg (2¼ - 2½ lb)
salt and pepper, to taste
4 tbsp oil
2 chopped shallots
100 ml (3 oz) white wine
3 tbsp paprika
1 litre (2 pt) double cream (whipping cream)
1 tbsp flour
100 ml (3 oz) Grand Marnier
100 ml (3 oz) whisky
50 g (1¾ oz) butter
8 orange halves, juice and pulp removed

Cut off the tail of the lobster, remove the legs, and break the claws to make it easier to remove the flesh after cooking. Split the case in 2, lengthwise, and remove the bag near the head. Set the intestines and coral aside. Season the lobster pieces with salt and pepper. Heat the oil in a frying pan over very high heat, add lobster pieces, and cook until flesh has become stiff and the shell red. Remove the grease. Add shallots, white wine, paprika, and cream. Let boil gently for about 15 minutes, then remove the lobster and take out the flesh.

To prepare the sauce: Thoroughly mash the reserved lobster intestines and coral. Mix in the flour to thicken it, then add Grand Marnier and whisky. Heat without boiling, then add butter.

Place the pieces of lobster in the empty half-orange peels, and pour the sauce over.
Suggestion: Serve with rice pilaff and quartered oranges.

Serves: 4

Chez Pointaire

46, rue de Villiers, 92300 Levallois-Perret
Tel: 757-4477
Proprietor/Chef: Alain Albert

Pierre Pointaire, an exceptional chef, will not be forgotten. When he left this little provincial restaurant, he knew that it would be in good hands — those of Alain Albert. This young chef and his pretty, young wife have made many of their dreams come true: a business clientele at midday, friends in the evening, always an atmosphere of camaraderie, and the respect for quality and intimacy from all.

The dining room and the salon are separated by the kitchens, where Alain prepares the famous Beuchelle Tourangelle, the masterpiece of Pointaire (sweetmeat stew, veal kidneys, truffles, etc.) and also Gratin of Lobster, Assorted Fish in Butter, Pheasant à la Brabançonne, and a marvellous dessert, La Marquise d'Anjou in Bitter Chocolate.

Assorted Fish in Butter

150 g (5¼ oz) fine green beans
100 g (3½ oz) onions
100 g (3½ oz) carrots
1 bouquet garni*
salt, to taste
200 ml (6 oz) white wine vinegar
1 pike perch (pike) of 1 kg (2¼ lb)
2 perch, 500 g (1 lb) each
3 grey shallots
100 ml (3 oz) Muscadet
1 tbsp double cream (whipping cream)
300 g (10½ oz) butter
cayenne pepper, to taste

Cook the green beans in a saucepan with water until tender but crisp. Prepare a court bouillon* with the onions, carrots, thyme, bay leaf, salt, and ½ the wine vinegar. Clean, draw, and fillet the fish. Chop the shallots very finely and let reduce in the remaining vinegar and Muscadet until liquid is almost completely evaporated. Poach the fillets in this mixture for about 5 minutes. Add cream and bring to a boil. When boiling, add the butter in small pieces and whisk thoroughly. (The butter should be almost frothy.) Season with cayenne pepper and salt. Remove the skin from the fillets.

Serve the fillets on individual plates with a few green beans on top of each and coated with butter.

Wine: *Muscadet*

Serves: 4

Bacon

Boulevard de la Garoupe, 06600 Cap d'Antibes
Tel: (93) 61-50-02
Proprietor: Mme. Sordello • Chef: Philippe Serge

Bacon is justly one of the most famous restaurants of the Riviera in Cap d'Antibes. Mme. Sordello is lucky in two ways: her fish are caught especially for her in the Mediterranean, and she employs a young chef, Philippe Serge, who skillfully takes care of them.

Doubtless one comes here for the bouillabaisse, but there are also lobster salad, *foie gras* salad, and, according to how the fishing goes (imported fish in blocks of ice are quite out of the question), the local fish (bass, sea bream, John Dory, lamprey, red mullet, etc.) cooked in basil or grilled in fennel or most deliciously with fresh, scented chervil. Add to that, fine desserts and wines, and you have the full range of a seafood symphony.

Bouillabaisse

500 g (1 lb) finely sliced onions
5 cloves garlic
500 g (1 lb) sliced tomatoes
1 stalk celery, sliced
2 carrots, sliced
pinch of saffron
100 ml (3 oz) olive oil
4 kg (8¾ lb) any rock fish (any Mediterranean fish such as scorpion fish, girella, wrasse, or striped bass)
3 kg (6½ lb) any larger fish such as porgy, John Dory, conger, anglerfish, sea bream, red gurnet, perch
250 g (½ lb) croutons
pimento-flavoured mayonnaise, as needed

Gently brown the finely sliced onions, garlic, tomatoes, celery, carrots, and saffron in oil, add the smaller rock fish, and cook until mixture becomes a thick purée. Boil for 10 minutes, then strain through a strainer. Add the larger fish to the strained stock and cook until they are pink to the bone. Serve the soup and the fish (bones removed) with croutons coated with pimento-flavoured mayonnaise.

Wine: *White Côte de Provence*

Serves: 4

Auberge Saint-Vincent

Place de la Halle, 21200 Beaune
Tel: (80) 22-42-34
Proprietor: Lucette Laurent • Chef: M. Saulnier

Beaune is known to some as the pearl of Burgundy. This old town comes alive each year for the sale of famous wines. Beaune is also the town where **Auberge Saint-Vincent** can be found. Situated in a restored 17th century house, this very rustic style auberge is where Chef Saulnier conjures up classical country-style food along with some surprises. For example, there are Jellied Ham with Parsley, Salad of Raw Salmon, Pike "Saint-Vincent" Style, Crayfish and Fillet of Sole Stew, Duck with Blackcurrants, and Veal Tournedos with Avocado Sauce.

Of course, there is a fine list of Burgundy wines because, as the menu says, "The greatest pleasures of eating would, in fact, have little attraction if fine wine could not light up the face of the one we love."

Crayfish and Fillet of Sole Stew

700 g (1½ lb) sole
¼ litre (½ pt) fish fumet* made from sole bones
250 g (½ lb) carrots
250 g (½ lb) turnips
1 cucumber
6 shallots, finely chopped
1 tbsp olive oil
¼ litre (½ pt) white wine
½ litre (1 pt) double cream (whipping cream)
salt and pepper, to taste
1 tsp butter
1 sprig tarragon
1 sprig thyme
1 clove garlic, crushed
1.2 kg (2½ lb) crayfish (or lobster tails)
70 g (2½ oz) butter, and as needed

Remove the fillets from the sole, cut into strips, and soak for ¼ hour in cool water. Prepare a fumet with the bones, keeping it thick. Cut the vegetables into little oval shapes, blanch them separately, and set aside.

To prepare the sauce: Sweat* 3 shallots in oil, add the fumet, and let reduce by ½. Add wine, then add cream, and reduce again by ½. Add salt and pepper, 1 tsp butter, and keep hot.

Steam the tarragon, thyme, remaining shallots, and garlic for 5 minutes.

Grill the crayfish, remove the heads, claws, and undershells, then place upside down around the serving dish. Cook the strips of sole and place around the edges of the dish also. Strain the vegetables, and then glaze them in a frying pan with butter. Put the vegetables in the middle of the serving dish.

Nap* the crayfish and the sole with the sauce and serve.

Wine: *Puligny Montrachet, 1978*

Serves: 4

Prunier "Madeleine"

9, rue Duphot, 75001 Paris
Tel: 260-3604
Proprietor: Aldo Funaro • Chef: Alain Mestas

"Dieppe" Style Casserole

1 fillet of sole of 800 g (1¾ lb)
1 young turbot of 800 g (1¾ lb)
1 red mullet of 600 g (1⅓ lb)
200 g (7 oz) butter
1 litre (2 pt) mussels
1 stalk celery
1 leek
4 shallots
1 large onion
1 bouquet garni*
½ litre (1 pt) double cream (whipping cream)
salt and pepper, to taste
1 sprig chervil

Draw, skin, and trim the sole; cut the flesh into 4 slices and reserve the trimmings. Remove the fillets from the turbot and skin them. Cut each fillet in half. Remove the scales from the red mullet, draw and cut off the head, and cut into 4 parts. Sweat* the fish trimmings in butter, moisten with the juice from the mussels, and cook with the celery, leek, shallots, onion, and bouquet garni for 30 minutes. Strain this stock into a saucepan, add all the fish, and cook for 3 minutes. Remove the fish, add the cream, and check the seasoning.

Serve the pieces of fish in a pot or deep dish, add the mussels, and pour the stock from the saucepan on top. Sprinkle with chervil and serve.

Suggestion: Serve with oven-dried or toasted croutons.

Serves: 4

This restaurant was created in 1872. In 1977, it was taken over by M. Aldo Funaro, who refurbished the 1925 decor, which is now full of charm, and reinstated the establishment's reputation for serving some of the finest seafood in France.

His fried fish dishes are worth noting — red mullet, young sole, and squid — as are his scallops with either sorrel, leeks, onions, or "Seaman" style. The turbot is served either with curry, butter sauce, or Hollandaise sauce, or is broiled; the anglerfish is served with saffron or is stewed; and there is a fine mixed seafood casserole. The fillet served with oysters is most tasty and is one of the rare homemade treats. There is also a wide choice of desserts and a very good wine cellar.

Ty-Coz

35, rue Saint-Georges, 75009 Paris
Tel: 878-4295
Proprietor/Chef: Jacqueline Libois

Cotriade "Ty-Coz" Style

12 Norway lobsters (or langoustines, lobster tails, spiny lobster)
1 kg (2¼ lb) large mussels
1 lobster tail or crayfish
1 litre (2 pt) fish fumet* made from a large variety of small fish
oil and butter, as needed
onions, to taste
4 potatoes, cut in round slices
100 ml (3 oz) Muscadet or any white wine
1 porgy or John Dory of 1.2 kg (2¾ lb)
1 anglerfish of 1 kg (2¼ lb)
1 bass or mullet of 600 g (1⅓ lb)
1 tbsp double cream (whipping cream)

Cook the shellfish in the fumet for 10 minutes. Heat a little oil and butter in a cooking pot and scald the onions and potato slices in it. After a few minutes, add white wine and fish fumet. Ten minutes before serving, cook the remaining fish in the fumet.

Serve the soup as follows: Put the fish, shellfish, and potatoes in a soup dish followed by the broth with cream mixed in to finish it.

Wine: *A Gamay or other light, chilled red wine*

Serves: 6

Fifty years ago, Jacqueline Libois started her first restaurant, her first **Ty-Coz**. In 1963, she moved to Saint-Georges and furnished a rustic auberge with old Breton furniture in order to offer her cooking "without meat and without complaint" to the gourmets of Paris. Start with buckwheat cakes as your apéritif and finish with dessert crepes, and I suggest a most admirable seafood dish — Cotriade (a fish soup from Brittany) as your main course. It comprises a whole array of fresh fish. The Brittany wines and cider make delicious company for this marvellous food. Jacqueline's recipes were handed down to her by her grandmother and, as she likes to say, her "childhood is imprinted with this cooking."

Le Soubise

62, rue de la République, 17780 Soubise
Tel: (46) 99-31-18 and 99-49-20
Proprietor: R. Benoît • Chef: Lilyane Benoît

Lilyane Benoît may be the prettiest and most cheerful of all chefs. In 1963, she and her husband opened this restaurant here in Soubise, the birthplace of M. Benoît, located between La Rochelle and Royan.

The people who stay in the few hotel rooms here are lucky, indeed, to be able to enjoy the soft and rustic decor and to be so close to the kitchen of this gifted chef. Lilyane Benoît has been a sort of ambassador for this regional style cuisine, sharing the secrets of typical dishes and recipes such as Young Eel "Charentes" Style, mussels, and Pork Stew with Fatted Duck, together with the classics such as Fish Soup with Foie Gras, Fisherman's Stew, Fillet of Beef in Green Peppers, and various desserts.

Fisherman's Stew

1 porgy or John Dory of 300 g (10½ oz)
1 large stockfish (hake, sea pike) of 500 g (1 lb)
2 whiting or little hake, 500 g (1 lb) each
1 kg (2¼ lb) flattened fillets of sole
1 large turbot of 1 kg (2¼ lb), filleted
Muscadet white wine, as needed
400 g (14 oz) green beans
400 g (14 oz) carrots
8 small leeks
4 white turnips
2 courgettes (zucchini)
4 lobsters, 400 g (14 oz) each
16 large scallops
1 tail of anglerfish (monkfish or cod)
100 g (3½ oz) butter
salt and pepper, to taste

Prepare a fumet* with the porgy or John Dory, stockfish, whiting, sole, and turbot. Add a mixture of ⅓ wine to ⅔ water to the fumet. Poach the green beans, carrots, leeks, turnips, and courgettes in separate saucepans, then add to the fish fumet. Poach the lobster, the turbot fillets, the flattened sole fillets, the scallops, and the anglerfish tail. When the fish have turned a pink colour, remove and keep hot.

Thicken the fumet sauce with butter and check the seasoning. Serve the fish layered with vegetables and coated with the buttered fumet.

Wine: *Muscadet*   Serves: 8

Le Restaurant Vendôme de l'Hôtel Ritz

15, place Vendôme, 75001 Paris
Tel: 260-3830
Proprietor: Frank Klein • Chef: Guy Lecat

Since 1898, just about all the crowned heads of Europe, along with such renowned figures as Marcel Proust, Ernest Hemingway, Charlie Chaplin, Winston Churchill, Rudolph Valentino, and Greta Garbo, have all enjoyed the very French style *dolce vita* in this, one of the great fabled luxury hotels of the world that is found in the Place Vendôme in Paris.

Cesar Ritz called upon the helping hand of the culinary genius August Escoffier at the turn of the century; the current owner, M. Klein, calls upon the gifted Guy Lecat to prepare the superb Sole "Escoffier" Style and Veal Sweetbreads "Ritz" Style, as well as other fine dishes such as Fish Fricassee with Pleurotus Mushrooms. As the saying goes: "The Ritz will always be the Ritz."

Fish Fricassee with Pleurotus Mushrooms

2 shallots, chopped
250 g (½ lb) softened butter
1 salmon steak of 200 g (7 oz), cut into 6 slices
1 sole of 200 g (7 oz), cut into 12 pieces, 3 per fillet
1 red mullet of 200 g (7 oz), each fillet cut into 3 pieces
200 g (7 oz) fillet of anglerfish (monkfish or cod), cut into 6 pieces
400 ml (¾ pt) red wine
few leaves thyme
3 bay leaves
salt and pepper, to taste
1 tbsp *beurre manié* (½ tbsp softened butter rubbed with ½ tbsp flour)
150 g (5¼ oz) butter
600 g (1⅓ lb) pleurotus mushrooms, washed, diced, and sautéed
1 bunch parsley
12 quails eggs, poached in red wine and kept warm
6 fried croutons

Sweat* the shallots in a pan with high sides in 50 g (1¾ oz) softened butter. Add all the fish, red wine, thyme, and bay leaves. Season with salt and pepper. Cover with greaseproof (wax) paper and bake at 350°F (175°C). When the juice starts to boil, let boil for 2 minutes, then remove the fish from the pan. Reduce just a little more than ¾ of the cooking liquid to sauce consistency, add *beurre manié*, then add 150 g (5¼ oz) butter. Check the seasoning. Strain through a sauce strainer and keep warm in a bain-marie* over boiling water.

Arrange the fish on a serving dish, place the mushrooms in little groups around them, and nap* all with the sauce. Sprinkle with parsley and place the warm quails eggs and croutons on top.

Serves: 2

L'Étoile d'Or

Hôtel Concorde-Lafayette, 3, Place de la Porte des Ternes, 75017 Paris
Tel: 758-1284
Proprietor: Hôtel Concorde-Lafayette • Chef: Joël Renty

Who has not, at some time, dreamed of dining in a place overlooking the roofs of Paris and superbly contemplating the lights of the city below? It would be ideal for starry-eyed romantics. Well, ascend to the top floor of the Concorde-Lafayette where it would definitely appear that all the stars are together as one — as in the name of this restaurant (translated as the Golden Star).

Those little stars will have to be cleared from your eyes, however, when Joël Renty presents you with his Red Mullet in Bone Marrow, his "Fish Merchant" Panache, or his warm tartlets. The view and the food are equally dazzling.

"Fish Merchant" Panache with Cucumbers

1 bass of 400 g (14 oz)
4 scallops
4 small red mullet, 60 g (2 oz) each
4 large mussels
50 g (1¾ oz) butter, and as needed
salt and ground pepper, to taste
800 g (1¾ lb) finely chopped shallots
4 fillets of sole
4 large Norway lobsters (or langoustines, lobster tails, spiny lobster), prepared for cooking
500 g (1 lb) cucumbers, julienne
50 ml (1½ oz) good white wine
50 ml (1½ oz) fumet*
200 ml (6 oz) double cream (whipping cream)
fine herbs, to garnish

Remove the fillets from the bass and shell the scallops. Clean the red mullet. Carefully scrape the outside of the mussel shells clean. Butter and season the bottom of a cooking dish, sprinkle with shallots, and place all the fish and shellfish in it. Cover the whole preparation with cucumber sticks and season with salt and pepper. Pour wine and fumet over all, then bake in the oven at 400°F (205°C) for 3 minutes. Steam the mussels separately in a covered pan with 60 ml (2 oz) water until they open (about 6 - 8 minutes).

Recover the stock from the fish and mussels and let reduce by ½. Add cream, bring to a boil, and thicken with butter.

Nap* the fish and cucumbers with sauce on a serving platter. Sprinkle fine herbs over all and serve.

Serves: 4

Christian Clément

58, rue du Pas-Saint-Georges, 33000 Bordeaux
Tel: (56) 81-01-39
Proprietor/Chef: Christian Clément

Christian Clément is at last in a place of his own, a fulfillment of a dream that began 17 years ago. His apprenticeship was served working in Laval, Nantes, the Orly Hilton, and finally with the Frantel establishment in Bordeaux. Since 1963, he had been hoping for the time when he would be home in his own place. His "home," which opened in April 1980, consists of 18th century stone walls, a large 18th century dining room, and a vaulted cellar, which is even older.

Christian operates with the help of his wife. The charming Mme. Clément ably welcomes their guests and describes the Cream of Pigeon "Malvoisie" Style, Lobster and Shrimp Fricassee, Fillet of Roast Anglerfish, Duck in Five Dressings, and Pear Caramel in Tea "Bergamote" Style, all prepared by her husband.

Lobster and Shrimp Fricassee

300 g (10½ oz) leeks
1 stalk fennel
4 mushrooms
3 tbsp olive oil
2 lobsters, 700 g (1½ lb) each
16 large shrimps
ground pepper, to taste
4 chopped shallots
1 bunch herbs, finely chopped
1 bouquet garni*
150 ml (5¼ oz) vermouth
½ clove crushed garlic
200 ml (6 oz) double cream (whipping cream)
100 ml (3 oz) veal stock*
pinch of crushed coriander seeds

Peel and finely slice the leeks, fennel, and mushrooms. Heat the olive oil in a thick frying pan on high heat. Cut up the lobsters and fry them quickly in the hot oil. Add shrimps and season with pepper. Let cook for 3 minutes, then add, in order, shallots, leeks, fennel, mixed herbs, bouquet garni, and mushrooms. Let thicken for 5 minutes. Add vermouth, let simmer for 3 minutes, then remove shrimps and add garlic, cream, veal stock, and coriander. Reduce to sauce consistency.

Place the lobsters and shrimps on a warm serving dish while the sauce reduces. Nap* with reduced sauce and serve very hot.

Wine: *Domaine de Chevalier, 1978 (Graves White)*

Serves: 4

Le Manoir d'Hastings

14970 Bénouville
Tel: (31) 93-30-89
Proprietor/Chef: Claude Scaviner

This famous restaurant is housed in what used to be a priory back in 1670 in this famous little Normandy village of Bénouville. Here, M. and Mme. Scaviner — he in the kitchens and she in the restaurant — take care of "you and your happiness when you are under their roof," as Brillat-Savarin might have said. Claude Scaviner cooks everything the sea can produce — such as Hot Oysters, Poached Scallops, Panache of Fish with Cucumber, Roast Anglerfish with Shallots, and Sole with Sorrel — but you will also be delighted with his Ham in Cider served with Blanquette of Potatoes with Leeks. "Good eating," as someone once said, "is one of the four goals of mankind. I have forgotten the other three." Had he or she just eaten in this restaurant?

Panache of Fish with Cucumber

1 young turbot of 800 g (1¾ lb)
1 sole of 600 g (1⅓ lb)
1 porgy or John Dory of 600 g (1⅓ lb)
1 carrot
1 small onion
1 stalk celery
1 bouquet garni*
¼ litre (1 cup) white wine
1 large cucumber
6 large scallops
salt and pepper, to taste
200 ml (6 oz) double cream (whipping cream)

Remove the fillets from the 3 fish and prepare a fumet* using the bones, carrot, onion, celery, bouquet garni, and wine. Peel the cucumber and cut into long, thin slices; reserve the peel. Open and trim the scallops. Cook the cucumber and peel in a few tablespoons of fumet. When the cucumber has become soft, add fish fillets and scallops. Poach quickly for a few minutes, keeping the fish cooked but firm. Season. Remove fish from the frying pan and place on a serving dish with cucumber slices between each.

Add the stock, which still contains the cucumber peel and the cream, to the pan. Bring to a boil and reduce by ½. The sauce should thicken slightly. Strain the sauce by pushing and squeezing the peel through a strainer to get a rich, creamy sauce. Reheat the fish, pour sauce over, check the seasoning, and serve.

Serves: 6

Le Galion

15, rue Saint-Guénole, 29110 Concarneau
Tel: (98) 97-30-16
Proprietor/Chef: Henri Gaonac'h

It was back in 1976 that M. and Mme. Gaonac'h took over **Le Galion**, a restaurant that was founded in 1972 in the town of Concarneau. This restaurant features the charm of an old, Breton dwelling and the cuisine of a fine chef. The restaurant has a quiet ambiance, with soft music and lighting to go with the discreet elegance of the menu and table settings. Fish prepared "Brittany" Style is the speciality, but there are also Cotriade (fish soup), Fricassee of Anglerfish, Turbot in Champagne, Sole and Scallop Stew, Salmon Steaks, etc. The smoked salmon is served with cucumbers in cream, the crawfish in aspic, the mussels in cider, and the oysters are stuffed ("Brittany" style, of course).

Sole and Scallop Stew with Vegetables

400 g (14 oz) large scallops
2 large sole, 500 g (1 lb) each
250 g (½ lb) green beans, julienne
2 carrots, julienne
400 g (14 oz) small turnips, julienne
50 g (1¾ oz) peeled shallots
100 ml (3 oz) white wine
200 g (7 oz) butter
1 tbsp double cream (whipping cream)
50 g (1¾ oz) mixed herbs: parsley, chervil, fennel, and tarragon

Clean the scallops thoroughly. Remove the fillets from the sole, roll into rolls and fasten with cocktail sticks (toothpicks). Cook the green beans, carrots, and turnips in 3 separate saucepans until tender. Do not overcook them.

In a frying pan, reduce the shallots and wine, then slowly add the melted butter and the cream. Steam the sole fillets and the scallops for 10-12 minutes. Serve the vegetables, fillets, and scallops in a dish, pour the butter/cream sauce over, and sprinkle with the mixed herbs.

Wine: *Sancerre or Macon White*

Serves: 2

Les Champs d'Ors

22, rue du Champ de Mars, 75007 Paris
Tel: 551-5269
Proprietor/Chef: Georges Cloët

Waterzoöi

½ stalk celery (the bottom half)
3 leek whites
1 fennel bulb
1 tsp butter
salt, as needed
250 ml (7½ oz) chicken consommé
1.2 kg (2¾ lb) fillets of white fish (sole, anglerfish, brill, porgy, or John Dory)
3 egg yolks
1 tbsp double cream (whipping cream)
6 large scallops, cooked

Heat the vegetables in a covered pot with butter, a little water, and a little salt. Spread the vegetables into a frying pan, add the consommé, and cook until the vegetables begin to swell. Place fish fillets on top, cover, and cook gently until fish flakes easily with a fork. Remove fillets and place on 6 hot plates.

Thicken the vegetable sauce with the egg yolks and the cream; stir well, but do not boil. Pour the sauce over the fish, place a scallop on each plate, and serve.

Wine: *White Burgundy*

Serves: 6

Georges Cloët was born in Normandy of Belgian parents. After working for a long time at Chez Les Anges, he left to go and find his own little "angel" in Belgium. Her name is Rosita. He then worked in Anvers, then Brussels, then in 1974, he decided to take over a little restaurant in Paris. It had opened in 1965 but had had little success. He turned it into a dainty little eating place with a warm and cosy decor, a perfect fit for the charm of Rosita. He works in the kitchens with his fish. There's a touch of Belgium in his Waterzoöi and a flair to his Salad of Warm Oysters. There are also some meat dishes, as well as very tasty desserts (Rhubard Mousseline with Cream "Peru" Style), and a pleasant wine cellar.

La Toison d'Or

Place Thiers, 11, rue Poincaré, 54000 Nancy
Tel: (28) 35-61-01
Proprietor: Frantel • Chef: Joël Roy

Smoked Pike Perch on Hot Crepes

1 pike perch (pike or perch) of 1.2 kg (2½ lb)
1.5 litres (3 pt) crepe batter*
75 g (2¾ oz) butter
1 bunch chives, and to garnish

Smoke the pike perch gradually, being careful not to dehydrate the flesh. Cook 12 crepes.* Cut the fish into thin strips and spread on top of the crepes. Pour hot, melted butter mixed with some chopped chives around the fish and serve on hot plates with a sprinkling of chives.

Serves: 6

If you are fond of towns that have a sense of history in their architecture and cuisine, you will certainly admire Nancy — this masterpiece from the 18th century — and the privilege of dining at **La Toison d'Or** in the middle of the Place Thiers, at the gates of the splendid Place Stanislas.

Here, Joël Roy, one of the hardest working people in France today, has thoughtfully elaborated on a whole series of dishes that are very firmly in the Lorraine tradition. They include Smoked Pike Perch on Crepes, Noisettes of Lamb in Onion Compote with Beer, Fine Pippin Apple Tart with Pruce Sauce, and Mirabelle Plum Flake, and they are all delicious. It's all quite sufficient to help you forget the region's rather unkind weather.

Delphin

Bellevue-Sainte-Luce-sur-Loire, 44470 Carquefou
Tel: (40) 49-04-13
Proprietor/Chef: Joseph Delphin

After four years working as a pastry chef, Joseph Delphin wanted to become a master chef in his own right. At the time, he was at the Aubergade de Pontchartrain, and later he moved on to the George V and the Bourgogne in Paris. Finally, in 1962, he settled down on the banks of the Loire. He was born in Voiron, a distant part of France, but as a true follower of the Tour de France he is at home anywhere — everywhere where people know their food. In his tasteful, pleasant restaurant, Joseph cooks with a subtle blend of flavours that ensures that each preparation has a real "soul." This soul is evident in the blueberry jelly for his *foie gras,* hazelnut butter for his warm oysters, vinaigrette of artichokes for his warm *foie gras* coated with honey, Sauterne wine sauce for his fresh salmon, etc.

Fresh Salmon in Sauterne Wine

1.25 kg (2¾ lb) salmon fillets
salt and pepper, to taste
400 g (14 oz) chopped leeks
250 g (½ lb) butter
4 seedless tomatoes, chopped
½ bottle Sauterne wine
½ litre (1 pt) double cream (whipping cream)
1 bunch watercress, chopped

Cut salmon into large dice of 1 cm (2½ in). Season with salt and pepper. Sweat* the leeks in 100 g (3½ oz) butter in a thick, cast-iron pot. Gently brown the salmon in the leek butter. Add tomatoes, wine, and bring to a boil. Let cool, off the heat, for 10 minutes.

Reduce the stock until it looks shiny. Add cream and let reduce until thick. Thicken again with the remaining butter and check the seasoning.

Coat the salmon with the sauce and place chopped watercress around the plate. Suggestion: Serve with fennel purée.

Wine: *Sauterne*   Serves: 4

La Rascasse

10, avenue de Madrid, 92200 Neuilly-sur-Seine
Tel: 624-0530
Proprietor: Louis Franza • Chef: Jean-Marc Tillay

La Rascasse used to be a Spanish restaurant. In 1975, Louis Franza, who had learned his trade in a once-famous restaurant, started working here. He created an atmosphere that is comfortable and pleasant, where the service is not overbearing, and where the attention is paid to what is served on your table, not what decorates the walls.

Louis Franza and his chef, Jean-Marc Tillay, prepare their fish in a most classical and reasonable way. The little note on the menu says: "With your fish we propose white butter, anchovy butter, sea urchin butter, Béarnaise sauce, Hollandaise sauce, or olive oil with basil." That's what one calls freedom of choice! The desserts are also good. Mme. Franza, at the bar and cash desk, is most charming.

Fresh Salmon with Cucumbers

3 cucumbers
4 egg yolks
½ litre (1 pt) double cream (whipping cream)
150 g (5¼ oz) butter, and as needed
3 tbsp fish velouté*
¼ litre (1 cup) white Sancerre wine
3 shallots, chopped
4 tbsp fumet*
salt and white pepper, to taste
1.8 kg (4 lb) fresh salmon

Peel the cucumbers, cut them lengthwise, and remove the seeds. Cut into thin slices, purée in a blender, and pass through a strainer. Set aside.

Mix the egg yolks with 3 tbsp cream and stir with a whisk over low heat until warm. Add 30 g (1 oz) butter and continue to stir. Keep warm.

Reduce the remaining cream and the fish velouté in a separate pan for 10 minutes.

Put the white wine, remaining butter, shallots, fumet, salt, and white pepper into a large, thick frying pan and heat very gently. Cut the salmon into fillets, remove the skin, and cut into thirds. Add the salmon to the wine mixture and cook on low heat for 8 minutes. Remove the salmon fillets, coat them with the cucumber purée, and bake at 350°F (175°C) for 4 minutes.

Strain the wine mixture that the salmon cooked in and mix it into the reduced cream and velouté mixture. Add the egg yolk and cream mixture and let reduce for 5 minutes. Remove from heat and pass through a sauce strainer. Serve the salmon in a serving dish coated with this sauce.

Wine: *Sancerre white wine*   Serves: 6

Lapérouse

51, quai des Grands Augustins, 75006 Paris
Tel: 326-9014 and 326-6804
Proprietor: Société Sogepan • Chef: M. Gravier

This old restaurant of the quays of Paris is historical, or rather, t is history itself. The private dining rooms, discreet as Victorian age adultery and as mysterious as any political intrigue, have played host to the cream of Parisian society for a hundred years. This old establishment has recently been taken over by new owners and started afresh with new menus and recipes. Nevertheless, it still retains its elegantly warm style — the calm serenity and discreet atmosphere of yester-year. It would be impossible to say which is better: the Scrambled Eggs "Lapérouse" Style, the Salmon Cream Slices with Endives, or the Fillet of Beef with Truffles, the Braised Veal Sweetmeats in Juice, the Truffled Lobster Pudding, or the Scallops of Salmon with Mustard

Scallops of Salmon with Mustard

150 ml (4½ oz) dry white wine
2 shallots
200 g (7 oz) butter, cut in pieces
salt and pepper, to taste
600 g (21 oz) scallops of salmon
5 tbsp oil
4 tsp mustard, Meaux preferred

Gently heat the white wine and shallots in a saucepan and let reduce to ⅔. Thoroughly whisk in the butter, piece by piece. Check the seasoning. Keep the sauce hot in a bain-marie.*

Sauté the salmon scallops in oil in a non-stick frying pan, 2 minutes per side.

Reheat the sauce, whisk in the mustard, and pour the sauce onto a serving dish. Place the scallops of salmon on top of the sauce and serve.

Serves: 2

Hôtel de France

Place de la Libération, 32000 Auch
Tel: (62) 05-00-44
Proprietor/Chef: André Daguin

Auch is the capital of Gascony. This is the land of musketeers and rugby teams. André Daguin, taking over from his parents, has made the **Hôtel de France** into a haven of fine food and friendship. When you ask him what sort of cooking he prepares, he replies, "Cooking that I love." When you ask him what his speciality is, he answers, "Imagination!" It is certainly true that even though he uses age-old recipes, he creates amazing dishes with the greatest inspiration, as his Cassoulet with Broad Beans and his Ice Cream Truffle prove. The Foie Gras with Garlic and Capers, the Sharp Sauce of his rabbit pâtés, his Gratin of Oysters, and his Smoked Salmon on Vinaigrette are other splended examples. There is a fine wine cellar of regional wines and wines from further afield, as well.

Smoked Salmon Scallops on Warm Vinaigrette

1.5 kg (3⅓ lb) salmon
100 ml (3 oz) wine vinegar
½ litre (1 pt) oil
1 tbsp truffle juice
1 tbsp double cream (whipping cream)
12 small carrots

Cut salmon into 6 equal-sized scallops and place them on the bottom of a smoking pot (a special utensil for smoking meats and fish). Prepare a mixture of ⅓ wine vinegar to ⅔ oil, then add truffle juice and cream. Set aside.

Steam cook the carrots whole with their tops for 15-20 minutes or until tender but crisp.

15 minutes before serving, put the smoking pot, firmly closed, on the heat. Just keep the heat hot and let the smoke out twice during cooking. Check if salmon is cooked by testing the suppleness of the fish with your fingers.

Place a generous spoonful of the vinegar mixture in the middle of each plate and 2-3 carrots around the edges. Serve the salmon on top of the vinaigrette.

Serves: 6

Le Monde des Chimères

69, rue Saint-Louis-en l'Isle, 75004 Paris
Tel: 354-4597
Proprietor: Jeannine Coureau • Chef: Christian Schuliar

Sea Bream in Pepper and Red Wine

1 pink sea bream (perch) of 500 g (1 lb)
100 g (3½ oz) butter
2 white mushrooms
1 stalk celery
1 carrot
1 green part of leek, finely shredded
1 sprig thyme
1 bay leaf
½ clove garlic, crushed
1 bottle light claret
25 g (¾ oz) crushed pepper
salt, as needed

Wash the bream, remove and skin the fillets. Keep the head and the backbone, which should be cleaned and used to prepare the fumet as follows: Brown the head and bone gently in 1 tsp butter with the mushrooms, onion, celery, carrot, leek, thyme, bay leaf, and garlic. Add the claret and let cook for 30 minutes on medium heat, stirring often.

Remove the small bones from the fillets. Coat the skin side of the fillets with crushed pepper and add a little salt. Gently fry the coated side only in a little butter, keeping the fish pink.

Serve the bream, coated side up, with the fumet sauce poured around it.

Wine: *A light claret*   Serves: 2

This is a situation that has only rarely been seen before: two pretty, young ladies, both students working for their degrees, suddenly become restaurant owners because the mother of one of them had a bistro on the Ile Saint Louis that she did not know what to do with! Jeannine and her friend, Francine, are now knowledgeable and have the knack for finding gifted chefs; their latest is Christian Schuliar. They have made this restaurant into one of friendliness, decorated with striking pictures on the old stone walls. This restaurant should be a stopping place for any gourmand because here, fresh fish are treated with the greatest respect, meals are prepared with the utmost originality, and the desserts (like all the cooking here) are exquisite.

Grandgousier

17, avenue Rachel, 75018 Paris
Tel: 387-6612
Proprietor/Chef: Jean-Pierre Vigato

Skate with Mustard and Lemon

1 skate of 3 kg (6½ lb)
3 litres (¾ gal) water
200 ml (6 oz) vinegar
1 kg (2¼ lb) spinach, and as needed to garnish
300 g (10½ oz) butter
juice of 1 large lemon
3 tbsp of 3 kinds of mustard, for example: white, Savora, and old-style Meaux

Cut the skate into pieces and soak in cold water for 6 hours. Cook the skate in the water and vinegar for 20 minutes.

Melt 1 tbsp butter with a drop of water on very high heat. Add spinach and stir with a fork until fully cooked.

Put the lemon juice and a little water into a saucepan on high heat. Add melted butter, then remove from heat and thoroughly whisk in the 3 mustards.

Place a little of the spinach stock on the bottom of each plate, place the strips of skate flesh on top, gently pour the sauce over, and decorate by sprinkling finely chopped spinach over all.

Wine: *Macon Blanc Uchizy or any other dry white wine*   Serves: 6

This little avenue Rachel, secretive, intimate, and just a stone's throw from the clamour of Montmartre, had the good fortune to welcome Jean-Pierre Vigato in 1979. Together with his young wife, he transformed an old establishment into a lovely restaurant with pastel colours and lighting as soft as the background music. It is very relaxing to be here; you really do feel at home. Jean-Pierre buys only top quality products, but not necessarily the most expensive ones. This means the bills are reasonable and the dishes are original. The Fricassee of Veal Kidney with Raw Spinach, Poultry Liver Mousse with Grapes, and Skate with Mustard and Lemon are only a few of the fine offerings.

Guerguy La Galère

La Galère, 06590 Théoule
Tel: (93) 90-33-90
Proprietor/Chef: Lucien Guerguy

Lucien Guerguy set up shop in 1957 near Théoule on a site with a panoramic view of the Riviera. Those who stay in the hotel's few rooms or who find themselves in the vicinity during eating hours are lucky indeed. The menu is full of classical recipes that have proved their durability.

Here, the real crowning piece is the Bourride (a special fish soup). People come to discover and rediscover the Bourride Guerguy from the four corners of France. It is the deification of Provençal cuisine prepared by a master. The Elixir of Rock Fish, the Supreme of Barbary Bitter Orange, Orange "Oriental" Style, and Fillets of Sole in Cocoons are also unforgettable, but not as well known, yet!

Fillets of Sole in Cocoons

1 litre (2 pt) milk
400 g (14 oz) flour
6 eggs
500 g (1 lb) anglerfish (perch or sea bream), flesh only
500 g (1 lb) fat from beef kidney
40 g (1½ oz) truffles
2 sole, 300 g (10½ oz) each, filleted
300 g (10 oz) prawns
200 g (7 oz) sliced white mushrooms
100 ml (3 oz) Béchamel sauce*
1 tbsp sauce Américaine*
100 ml (3 oz) double cream (whipping cream)
salt, pepper, and nutmeg, to taste

Whisk the milk, flour, and 1 egg together, then knead until you have about 500 g (1 lb) of thick, pastry dough. Mix in the anglerfish, kidney fat, remaining eggs, and ½ the truffles. Roll out the dough to 15 by 15 by 1 cm (6 by 6 by ½ in). Roll the sole fillets and place the rolls on the dough 3 cm (1¼ in) apart. Fold dough over and press down well to outline the fillets. Poach in boiling water for 7-8 minutes.

Sweat* the prawns in a pan, then add mushrooms, Béchamel sauce, sauce Américaine, and cream. Thicken over gentle heat to sauce consistency. Season with salt, pepper, and nutmeg. Nap* the cocoons of sole with the sauce and serve.

Serves: 4

Drouant

Place Gaillon, 75002 Paris
Tel: 742-5661
Proprietor: Robert Pascal • Chef: Michel Moreau

Drouant is a name that is inseparable from international literature because the headquarters of the Académie Goncourt is located here. This establishment dates back to the 1880s, but at that time it was only a modest bistro frequented by writers and artists. With success came periodic expansions of the building, and in 1925, there was a change of decor, which Robert Pascal, the present owner, has kept. On the ground floor are the grill room and the main restaurant; on the first floor is the famous Salon des Goncourt.

Robert Pascal arrived in 1946 and bought the establishment in 1976. His chef, Michel Moreau, has remained faithful to classical cuisine. The Whiting "Colbert" Style and the Fillets of Sole "Drouant" Style have never been better.

Fillets of Sole "Drouant" Style

8 fillets of sole, 400 g (14 oz) each
125 g (¼ lb) butter
salt and pepper, to taste
2 chopped shallots
100 ml (3 oz) white wine
1 litre (2 pt) mussels, cooked and cooking liquid reserved
¼ litre (½ pt) double cream (whipping cream)
¼ litre (½ pt) sauce Américaine*
3 egg yolks, whisked
125 g (¼ lb) shelled, pink, cooked shrimps
150 g (5¼ oz) cooked white mushrooms

Place the fillets in a buttered dish and season with salt, pepper, and shallots. Moisten with white wine and a little cooking liquid from the mussels. Cover and bake at 350°F (175°C) in the oven for 10 minutes. Remove the fillets and reduce the liquid in the pan by ½. Add cream and reduce again by ½. Remove from heat, mix in the butter, sauce Américaine, and egg yolks. Check the seasoning and pass through a sauce strainer.

Place shrimps, mussels, and mushrooms around the sole fillets on a serving dish. Coat fillets with sauce, glaze under a hot broiler for 2 minutes, and serve.

Wine: *Dry white wine (Sancerre, Pouilly Fumé, Chablis)*　　　Serves: 4

L'Ane Rouge

7, quai des Deux-Emmanuel, 06000 Nice
Tel: (93) 89-49-63
Proprietor/Chef: M. Vidalot

In Nice, a cosmopolitan and sometimes pompous town, this spruce little dining room on the quai des Deux-Emmanuel is a dedicated fish restaurant. If M. Vidalot, who is in the kitchen, has the time, he might explain why he named his restaurant The Red Donkey. On the other hand, with him we are better off talking about cooking and trying to find out the secret of his Stuffed Mussels "Ane Rouge" Style or his Special Crawfish.

Here, bouillabaisse and bourride (both special fish soup dishes) are rich with the flavour of the Riviera, as is his Fillets of Sole "Menton" Style — a new creation of which he is quite rightly most proud. The *foie gras* is from Alsace, and his Young Turbot "Val de Loire" is also delicious. In fact, this seasoned chef cooks everything well.

Fillets of Sole "Menton" Style

4 fillets of sole, 400 g (14 oz) each
4 large scallops
2 shallots
200 g (7 oz) butter, and as needed
200 ml (6 oz) fish fumet*
50 ml (1½ oz) double cream (whipping cream)
juice of 1 lemon
zest* of 1 lemon and 1 orange, scalded
2 tbsp Hollandaise sauce*

Beat and flatten the fillets. Cook the scallops with the shallots, butter, and the fumet until they are sufficiently stiff. Remove the scallops, reserve the liquid, let cool, then wrap in the fillets. Place the stuffed fillets in the cooking liquid from the scallops and bake at 450°F (230°C) for 10 minutes. Remove the fillets and keep hot.

Reduce the stock in the pan to sauce consistency. Add butter, cream, lemon juice, and orange and lemon zests. Add Hollandaise sauce.

Nap* the fillets with the sauce and serve on a hot dish with the squeezed lemon halves around them.

Suggestion: Serve with mashed potatoes flavoured with zest of lemon and sprinkled with a few chives and chervil.

Wine: *Sancerre white*   Serves: 2

Dodin-Bouffant

25, rue Frédéric-Sauton, 75005 Paris
Tel: 325-2514
Proprietor: Jacques Manière • Chef: Jean-Marie Clément

Thirteen years ago, Jacques Manière opened **Dodin-Bouffant** and chose as his trademark the name of Marcel Rouff's novel, which is the name of a Roman epicurean. It is one of the most savoury restaurants in town. Dodin-Bouffant is well illuminated, elegant (without being snobbish), joyous, and alive. On the first floor, there is a special room for banquets where fresh seafood, accompanied by excellent wine, is served at a fixed price.

The regular menu is full of surprises, expressing the imagination of the owner and the extraordinary talents of the chef, his associate since the restaurant opened, and includes Tripe Cassoulets with Sherry, Fillet of Duck, Eggs with Caviar, and a fillet of sole dish that I was honoured to have named after me.

Fillets of Sole "Robert Courtine"

fillets of 7 sole, 450 g (1 lb) each
mirepoix* of vegetables and parings of mushrooms
70 ml (2 oz) champagne
salt and pepper, to taste
30 g (1 oz) butter
1 tbsp flour
250 ml (1 cup) double cream (whipping cream)
125 g (¼ lb) caviar
1 chopped shallot
90 ml (2¾ oz) vermouth
2 eggs
4 sea urchins (optional)
1 handful seaweed

To prepare the sauce: Make a clear, strong fish stock from the bones of the soles, vegetable mirepoix, champagne, a little salt and pepper, and ½ litre (1 pt) water by bringing the mixture to a boil then reducing it to ¼ litre (1 cup). Melt the butter in a saucepan. Add flour and stir. Strain onto the reduced stock. Bring to a boil, stirring constantly. Season with salt and pepper. Reduce by ¼. Add ¼ of the cream. Reduce by ⅓ and strain. Add the caviar.

To prepare the stuffing: Sweat* the shallot in vermouth. Place in a food processor with 3 fillets of sole, eggs, sea urchins (if desired), salt, and pepper. Blend, then thoroughly mix in remaining cream. Divide the stuffing among the remaining 4 fillets. Roll each fillet around its stuffing. Place in a steamer on a bed of seaweed and steam for 8-10 minutes.

To serve: Arrange the fish on a plate, cover with sauce, and serve hot.

Serves: 4

Lucas-Carton

9, Place de la Madeleine, 75008 Paris
Tel: 265-2290
Proprietor: Mme. Allegrier-Carton • Chef: Michel Comby

Lucas Sole Delight

3 sole, 500 - 600 g (1 - 1⅓ lb) each
1 medium-sized onion, chopped
1 sprig parsley
200 g (7 oz) butter
100 ml (3 oz) Pouilly wine (or other dry white wine)
salt and pepper, to taste
2 medium-sized ripe tomatoes, skinned, seeded, and crushed
80 g (2¾ oz) white Paris mushrooms, thickly sliced
100 ml (3 oz) double cream (whipping cream)

Skin the sole, draw and wash them; remove the fillets, and dress and trim them. Soak fillets and bones in cold water for 1 hour. Cut the bones into 4 - 5 pieces. Sweat* bones in a saucepan with onion, parsley, and 1 tsp butter for 6 - 8 minutes. Moisten with wine and 100 ml (3 oz) water. Bring to a boil, skim, and let simmer for 10 - 20 minutes.

Generously butter a rectangular casserole. Place the fillets in the casserole and season with salt and pepper. Sprinkle the tomatoes and mushrooms on top of the fillets, moisten with the stock obtained from cooking the bones, cover with buttered greaseproof (wax) paper, and bring to a boil. Cook for 7 - 8 minutes.

Pour the resulting juices into a saucepan, add cream and cook to the desired consistency. Add the remaining butter in small pieces, stirring all the time, without boiling. Coat the fillets with the sauce, brown under a hot broiler, and serve.

Serves: 6

Dining here is time well spent! Lucas, an Englishman, settled here towards the end of the 19th century. Francis Carton took over the establishment, which then became known as **Lucas-Carton**. The pure and elegant decor makes the restaurant (often a venue for political meetings) a "souvenir" of Paris during *La Belle Epoch*.

Mme. Allegrier, the daughter of Francis Carton, now manages the restaurant, ably assisted by Chef Michel Comby. Under the panelled ceilings, devoted gourmets treat themselves to Whiting "en Colère," Germiny Soup (from the name of the former governor of the Bank of France), Bresse Poultry Stewed in Port, Lucas Kidneys "Flambé," Lucas Sole Delight, Lime Sorbet with Champagne, etc. There's a very good wine cellar, too.

Hôtel d'Espagne

9, rue de Château, 36600 Valençay
Tel: (54) 00-00-02
Proprietor/Chef: Maurice Fourré

Sole "Arsène Avignon" Style

125 g (¼ lb) onions
125 g (¼ lb) carrots
125 g (¼ lb) leeks
125 g (¼ lb) celery sticks
60 g (2 oz) butter
2 sole, 300 g (10½ oz) each, filleted
150 ml (¼ cup) fish fumet*
¼ litre (½ pt) white wine
¼ litre (½ pt) double cream (whipping cream)
2 egg yolks
salt and pepper, to taste

Peel the onions, carrots, leeks, and celery and sweat* them in a little butter on low heat. Add the sole fillets to this vegetable dressing. Moisten with fish fumet and wine. When the fish flakes easily with a fork, remove them and set them aside.

Reduce the remaining mixture on high heat to sauce consistency; thicken with the cream and the egg yolks at the last moment. Check the seasoning.

Serve the sole and sauce separately.

Wine: *Sancerre white*

Serves: 4

Valençay, encircled by forests, is proud of its historic chateau, the residence of Talleyrand in 1803. (He is buried in the crypt of the chapel.) A short distance from the chateau is the **Hôtel d'Espagne**, named in memory of the Princes of Spain who were Napoleon's prisoners here from 1808 to 1814. This has been a family hotel since 1875. Pierre Fourré runs the restaurant with his sons, who graduated from L'École Hôtelière of Thonon-Les-Bains. Philippe Fourré looks after the dining room and the wine cellar and selects the marvellous goats cheese from the local farms. Maurice Fourré, in the kitchen, will delight you with his very provincial approach to cooking, an example of which is his Sole "Arsène Avignon" Style, named after the former chef of the London Ritz.

Lapérouse

Laurent

La Mère Blanc

Auberge Les Santons

Colline de l'Annonciade, 06500 Menton
Tel: (93) 35-94-10
Proprietor/Chef: Bernard Simon

There's nothing dishonourable in having doubts about yourself at the age of 28, especially for a chef who has just met up with André Guillot, a master among chefs. Bernard Simon admits his insecurity and adds, "Cooking is not so much a speciality, it's more a kind of religion," but the quality of his dishes should give him confidence.

He is the owner and chef of **Auberge Les Santons**, an auberge way up on a hill overlooking Menton that offers a simple and restful decor (and a splendid view from the terrace). This chef will not disappoint you. His Sole "Riviera" Style and Mousseline of Scorpion Fish, as well as any of his daily specials (such as Brains Truffled with Lentils) are dishes worthy of André Guillot's phrase: "Cooking is a technique of execution but also an art of inspiration and intuition."

Sole "Riviera" Style

2 sole, 400 g (14 oz) each, filleted and bones reserved
salt and pepper, as needed
lemon and orange juice, to taste
few sprigs fresh thyme
1 tbsp olive oil
2 unpeeled courgettes (zucchini)
2 large, seeded tomatoes
12 leaves basil
60 g (2 oz) butter

Place the fillets of sole in a dish, season with a little salt and pepper, then sprinkle on lemon and orange juice, thyme, and olive oil. Let marinate overnight in a cool place, covered with greaseproof (wax) paper.

Prepare a sole fumet* from the reserved fish bones and strain. Cut the courgettes into 2 cm (¾ in) slices without cutting into the seeds. Put the sole fumet into a wide saucepan and check the seasoning. Add the courgette slices, tomatoes, and basil and cook gently without boiling.

Bring the water in the bottom of a double-boiler to a boil. Cut the fillets diagonally into slices (4-5 per fillet) and place in the upper part of the double-boiler (the fillets should not touch each other or they won't cook evenly). Cover the double-boiler and let cook for 2-3 minutes. Place the sole portions onto individual serving plates and keep hot.

Thicken the sauce in the saucepan with the butter and the marinade in which the fillets were left overnight. Heat the sauce, without boiling, and serve on top of the sole slices.

Wine: *A white wine from Provence*   Serves: 4

Ledoyen

Carré des Champs Élysées, 75008 Paris
Tel: 266-5477
Proprietor: Gilbert Lejeune • Chef: Francis Trocellier

Marie de Medici was responsible for converting wooded marshlands into the "Queen's Alleys," which later became the famous Champs Élysées. In 1792, Nicolas le Doyen, with his revolutionary culinary innovations, opened this restaurant and made this establishment into a veritable high spot for gastronomy (and a popular meeting place for duellists).

Today, Gilbert Lejeune is ready to welcome you to this historic restaurant, which is decorated with lace and vermeil. Be sure to taste the Truffle Salad, the Scallops in Fennel, and the Sole Soufflé. Follow the advice of the attentive sommelier who almost religiously takes the temperature of the wine in his special medieval ewer.

Sole Soufflé "Ledoyen" Style

350 g (¾ lb) lobster flesh
350 g (¾ lb) pike flesh
coral of lobster
salt and cayenne pepper, to taste
2 egg whites
750 ml (1½ pt) double cream (whipping cream)
10 sole, 350 g (¾ lb) each
100 ml (3 oz) white wine
100 ml (3 oz) fish fumet*
2 tsp butter

To prepare lobster and pike mousse: Crush the lobster, pike, and coral in a mortar (if possible, or use a fine mesh mincer). Sieve the stuffing to eliminate the small pike bones and to make a smooth paste. Put paste in a thick frying pan placed in ice and start to mix with a wooden spatula. Add salt, cayenne pepper, egg whites, and, gradually, the cream. Let stuffing (mousse) rest at least 1 hour.

Remove the dark skin and scales from the light skin of the sole and remove the backbone by cutting the fish in half lengthwise. Wash fillets carefully; do not detach the edges. Stuff the sole with the lobster and pike mousse and place on a buttered ovenproof dish, stuffing side up. Moisten with the wine and fumet, cover with buttered, greaseproof (wax) paper, and bake in the oven for 6-8 minutes at 375°F (190°C). Stuffing should look pink.

Suggestion: Serve each sole on a plate coated with sauce Américaine,* and with a round slice of lobster on top. Put a skewer through the head of each sole for presentation purposes.

Wine: *Pouilly-Fuissé, Chablis*   Serves: 10

Auberge Vaugrain

13, rue Jacques-Amyot, 77000 Melun
Tel: 452-0823
Proprietor/Chef: Francis Desroys du Roure

Sole "Vaugrain" Style

250 g (½ lb) mushrooms
juice of ½ lemon
40 g (1⅓ oz) butter
1 clove garlic
2 shallots
10 g (⅓ oz) parsley
2 slices white bread, crusts removed
250 ml (1 cup) double cream (whipping cream)
1 egg
salt and pepper, to taste
4 sole, 200 - 250 g (7 - 8 oz) each
1 litre (2 pt) fish fumet*
1 litre (2 pt) Sancerre white wine
10 g (⅓ oz) bread crumbs

To prepare the stuffing: Sauté the mushrooms in ¼ of the butter and the lemon juice, then chop finely with garlic, shallots, parsley, and white bread. Cook the mixture for 20 minutes on gentle heat, then add ⅓ of the cream and the egg. Season with salt and pepper. Remove from heat and let cool.

Skin the sole and remove the bones, taking care to preserve each head and tail so the fish shape remains. Stuff the sole with the stuffing and place on a baking tray. Cover the fish, halfway up, with a mixture of equal parts fumet and Sancerre. Bake in the oven at 375°F (190°C) for 10 minutes. Remove the fish and keep hot. Coat the fish lightly with bread crumbs and then brown them under a hot broiler. Check the seasoning of the cooking juices in the pan, then whisk in the butter and the remaining cream to thicken it. Serve the sauce on each plate with a sole on top.

Wine: *Sancerre or Pouilly Fumé*   Serves: 4

After having been graduated from the renowned École Hôtelière in Strasbourg, Francis Desroys du Roure worked for a few years in his parents' family restaurant in Samois. Finally, in 1968, he created his own restaurant, a 16th century establishment with a vaulted wine cellar and antique furniture, which looks its best in the filtered, relaxed atmosphere of its candlelight.

Within this chic, yet comfortable, Louis XIII decor, the cooking of Francis Desroys du Roure is properly classical. Some of his most popular dishes are Sole "Vaugrain" Style (from an old family recipe), Oxtail Compote, and the "Beuchelle Tourangelle," a creation of Edouard Nignon, a great chef from the last century. The desserts are also excellent, and the wine cellar features some very good wines.

Le Flambard

79, rue d'Angleterre, 59800 Lille
Tel: (20) 51-00-06
Proprietor/Chef: Robert Bardot

Sole with Baby Artichokes

4 soles, 800 g (1¾ lb) each
8 baby artichokes
juice of ½ lemon, and as needed
1 large sliced onion
1 carrot, sliced
150 ml (½ cup) olive oil
1 bouquet garni*

salt and pepper, to taste
100 ml (3 oz) white wine
300 g (10½ oz) mushrooms
butter, as needed
125 g (¼ lb) smoked bacon, blanched
125 g (¼ lb) tomatoes, chopped finely

Fillet the soles. Cut each fillet into 3 slices. Keep them in the refrigerator.

Remove the tough outer leaves from the artichokes. Cut off the tops about halfway down and trim the bases. Remove the chokes. Wash the artichokes in water with a little lemon juice. Colour the onion and carrot in ⅔ of the olive oil. Add the artichokes, bouquet garni, salt, pepper, and white wine. Barely cover with water. Boil rapidly for 20 minutes. If the cooking liquid has not acquired a slightly creamy consistency, continue to reduce it. Correct the seasoning.

Cook the mushrooms rapidly in a little water, butter, salt, and pepper. Drain and chop. Purée them in a blender with remaining olive oil. Cut the bacon into very fine dice and add to the mushrooms. Stuff the artichokes with this mixture.

Season the strips of sole and place them on a buttered baking dish. Moisten with a little of the artichoke cooking liquid. Cover with greaseproof (wax) paper and a lid. Bake in the oven at 350°F (175°C) for about 8 minutes. Keep hot.

Mix the cooking juices of the sole with the remaining artichoke liquid and add the tomatoes. Correct the seasoning and add lemon juice to taste.

On a serving platter, surround the artichokes with the sole covered with sauce and serve.

Serves: 8

This was once a private hotel; it dates back to 1691. **Le Flambard** is now classified as a monument, and Robert Bardot has turned it into a patio, bar, and dining rooms. It is a beautiful restaurant that would make any restaurateur proud.

Robert is also the chef and has been publicly recognized for his culinary achievements. He offers an elaborate and original variety of dishes: Turbot Terrine with Aspic, Foie Gras with Garlic, Salmon Pot-au-Feu with Basil, Turbot with Mustard and Cucumbers, Filet Mignon with Preserved Garlic, Veal Kidneys and Sweetbreads with Herbs, and delicious Sole with Baby Artichokes. The desserts are also sublime. The menu is truly created for gourmands.

Château de la Corniche

Route de la Corniche, 78000 Rolleboise
Tel: 093-2124
Proprietors: Jean Picard, Janine Bourdrez • Chef: Pierre Blanchard

This is an ideal place for romantics and sentimentalists. The building faces the meandering Seine, and it is easy to imagine the view as it was in the 19th century — canoes floating down the river, as in a Renoir painting, and the barges of Simenon passing by. This location has a very special feeling. In 1920, this house in the country was a stopping place for travellers. In 1975, Jean Picard discovered it and realised its potential. He purchased the establishment, hired an elegant chef, Pierre Blanchard, and made the relais into a renowned restaurant. **Château de la Corniche**, with its perfect setting, is also an epicurean's dream come true. Pierre creates marvellous things in his kitchen, such as Turbot with Rhubard, "Beautiful Normandy" Salmon Trout, and Anglerfish Stewed in Wine.

"Beautiful Normandy" Salmon Trout

1 salmon trout (lake trout) of 2.5 kg (5½ lb), boned but not skinned	8 large scallops
salt and pepper, to taste	8 oysters
pinch of cayenne pepper	¼ litre (1 cup) double cream (whipping cream)
pinch of curry powder	4 apples, peeled and cored
125 g (¼ lb) butter	1 tbsp sugar
200 g (7 oz) shallots, chopped	100 ml (3 oz) cider vinegar
½ bottle cider	1 tbsp chervil

Season the trout with salt, pepper, cayenne pepper, and curry powder. Butter a sheet of aluminum foil. Place the trout on the foil, sprinkle with ⅔ of the shallots. Add 100 ml (3 oz) cider and some butter. Seal foil well. Cook in the oven at 350°F (175°C) for 30 minutes. Poach the scallops in a saucepan with ½ the remaining shallots. Cover with 60 ml (2 oz) cider. Cook over low heat for a few minutes, but do not boil. Drain and keep warm. Poach the oysters the same way, but use less cider and a shorter cooking time. Remove trout from oven. Pour out juice (reserve) and reseal aluminum foil to keep trout warm. Mix the cooking juice from the trout with the cooking juices from the scallops and oysters. Reduce to half. Add cream and reduce, again, to half over high heat. With a scoop, scoop out small round balls from the apples. Sugar them slightly and roll in butter. Caramelise in a saucepan. Deglaze the pan with cider vinegar and keep warm. Add the scallops and oysters to the sauce. Correct the seasoning. Skin the trout and cover with sauce. Sprinkle with chervil, arrange on a plate with the apple balls, and serve.

Serves: 8

Hostellerie Fiard

Rue de la République and Quai des Terreux, 38270 Beaurepaire d'Isère
Tel: (74) 84-62-02
Proprietor/Chef: Jean-Claude Zorelle

Beaurepaire, in the Isère, is not quite mountain country; it's just on the way to mountain country. After leaving Vienne (and Chez Point), you should drive towards Grenoble (and Chavant), but on the way there, do stop and visit with Jean-Claude Zorelle, the owner and chef of this tranquil little place called **Hostellerie Fiard**. Here you can enjoy such gourmet specialities as Truffle Rissoles, Loin of Lamb Roasted in Provence Herbs, Chicken Indienne, Guinea Fowl Truffled with Morels, Cockerel with Old Chambertin, Mousseline of Trout with Crayfish, Crayfish Gastronome, and so on. Here, it's classicism, through and through, which appeals to the more conservative guests. The Crepes Suzette and the Peach Melba are two such classic recipes that perfectly top off any meal served here.

Mousseline of Trout with Crayfish

600 g (1⅓ lb) salmon trout (lake trout) flesh	1 kg (2¼ lb) crayfish
salt and 4 spices, to taste	2 tbsp oil
250 g (½ lb) butter	3 chopped shallots
6 whole eggs	100 ml (3 oz) cognac
400 g (14 oz) double cream (whipping cream)	140 ml (4 oz) white wine
	salt and pepper, to taste
	1 tbsp tomato paste

To prepare the mousseline: Cut up the trout flesh very finely, then add salt, spices, and butter. Add the eggs, 2 by 2, and mix until a smooth consistency is reached. Quickly add cream and refrigerate. When set, mould into quenelle shapes, wrap with buttered greaseproof (wax) paper, tie up the ends, and poach for 10-15 minutes on low heat. Do not boil.

Gently brown the crayfish in a thick frying pan with oil and shallots, then flame with cognac. Add wine and water, season with salt, pepper, and tomato paste, and let simmer for 5 minutes. Reserve about 12 crayfish to garnish the dish; shell the rest and keep the tails for garniture.

Crush the shelled crayfish very thoroughly in its stock. Add the bones from the turbot and cook for 15 minutes on medium heat. Put the preparation through a conical strainer, let reduce to sauce consistency, then remove from heat and whisk in butter.

Take the quenelles out of the paper and put them on an ovenproof serving dish. Place the reserved whole crayfish and the crayfish tails around the quenelles, nap[*] with sauce, and place in the oven at 450°F (230°C) for 5 minutes before serving.

Serves: 12

Moulin de Mombreux

62380 Lumbres
Tel: (21) 39-62-44
Proprietor/Chef: Jean-Marc Gaudry

In 1968, from the ruins of a former mill dating from the 17th century, Jean-Marc Gaudry created a rustic, warmly comfortable, and very attractive auberge located on the banks of a drowsy river. Classical cooking, a warm welcome from Jean-Marc's friendly wife, and the attraction of a fine wine list that is particularly rich in clarets and champagnes make this a marvellous little country stopping off place. The connoisseurs will certainly take note of the Turbot in Broccoli Terrine, Stuffed Trout Braised in Champagne, and, in season, Young Rooster Cooked in Fresh Truffles. The amateurs among us will go in for the Duck Foie Gras, and no one will say no to the array of sweet pastries. This mill could be just the place for a dream weekend.

Stuffed Trout Braised in Champagne

1 trout of 1.4 kg (3 lb)
6 large whole scallops,* coral removed and reserved
1 egg white
salt and pepper, to taste
½ litre (1 pt) double cream (whipping cream)
1 head lettuce
250 - 300 g (8 - 10 oz) butter
½ bottle dry champgane
300 ml (9 oz) fumet*
4 shallots, chopped

Carefully remove the bones and flesh from the trout without destroying the skin. Crush the flesh of the trout in a mortar with the coral from the scallops and then mix in the egg white, salt, and pepper. Finely sieve this stuffing into an earthenware dish and place on crushed ice.

Season the inside of the trout slightly with salt and pepper, then put in ½ the stuffing, the kernels of scallops, cut in thirds, and then the remainder of the stuffing. Wrap the trout in lettuce leaves and put on a buttered baking dish. Add the champagne, fumet, shallots, and 20 g (¾ oz) butter. Cover with greaseproof (wax) paper and cook in the oven at 350°F (175°C) for 30-35 minutes, basting frequently. When cooked, take the trout out of the oven, and place on a serving dish, cover, and keep hot.

Pour the liquid in the baking dish into a thick frying pan, add the cream, and reduce to the desired sauce consistency. Strain the sauce through a strainer onto the trout.

Suggestion: Serve with poached broccoli.

Wine: *Pouilly Fuissé*   Serves: 2-3

La Chaumière des Gourmets

22, Place Denfert Rochereau, 75014 Paris
Tel: 321-2608
Proprietor: Simone Bequet • Chef: Jean Bequet

A *chaumière* is a thatched cottage indigenous to Normandy where Jean Bequet, the son of an excellent cook, spent all his early years. There, in Deauville, he watched his father and learned from him. Then Jean came to Paris where he worked for the Prunier and Maxim's before taking over a very ordinary local restaurant in 1965. At that time, meat was very much the number one dish there. He arrived, as he says, "with my arms loaded with fish and shellfish and the idea of winning over the gourmands of Paris."

When you ask him if his cooking is *la nouvelle cuisine,* Bequet replies, "It doesn't exist. My recipes are as they have always been in Normandy, made with local cream, but I do my utmost to keep my sauces light." He succeeds very well.

Braised Turbot in Mustard

1 young turbot of 2 kg (4½ lb)
200 g (7 oz) butter
Dijon mustard, enough to coat the fillets
4 slices of seedless tomato
1 tsp thyme
salt and pepper, to taste
200 ml (6 oz) fish fumet*
1 tbsp chives

Fillet and skin the turbot. Place fillets in a buttered dish. Coat each fillet with mustard and put 2 round slices of tomato on each. Add thyme, salt, pepper, and the fumet. Cook in the oven at 375°F (190°C) for 15 minutes, then place the fillets onto a serving dish and keep hot.

To prepare the sauce: Pour the cooking liquid into a thick frying pan and reduce by ¾, then whisk in the remaining butter.

Coat the fillets with sauce, sprinkle the chives on top, and serve very hot.

Wine: *Macon Village, Pouilly Fuissé*   Serves: 4

Restaurant du Parc

1, rue Marc-Viéville, 93250 Villemomble
Tel: 854-1624
Proprietor/Chef: Mme. Fath-Conticini

Christiane Fath-Conticini is a naturally good cook, but this did not prevent her from taking a few months of lessons with the great Jacques Manière, a man for whom she has a great admiration. From an ordinary building in a popular suburb, she has created a chic restaurant with a Louis XIII style salon and an ever-changing menu that includes Flan of Scorpion Fish, Angler in Sweet Garlic, Fillet of Turbot with Cucumber, Salmon Pastry in Spinach, Sole and Mushrooms Soufflé, Veal Kidney with Artichokes, Fillet of Beef in Reduced Red Wine, and Fillet of Veal in Mushroom Sauce. The homemade *foie gras* is especially good, either with a salad, confit, or scrambled eggs. The desserts (especially the Iced Coffee Mousse with Nuts and the Chocolate Mousse with Warm Brioche) are also fine.

Fillet of Turbot with Cucumber

200 g (7 oz) turbot
butter, as needed
4 peeled shallots
salt and pepper, to taste
200 ml (6 oz) white wine
500 ml (1 pt) double cream (whipping cream)
1 cucumber
chives, to garnish

Lift the fillets from the turbot and place them in a buttered ovenproof dish with the shallots, salt, pepper, and white wine. Let cook in the oven at 400°F (205°C) for 8 minutes, then remove the fillets and keep hot. Reduce cooking liquid stock to ¾, add cream, and reduce to half.

Cut the cucumber into long, thin slices. In a separate saucepan, blanch them for about 2 minutes in boiling water, strain, and then add to the sauce.

Serve the fillets of turbot coated with sauce and with chives sprinkled on top.

Wine: *Dry, white wine*   Serves: 4

La Métairie

Mauzac, 24150 Lalinde
Tel: (53) 61-50-47
Proprietor: Françoise Vigneron • Chef: Gérard Culis

This restaurant, full of the charm and tranquillity of the rural Périgord countryside, seems to be surrounded by lush greenery and flowers.

At **La Métairie**, you are entertained by Françoise Vigneron in a warm and rustic atmosphere and treated to dishes such as Turbot "Emperor" Style (a well deserved name). At the ovens, there is a young, talented chef who just might keep you from leaving too quickly to continue your tour of French gastronomy, especially if you order his Fresh Cèpe Mushroom Omelette, a fabulous Confit of Duck, and to finish, an enormous "Périgord" Style Nut Gâteau.

Turbot "Emperor" Style

1 turbot of 1 kg (2¼ lb)
200 g (7 oz) salmon
200 g (7 oz) pike
150 ml (4½ oz) double cream (whipping cream), and as needed
salt and pepper, as needed
1 tbsp butter
100 ml (3 oz) dry white wine
100 ml (3 oz) fish fumet*

100 ml (3 oz) red vermouth
400 g (14 oz) large scallops, poached and diced
6 Norway lobster tails (langoustines, lobster tails, or spiny lobster), cooked and shelled
100 ml (3 oz) Armagnac
200 g (7 oz) mushrooms, sautéed
mixed herbs, to taste

Remove the bones from the turbot. Remove the bones from the salmon and pike and mash the flesh from these two together with ⅓ of the cream and a little salt and pepper to make a stuffing. Stuff the turbot, then bake it on a buttered tray with salt, pepper, and white wine at 350°F (175°C) for 30-35 minutes.

To prepare the sauce: Mix the fumet, remaining cream, and vermouth together and heat. Add the diced scallops to the sauce.

Flame the lobster tails with Armagnac and cut into round slices.

Serve the turbot on a plate coated with the sauce. Decorate the dish with slices of lobster, mushrooms, and a sprinkling of mixed herbs.

Wine: *A dry, white Bordeaux or Bergerac*   Serves: 4

Pantagruel

20, rue de l'Exposition, 75007 Paris
Tel: 551-7996
Proprietor/Chef: Freddy Israël

This is one of the smallest restaurants in Paris. Freddy Israël set up shop here back in 1972. He wanted a rustic style, intimate restaurant that had flowers just about everywhere. He wanted to create a place where his customers felt at ease and could just sit back and enjoy the cooking. He succeeded.

Freddy defines cooking by saying, "It's not enough for sauces to be fine and delicate; you have to have enough on your plate not to go away hungry."

His Soufflé of Sea Urchin, his Turbot in Bouzy Red Wine, his game, his salads in truffle oil, his Duckling in Peaches, and his very long dessert menu all bear witness to this phrase from Curnonsky, which Freddy takes to heart: "Cooking is an art, and all art is patience."

Turbot in Bouzy Red Wine

1 turbot of 2 kg (4½ lb)
50 g (1¾ oz) butter, and as needed to grease
1 shallot
4 mushrooms
salt and pepper, to taste
300 ml (9 oz) double cream (whipping cream)
½ bottle Bouzy (or use any sparkling red wine)

Clean the turbot, lift off the fillets, and remove the skin. Butter an ovenproof dish and put the shallot, turbot fillets, and mushrooms on it. Season to taste. Cover these ingredients with ½ the cream and the wine, then cover with aluminum foil. Cook in the oven at 400°F (205°C) for 15 minutes. Remove the turbot and the mushrooms and keep warm.

To prepare the sauce: Heat and reduce the stock to ⅔. Add the remaining cream and boil for 3 minutes. Remove the pan from heat and whisk in the butter. Strain the sauce and check the seasoning. Coat the turbot with sauce on a serving dish and serve.

Suggestion: Serve with rice pilaff.

Wine: *Red Bouzy or Champagne*   Serves: 4

Chantecler

Hôtel Négresco, 7, promenade des Anglais, 06000 Nice
Tel: (93) 88-39-51
Proprietors: M. and Mme. Augier • Chef: Jacques Maximin

In 1912, M. Négresco completed the construction of one of the most beautiful hotels on the Riviera. The Négresco remains one of the few truly luxurious hotels in France through the grace of its current owners, M. and Mme. Augier. Owning an exquisite hotel wasn't enough. They also sought a first-class restaurant, so in 1976 they hired Jacques Maximin. Under the direction of this talented chef, **Chantecler** has become a synonym for high quality. His dishes are prepared with the finest local products, and his interpretations of contemporary cuisine have a genuine touch of genius. You will embark on a grand gourmand adventure when you sample his speciality dishes such as the delicious Turbot in Red Stock. Dining at Chantecler is a truly memorable gastronomic experience.

Turbot in Red Stock

8 leaves cabbage
530 g (1¼ lb) butter, and as needed
12 mushrooms
16 small onions
2 sprigs chervil
125 g (¼ lb) smoked bacon
20 g (¾ oz) anchovy purée
4 small, cold croutons, cut in triangles
800 g (1¾ lb) turbot fillets
salt and pepper, to taste
100 ml (3 oz) fish stock,* and as needed
½ litre (1 pt) veal stock*

Blanch the cabbage leaves. In a pan with some butter and water, cook the mushrooms and onions with ½ the chervil. Rapidly boil the bacon in water; drain and cut into 4 pieces; brown the pieces in butter. Prepare anchovy butter by mixing the anchovy purée with 80 g (2¾ oz) butter. Cover the croutons with this mixture. Cut the turbot into pieces. Season with salt and pepper. Quickly brown the fillets in a sautée pan, then drain. Reduce the fish stock to ½ and add to the sautée pan. Add the veal stock. Let cook slowly, adding 150 g (5¼ oz) butter and the sautéed pieces of turbot. Set aside.

Quickly heat the cabbage leaves in the remaining butter. Heat the onions and mushrooms. Divide everything into 4 portions. Arrange the turbot pieces on 4 plates, covered with sauce, and sprinkle with remaining chervil. Serve hot with the croutons covered with anchovy butter.

Serves: 4

La Bretèche

171, quai de Bonneuil, 94210 La Varenne-Saint-Hilaire
Tel: 883-3873
Proprietor: M. Lamoureux • Chef: M. Morin

La Bretèche is a very pleasant suburban restaurant with a medieval, Brittany
name. Today, the Marne River is no longer
what it used to be, and in 1968, when
M. Lamoureux settled here with Chef
Morin, the Sunday afternoon boaters were
already fewer in number, fleeing in the face
of the overhead express Metro trains.

At least here, one is very well entertained
and rewarded for the journey. The classical
cooking with a tinge of modern influence is
just right. The Terrine of Anglerfish with
Vegetables, Warm Bass Salad, Turbot in
Charente Pineau Liqueur, Turbot with
Leeks, and Pullet with Leeks all make the
trip worthwhile as do the fine desserts, including the top quality sorbets (sherbets).

Turbot with Leeks

4 kg (8¾ lb) turbot
1 large chopped shallot
2 tbsp butter
250 g (½ lb) softened butter
100 ml (3 oz) fruit liqueur, Pineau preferred
2 small finely sliced leeks
2 finely sliced carrots
125 g (¼ lb) finely sliced green beans
1 finely sliced courgette (zucchini)
1 finely sliced aubergine (eggplant)
salt and pepper, to taste

Remove the fillets from the turbot and leave to steep in cold water the morning of use.

To prepare the sauce: Gently brown the shallot with 1 tbsp of butter, add the liqueur, and reduce to a syrup-like thickness. Let cool slightly. Thoroughly whisk the softened butter while gradually adding the syrup-like mixture to it. Set aside.

Use one sheet of aluminum foil (30 cm or 12 in square) for each turbot fillet. Put the fillet, some vegetables, a little salt and pepper, and 1 tbsp of butter in the foil, then cover with another piece of foil of the same size, rolling the edges on top of each other to seal. Bake in the oven at 375°F (190°C) for 20 minutes.

Suggestion: Each piece of foil should be opened at the table and served with the whisked butter sauce.

Wine: *Meursault Blagny White*

Serves: 6

Le Bernadin

18, rue Troyon, 75017 Paris
Tel: 380-4061 and 380-3622
Proprietor/Chef: Gilbert Le Coze

If he's not cooking in the kitchen of his
restaurant, you are likely to see Gilbert Le
Coze at the Rungis food market in the early
hours of the morning. To talk about fresh
seafood and **Le Bernadin** in one phrase is
something of a pleonasm.

Young Turbot with Parsley, Anglerfish
Saffron, Sole Meunière — you could name
a whole list of seafood dishes and you will
probably find most of them on the menu.
Not one will disappoint you. In fact, everything Gilbert cooks is delightful, as are the
wines he serves you.

Young Turbot in Parsley

2 small turbot, 800 g - 1 kg (1¾ - 2¼ lb) each
2 bunches parsley
1 litre (2 pt) fish stock*
2 tbsp olive oil
3 tbsp flour
200 g (7 oz) butter

Remove the skin from the turbot and cut off the 4 fillets. Prepare and wash the parsley, keeping a little to one side to be very finely chopped. Heat the fish stock until almost boiling and cook the parsley leaves in it for a few minutes. Remove and strain the parsley and make little beds of it on each of 4 plates.

Heat the olive oil in a thick frying pan, roll the fillets in flour, and when the oil is hot, cook the fillets on each side for 3 - 5 minutes. Remove the fat, leaving the fillets in the pan, then put pan on high heat and add butter, the reserved finely chopped parsley, and a ladle of fish stock.

Nap* the fillets with the sauce and serve on the beds of parsley.

Serves: 4

Le Verger de Montmartre

37, rue Lamarck, 75018 Paris
Tel: 252-1270
Proprietor/Chef: Michel Morazin

Fresh Artichoke Gâteau

6 artichokes
½ litre (1 pt) milk
6 eggs
salt and pepper, to taste
50 g (1¾ oz) butter
6 heaped tbsp vinaigrette dressing:* 1 part vinegar to 3 parts olive oil to
**   1 part mustard and seasoning to taste**
chopped chives, to garnish

Cook the artichokes in boiling water for 45 minutes. Separate the leaves from the hearts. Remove the choke. Cut the hearts into cubes, scrape the flesh off the leaves, and mix all together. Add milk, eggs, salt, and pepper. Blend well. Mixture should be creamy.

Fill 6 small, well-buttered soufflé moulds with the mixture; then cook in a bain-marie* in the oven at 415°F (210°C) for 45 minutes.

To serve: Unmould the gâteaux onto 6 plates. Cover each with a generous spoonful of vinaigrette dressing, and serve hot with a sprinkling of chopped chives for decoration.

Serves: 6

Dining at **Le Verger de Montmartre** is a fabulous treat. Michel Morazin wants to please his customers and he does so by preparing and serving truly fine food. His philosophy is "If I work hard to please, it will be worth everyone's time to dine at my place."

It is a genuine pleasure to dine at Michel's and feast on such outstanding dishes as his Artichoke Gâteau or his Crayfish Boudinet de Chair. In addition to the food, you will also enjoy the magnificent view from the restaurant of the Sacre Coeur on the Parisian skyline.

Aux Mets de Provence

11, quai de Rive-Neuve, 13000 Marseilles
Tel: (91) 33-35-38
Proprietor/Chef: Maurice Brun

Hearts of Artichokes with Mushrooms

8 small artichokes
100 ml (3 oz) olive oil
500 g (1 lb) white mushrooms, sliced
salt and pepper, to taste
2 cloves garlic, minced

Clean the artichokes and remove the hearts. Discard the rest.

Place the mushrooms, salt, and pepper in a skillet with olive oil. Put the artichoke hearts and garlic over the mushrooms, then add 2.5 cm (1 in) boiling water to the pan. Boil over high heat until the artichokes are tender and the water has evaporated (about 20 minutes). Place the cooked artichokes on a plate and cover with the cooked mushrooms from the pan.

Suggestion: Garnish with raw or cooked sliced truffles.

Serves: 8

Aux Mets de Provence has been in business many years, with many fine talented people owning it and cooking in it. Maurice Brun was trained in this respected establishment, and today he follows the same formula for success: offer a unique menu with fine hors d'oeuvres, main courses (featuring roasted dishes), fresh vegetables, cheeses, salads, and desserts, and a selection of wines from Provence that will make a meal perfect.

Maurice also offers a marvellous bouillabaisse and special snack treats. Have you ever eaten an olive oil gelatine tartine? This is a fabulous place to satisfy a hearty appetite as well as to sample something new.

Le Prieuré

30400 Villeneuve-Les-Avignon
Tel: (90) 81-76-31
Proprietor: Jacques Mille • Chef: Michel Gonod

Aubergine (Eggplant) à la Provençale

3 aubergines (eggplants)
½ litre (1 pt) peanut oil
salt, to taste
1 kg (2¼ lb) tomato concasse*
parsley, to taste
100 ml (3 oz) olive oil
pepper, to taste

Cut the aubergines lengthwise into 1 cm (½ in) slices. Put slices into a dish with enough peanut oil to cover them, then sprinkle with salt. Let them soak up the oil, then drain them completely.

Mix the tomato concasse with parsley and cook in a skillet in the olive oil. Simmer gently for about 1 hour. Season with salt and pepper.

Heat the remaining peanut oil in a sauté pan and fry the aubergine slices until well coloured. Drain them and put on a serving plate.

Cover the aubergine slices with a thick layer of the tomato and parsley mixture and serve.

Serves: 4

Villeneuve-Les-Avignon is the well-known city in a famous French song. You must cross a few bridges to reach **Le Prieuré**, this quaint and elegant provincial restaurant. Since 1943, the Mille family has been serving classic meals here. Jacques Mille came to Avignon in 1929 with his wife, Marie-France, and his son (who is now a chef).

With his chef, Michel Gonod, who worked in Pic in Valence and the Plaza in Paris, Jacques has made this restaurant a modern establishment with excellent cuisine and a festive, summer atmosphere.

The wine list is also quite impressive, containing some very unusual vintages.

La Tupina

6, rue de la Porte de la Monnaie, 33000 Bordeaux
Tel: (56) 91-15-37
Proprietor/Chef: Jean-Pierre Xiradakis

Broad Bean Stew with Duck Gizzards

15 g (½ oz) lard, diced
6 small white onions
100 ml (3 oz) chicken stock*
1 sliced carrot
1 heart of lettuce
3 duck gizzards
1 small piece fennel
200 g (7 oz) fresh broad beans, peeled

Brown the lard dice and the small onions together in a pan. Add chicken stock, carrot, lettuce, gizzards, and the fennel. Let reduce for 10 minutes.

Immerse the beans in water in a separate pot, bring to a boil and simmer for 5 minutes.

Place contents of both pots in a clay dish and bake in the oven at 350°F (175°C) for 8 minutes. Serve hot.

Wine: *Haut Bages Averens, 1976*

Serves: 4

A "tupina" is a country style stock-pot that, in this restaurant, symbolises simple and wholesome country cooking without any pretentious, fashionable frills. Back in 1970, when this restaurant opened, I indicated that **La Tupina** was one of the best restaurants in Bordeaux.

The menu offered by Jean-Pierre Xiradakis (who is the closest thing there is to a Bordeaux Greek) includes Vegetable Soup, Fried Pigs Feet, Veal Stomach with Stuffed Peppers, Duck Leg Cooked in Stew, Broad Bean Stew, Garlic Soup, Giblet Stew with Spring Onions (Scallions), and Duck Hearts on Skewers — in short, dishes which are not found on any ordinary menu. I have not changed my mind about this restaurant.

Restaurant Michel Pasquet

59, rue La Fontaine, 75116 Paris
Tel: 288-5001
Proprietor/Chef: Michel Pasquet

Broccoli au Gratin

2 kg (4½ lb) broccoli
½ litre (2 pt) double cream (whipping cream)
250 g (½ lb) grated Emmenthal cheese (or Swiss or Gruyère)
salt and pepper, to taste
pinch of nutmeg

Wash the broccoli and break apart into little bouquets. Boil in salted water, but keep crisp. Cool under running cold water to keep the bright green colour. Boil the cream to make it thick. Add the broccoli. Season with salt, pepper, and nutmeg.

Fill 4 small ovenproof dishes with the mixture and sprinkle with the cheese. Put dishes in the oven at 400°F (205°C) until the cheese topping becomes golden in colour.

This goes well with meat or fish dishes.

Serves: 4

An elegant restaurant, with the finest sophistication and class, is **Restaurant Michel Pasquet**. Michel converted a small, dusty, empty space into a most pleasant and beautiful restaurant that is decorated with rose- and gold-coloured Louis XVI furniture.

The cuisine here is of the highest quality and delicacy. There are fine Warm Oysters with Herbs and Vermouth Cream, Broccoli au Gratin, and Quail with Sour Grapes. For dessert, try the Iced Chestnut Bavarois, Arquebuse Parfait with Hot Chocolate, or an assortment of fresh fruits.

Maison Kammerzell

16, place de la Cathédrale, 67000 Strasbourg
Tel: (88) 32-42-14
Proprietor/Chef: Paul Schloesser

Sauerkraut Formidable

3 kg (6½ lb) sauerkraut
1 litre (2 pt) Riesling wine
½ litre (1 pt) veal stock*
½ litre (1 pt) water
500 g (1 lb) onions
125 g (¼ lb) garlic
1 pinch rock salt
10 crushed peppercorns
2 sprigs thyme
a few juniper berries
2 bay leaves
coriander, to taste
1 kg (2¼ lb) salted bacon
1 kg (2¼ lb) bacon fat
1 kg (2¼ lb) smoked bacon

Blanch the sauerkraut. Drain and press out all moisture. Place the sauerkraut in a pot with the Riesling, stock, water, onions, garlic, salt, peppercorns, thyme, juniper berries, bay leaf, and coriander. Bring to boil. Add the salted bacon, bacon fat, and smoked bacon. Let simmer for 1½ hours. Serve hot.

Wine: *Riesling or Pinot Blanc*

Serves: 8

Strasbourg is an eastern city in France that is renowned for its famous cathedrals and hotel school. Here, in the region of Alsace, the cooking is hearty and the people enjoy robust and authentic food and wine. Of course, the most famous dish is the *choucroute Alsacienne* (sauerkraut) accompanied by the famous wine from Alsace. It is an authentic meal, which, here, means that it has been prepared the same way for centuries. Alsace is a very colourful region of France. Some say it's due to its Germanic influences. Yet, the people here are very down-to-earth and warm. Don't pass by **Maison Kammerzell**; not only does it serve a fantastic Alsatian choucroute, but it has other vigorous and delicious dishes on its menu that will introduce you properly to the flavours of the region.

Chez Toutoune

5, rue de Pontoise, 75005 Paris
Tel: 326-5681
Proprietor: Colette Dejean • Chef: Jean-Louis Huclin

"Toutoune" is Colette Dejean, a baker's granddaughter, a cook's daughter, and a sister of a restaurateur. Three years ago, she discovered this bistro on a Parisian street corner. She then purchased the establishment and created **Toutoune**.

Toutoune offers good cuisine for a good price. There are also family dinners. The atmosphere is casual, very Parisian, and comfortable.

Start out with the chef's soup, then go on to a pork dish, a leek tart, a fish salad, or a stuffed cabbage, for example, and finish with a good cheese and a delicious dessert. You'll like this place.

"Grandmother's" Cabbage

200 g (6 oz) white beans
1 large cabbage
200 g (6 oz) carrots, julienne
100 g (¼ lb) turnips, julienne
1 leek, julienne
150 g (5¼ oz) pork chine (spare ribs or pork loin chops), boned
1 slice ham, 2 cm (¾ in) thick
2 shallots, chopped
1 clove garlic, chopped
2 onions, chopped
200 g (7 oz) white mushrooms, sliced
¼ litre (1 cup) bread crumbs
¼ litre (1 cup) milk
salt and pepper, to taste
chopped parsley, chervil, and thyme, to taste
200 ml (6 oz) double cream (whipping cream)
2 eggs
1 litre (2 pt) white wine
½ litre (1 pt) chicken stock*

Soak the beans in water for 6 hours, then cut them julienne and cook in boiling water for 1 hour. Blanch the cabbage, carrots, turnips, and leek.

To prepare the stuffing: Coarsely chop the pork; cut the ham into large dice. Mix pork and ham with shallots, garlic, onions, carrots, turnips, leek, mushrooms, bread crumbs soaked in milk, salt, pepper, chopped herbs, and cream. Thoroughly mix the eggs into this mixture.

Spread the cabbage leaves to reveal the hearts. Remove a little of the hearts to make room for the stuffing. Pile stuffing into the centre of each cabbage and replace leaves to make into a round shape.

Line an ovenproof casserole with bacon. Put the cabbages into the casserole and add wine and stock. Braise in the oven, uncovered, for 1 hour at 300°F (150°C), then add the beans and vegetables. Cook for 1½ hours more and serve.

Wine: *Graves rouge*

Serves: 4

Auberge des Deux Signes

46, rue Galande, 75005 Paris
Tel: 325-4545 and 325-0646
Proprietor: Georges Dhulster • Chef: Henri Guitonneau

Auberge des Deux Signes can really create a feeling of nostalgia, not for days past, but, rather, for centuries past. The crackling fireplace, background music (classical, of course), candlelight, crystal, silverware, and the majestic Notre Dame in the background make for a most beautiful atmosphere. You can almost imagine that a horse-drawn carriage is coming to pick you up.

The decor is medieval, and the cuisine features dishes reminiscent of the Middle Ages, such as La Talmousse François Villon.

Cheese Tartlets

800 g (1¾ lb) puff pastry dough*
60 g (2 oz) butter
½ litre (1 pt) Béchamel sauce*
2 egg yolks
250 g (½ lb) Cantal or Gruyère cheese

Roll out the dough to 5 mm (¼ in) thick, then cut it into 10 squares of 10 cm (4 in) each. Blend the butter, Béchamel sauce, egg yolks, and the cheese together very well. Place some of the mixture in the centre of each puff pastry square; bring the edges up as if to make an envelope. Seal the edges with your fingers.

Put the envelopes on a cooking sheet and place into the oven. Bake for 15 - 20 minutes at 475°F (250°C) and serve.

Yields: 10 pieces

La Mourrachonne

Route de Pégomas, 06370 Mouans-Sartoux
Tel: (93) 75-69-88
Proprietors/Chefs: Jean André, Guy Tricon

La Mourrachonne is the creation of two friends who united in an effort to establish a restaurant-hotel worthy of international praise. In 1972, Jean and Guy opened their provincial restaurant, set in a calm, beautiful area near Cannes. They specialise in *la nouvelle cuisine* to keep up with modern trends, however each dish is prepared with elegance and sophistication.

The menu does offer both traditional and new cuisine. Regional Courgettes (Zucchini) with Spaghetti, Baked Red Mullet Wrapped in Spinach or Beets, Guinea Fowl with Lavender Honey, and Noisettes of Lamb with Garlic Cream Sauce are all splendid treats.

Courgette (Zucchini) Slices with Chives

4 courgettes (zucchin), 150 g (5¼ oz) each
1 tbsp oil
50 g (1¾ oz) butter, and as needed
125 g (¼ lb) mirepoix*
1 sprig thyme
1 bay leaf
100 ml (3 oz) dry white wine
½ litre (1 pt) cream
2 bunches chives, chopped
salt and pepper, to taste
juice of ½ lemon

Slice the unpeeled courgettes lengthwise to make thin strips about 7 mm (¼ in) thick. Heat the oil and butter together in a saucepan. Add the mirepoix, thyme, and bay leaf. Let simmer a few minutes. Reduce with white wine until only 1 tbsp remains.

Add the cream, bring to a boil, and boil for 2 minutes. Pass mixture through a strainer into a pot containing the chopped chives. Add salt, pepper, and lemon juice. Keep this mixture warm.

In a pan, sauté the courgette strips in butter for 2 minutes. Season with salt and pepper.

To serve: Pile the courgettes on the centre of a serving plate and pour the sauce around them.

Suggestion: Serve topped with stewed tomatoes and sautéed basil.

Serves: 4

Jacqueline Fénix

42, avenue Charles-de-Gaulle, 92000 Neuille-sur-Seine
Tel: 624-4261
Proprietor: Jacqueline Fénix • Chef: Michel Rubod

Jacqueline Fénix is one of the very few lady proprietors in Paris. She is fresh, gay, and dazzling — so she built her restaurant to reflect this image. Michel is her assistant who prepares all the excellent dishes.

Jacqueline's restaurant is charming and fancy; so is the food she serves. You will appreciate the elegance of the Leeks in Chervil with Smoked Salmon, her Beurre Blanc Sauce that is a classic marvel, the subtlety of the Nut Sauce that accompanies the Challans Duck, and her own sublime invention, a Chocolate Brioche with Iced Coffee. Everything about the cuisine is delicate to the palate and pleasing to the tastebuds.

Leeks in Chervil with Smoked Salmon

20 small leeks
300 g (10½ oz) smoked salmon
½ litre (1 pt) peanut oil
100 ml (3 oz) oyster juice
salt and pepper, to taste
juice of 1 lemon
2 tbsp sherry wine vinegar
1 bunch chervil

Wash the leeks well. Divide them in two and boil in salted water for 10 minutes. Drain and let cool completely, but do not refrigerate. Grind 50 g (1¾ oz) smoked salmon with the oyster juice, salt, pepper, lemon juice, and vinegar. Blend together well, then add the chervil.

To serve: Place the leeks on a plate and cover with the sauce. Surround with the remaining salmon cut julienne and serve.

Serves: 4

Hostellerie du Maine Brun

162900 Asnières-sur-Nouère
Tel: (45) 96-92-62
Proprietor/Chef: Michel Ménager

Between Angoulême and Cognac, in the heart of the Charentaise region, there is an old mill that has been converted into a chateau-hotel. Here, in this peaceful countryside, away from all the noise of the cities, it is a privilege to spend time in a tranquil place that offers Fresh Duck Foie Gras in Cognac, Ham from Charente, Beef à la Charentaise, and, of course, modern cuisine for those with less robust appetites.

There is a fine collection of mineral waters and fabulous wines, a choice of which will complement any dinner.

Leeks in Chervil Sauce

1 kg (2¼ lb) leeks
70 g (2½ oz) butter
1 bunch chervil
150 ml (4½ oz) double cream (whipping cream)
salt and pepper, to taste
4 warm pastry shells, prepared or purchased

Clean the leeks, keeping only the white part. Cut into 2 cm (¾ in) strips. In a saucepan, melt the butter; add the leeks, and cook uncovered for 15 minutes. Grind the chervil in a bit of water in a food processor.

In a pan, reduce the cream, then add the chervil. Season with salt and pepper, then cook without boiling.

To serve: Spread the leeks over the pastry shells and cover them with the chervil cream sauce.

Wine: *Chablis, 1979*

Serves: 4

Delanné

10, rue Paul-Guillon, 86000 Poitiers
Tel: (49) 41-20-86
Proprietors: M. and Mme. Delanné • Chef: Jean-François Delanné

The Delannés are new to Poitiers. They have just established themselves, but they have brought with them some considerable professional training; Jean-François worked in four very respectable restaurants (Artigny, Château Besset, Gérard Vié, and Les Trois-gros) before opening his own establishment.

Jean's restaurant is small and modern, with soft background music and a small salon with round and oval tables for banquets. The cuisine is modern, however Jean doesn't completely exclude regional dishes from his fine menu.

Leeks with Mustard Sauce

3 kg (6½ lb) leeks, white parts only
salt and pepper, to taste
160 g (⅓ lb) butter
2 kg (4½ lb) tomatoes
125 g (¼ lb) onions, minced
1 clove garlic, minced
2 egg yolks
1 tbsp strong mustard

Cut the leek whites into 4-5 cm (1½-2 in) long strips, then gently cook with salt and pepper and 60 g (2 oz) butter in an ovenproof saucepan for 8 minutes. Cover the pan with aluminum foil and bake at 400°F (205°C) until the liquid is reduced. The leeks should remain firm.

Clean and empty the tomatoes of seeds. Simmer the minced onions and garlic in the remaining butter until transparent, then add the tomatoes and simmer over low heat for 5 minutes.

Make a sabayon by beating a little water and the egg yolks together. Heat in the top of a double-boiler and continue beating. Beat in the mustard, blend well, and continue to heat until thick.

In a pan, briefly sauté the leeks, then place them on the centre of a plate. Place the tomatoes on top of the leeks, surround with the sabayon, and serve.

Wine: *A delicate red wine*   Serves: 4

Le Lord Gourmand

9, rue Lord-Byron, 75008 Paris
Tel: 359-0727 and 562-6606
Proprietor/Chef: Daniel Météry

Daniel Météry planted his roots two steps away from the Champs Élysées, after spending an initiation period with Les Trois-gros in Roanne, the Paris Hôtel Windsor, and Paul Bocuse of Lyon. He then transformed a nice, ground level suite of rooms into an elegant restaurant, complete with a foyer.

The colours here are warm, the paintings are amusing, and the lighting is perfect. In fact, everything is perfect for tasting the freshness and quality of the fine food he serves. The Anglerfish Terrine with Citrus Fruits, Vegetable Timbales with Tomato Sauce, Haddock in Raspberry Vinegar, Crown Shaped Kidneys "Dijonnaise," Sautéed Beef Tidbits with pasta, and everything else the **Lord Gourmand** has to offer is worthy of its name.

Vegetable Timbales with Tomato Sauce

¼ bell pepper, sliced thinly
½ onion, sliced
1 sliced courgette (zucchini) plus
  220 g (½ lb) diced
1 aubergine (eggplant), sliced
6 tomatoes, peeled, seeded, and chopped
olive oil, to sauté
2 cloves garlic, chopped
1 tbsp tomato purée
160 g (6 oz) white mushrooms, diced
75 g (2½ oz) butter, and as needed
¼ bulb fennel, boiled and chopped
salt and pepper, to taste
4 eggs, beaten
125 g (¼ lb) ham, chopped
300 ml (9 oz) double cream
  (whipping cream)
2 shallots, finely chopped

To prepare the ratatouille: Stew the bell pepper, onion, sliced courgette, aubergine, and 2 tomatoes in olive oil. Add garlic and tomato purée. Cook gently for 20 minutes. Sauté the diced mushrooms and courgettes separately in butter.

Mix 4 tbsp of the ratatouille with all the remaining ingredients except the shallots and the remaining 4 tomatoes. Fill 6 small, buttered timbales with the mixture. Bake in a bain-marie* in the oven at 300°F (150°C) for 1 hour.

To prepare the sauce: Sweat* the shallots in butter, add the remaining tomatoes, and cook gently for 20 minutes. Stir in a spoonful of butter.

Unmould the timbales, cover with sauce, and serve.

Wine: *A light red wine*   Serves: 6

Les Princes

Hôtel George V, 31, avenue George V, 75008 Paris
Tel: 723-5400
General Manager: Christian Falcucci • Chef: Jean Carrat

This is the restaurant of the Hôtel George V, one of the great hotels of Paris. It combines a luxurious decor (the hotel is also a mini-museum) and excellent service. Christian Falcucci, the General Manager, and M. Frison, the restaurant supervisor, have made **Les Princes** into what they call "the most Parisian of the restaurants in Paris." The long dining room, draped in blue and decorated with paintings from the Findlay Gallery, looks out onto hanging gardens. In the summer, tables are set out in the open air. The menu is elegantly classical and offers the rull range of the art of fine cuisine, from the vast array of seafood starters to the marvellous desserts. I know of one gourmand who comes here just for their Macaroni au Gratin, a truly royal dish that is impossible to find elsewhere.

Macaroni au Gratin

500 g (1 lb) macaroni
200 ml (6 oz) double cream (whipping cream)
125 g (¼ lb) grated cheese (Parmesan, Swiss, etc.)
50 g (1¾ oz) Béchamel sauce*
50 g (1¾ oz) butter

Cook the macaroni in boiling salted water for 7-9 minutes; drain. Heat the cream to thicken it, then add almost all of the grated cheese and the Béchamel sauce. Bring to a boil, then remove to an ovenproof serving dish and mix with the cooked macaroni.

Sprinkle the remaining grated cheese on top of the macaroni mixture, dot with butter, and brown under a hot broiler. Serve hot.

La Petite Tour

11, rue de la Tour, 75016 Paris
Proprietors: M. and Mme. Trebuchon • Chef: Marinette Trebuchon

I don't know who said that the cooking of Marinette was "cooking from the heart." Perhaps it was Peter Ustinov, who is a loyal customer of **La Petite Tour**. In this chic quarter of Passy, this little lady from Auvergne, who came to the city at an early age to earn a living as a waitress, has crowned her success by opening a small, elegantly simple restaurant.

Marinette leaves her husband, Lucien, to look after the wine cellar while she goes off to the market to buy the fresh produce that will be used in the preparation of her superb provincial French dishes. Her trolley of hors d'oeuvres, lobster, Anglerfish with Américaine Sauce, Aligot, Pickled Pork with Lentils, and Curry Chicken are all brilliant.

Aligot "Petite Tour" Style

1.5 kg (3⅓ lb) potatoes, peeled
salt and pepper, to taste
½ clove garlic, crushed
1 tbsp double cream (whipping cream)
¼ litre (1 cup) boiling milk
125 g (4 oz) softened butter
500 g (1 lb) fresh Aubrac or Laguiole tomme cheese (or any soft, white cheese)

Cook the potatoes in water with salt and pepper. Strain. Mash the potatoes with the garlic and cream. Place in a copper saucepan (or any other thick pan) and mix in the boiling milk and softened butter. Cut the cheese into very fine slices, put the mashed potatoes into a bain-marie.* Slowly add the cheese, stirring frequently with a wooden spatula. When the mixture is smooth and even, the aligot is ready to serve.

Lift up the paste with a spatula and cut each portion off onto individual plates using scissors.

Suggestion: Aligot complements calf's liver "Auvergne style" (fried in butter with shallots and chopped parsley, pan deglazed with wine vinegar).

Serves: 4

Ambassade d'Auvergne

22, rue du Grenier-Saint-Lazare, 75003 Paris
Tel: 272-3122
Proprietor: Joseph Petrucci • Chef: Emmanuel Moulier

Aligot

1 kg (2¼ lb) potatoes
¼ litre (½ pt) whole milk
400 g (14 oz) fresh Cantal (Swiss or Gruyère) cheese, sliced
150 ml (½ cup) double cream (whipping cream)
1 clove garlic, minced
salt and pepper, to taste

Wash the potatoes, then boil them in salted water until soft (20-40 minutes).

Boil the sliced Cantal cheese in the milk in a separate pan. Remove and reserve both milk and cheese.

Drain the potatoes. Peel and mash them, then let the potatoes dry a bit. Add the cream and the reserved hot milk, and mix with a spatula. Once mixed and very warm, blend in the Cantal cheese. Add garlic. Season with salt and pepper and serve.

Suggestion: This dish goes well with Grilled Pigs Feet.

Joseph Petrucci opened **Ambassade d'Auvergne** in the old quarter of Paris, not too far from the famous marketplace. Here, in this old house with its rustic furniture and hams hanging from the ceiling, you will be deliciously surprised by the excellent and sumptuous cuisine. Joseph's son-in-law demonstrates an original talent for culinary creativity.

Joseph and Emmanuel offer a wide range of regional dishes. Duck Stew with Fresh Batter, Potée with Cabbage, Stuffed Cabbage, Lentil Cassoulet, Pigs Feet Salad, Fresh Duck Liver, Sheep Tripe in Paquets, Aligot (the most sublime because it uses fresh regional potatoes), and of course, the exceptional Pork Sausage are all delicacies to be savoured here.

Le Mazagran

6, rue Chauveau-Lagarde, 75008 Paris
Tel: 265-7438
Proprietor: Michelle Mealle • Chef: Guy Ducrest

"Burgundy" Style Potatoes

650 g (1½ lb) smoked bacon
575 g (1¼ lb) potatoes, cut .5 cm (¼ in) thick
150 g (5¾ oz) grated Gruyère cheese
pinch of pepper

Mince 400 g (14 oz) of the bacon and slice the rest.

In a heavy pot or ovenproof dish, make layers beginning with 175 g (6 oz) minced smoked bacon, then 225 g (½ lb) sliced potatoes, 50 g (2 oz) grated Gruyère, 150 g (5 oz) sliced bacon, 225 g (½ lb) potatoes, 50 g (2 oz) Gruyère, 225 g (½ lb) minced smoked bacon, and finally a pinch of pepper. Cook in the oven for 1¼ hours at 475°F (250°C). Unmould the mixture onto a plate and serve.

Suggestion: Serve this robust dish with a leg of lamb.

Wine: *St. Émilion, 1964*

Le Mazagran restaurant is located inside the Hôtel Roblin. The decor is elegant and flowered, the ambiance calm, and the dining room is furnished in Louis XVI style. Everything here is delicate and subtle.

Michelle Mealle really triumphed when she employed a chef with a distinguished background. Guy Ducrest previously worked in France and England in some of the most famous hotels in each country. He has composed a very rich menu for her that offers sumptuous food. The Veal Kidney and Sweetbread Rennet, Escalope of Turbot "Wagram," and Veal with Cèpe Mushrooms are all delicious. Definitely taste the Chocolate Soufflé; it is an unforgettable treat. It is apparent from the quality of the food here that Guy loves to cook.

Le Cabestan

Boulevard de la Garoupe, 06600 Cap-d'Antibes
Tel: (93) 61-77-70
Proprietor/Chef: Odette Guérin

What a location! Directly facing the Garoupe, **Le Cabestan** sits on a huge terrace with patios and large windows that reflect the beauty of daytime sunshine and the nighttime glow of the moon. Odette Guérin had been in the restaurant business for at least ten years before opening Le Cabestan in 1977. Odette's excellent assistant chef had worked at La Chèvre d'Or and Le Négresco before proving his talent here.

You will appreciate the Anglerfish with Rose Berries (not with pepper as is generally served elsewhere) and the Steamed Seaweed. It is evident that seafood is the priority here, but the meats, poultry, side dishes, and desserts on the menu don't suffer. The Chocolate Cake is anything but a conventional recipe.

Chocolate Cake "Cabestan" Style

125 g (¼ lb) cooking chocolate
3 tbsp water
125 g (¼ lb) sugar
125 g (¼ lb) butter
3 egg yolks
50 g (1¾ oz) flour
3 egg whites
500 g (1 lb) sweet chocolate
½ litre (1 pt) double cream (whipping cream)

Melt the cooking chocolate in a bain-marie* over boiling water with the water and sugar. When mixture is lukewarm, mix in butter, then the egg yolks, one by one. Mix each yolk in thoroughly before adding the next. Fold in the flour.

Beat the egg whites until they form stiff peaks. Fold them carefully into the first mixture to retain the maximum volume. Pour into a 23 cm (9 in) cake pan and bake in the oven at 275°F (135°C) for 35 minutes. The cake will be creamy at the centre but should not stick to the skewer or cocktail stick (toothpick) used to test if it is done.

To prepare the *ganache* (icing): Melt the sweet chocolate in a bain-marie over boiling water. When melted, add the cream and mix well. Remove from heat and whisk until the cream stiffens. Reserve one cupful.

When the *ganache* achieves a creamy, spreading consistency, cover the cake with a layer of it. Place the cake in the refrigerator. Barely melt the reserved *ganache* in a bain-marie over hot water, pour over the cold cake, and serve.

La Renaissance

58470, Magny, Cours
Tel: (86) 58-10-40
Proprietor/Chef: Jean-Claude Dray

On the Nationale 7, between Nevers and Moulins, there is a detour that will lead you directly to a beautifully flowered façade and a perfectly arranged garden all belonging to **La Renaissance**, where Jean-Claude Dray and his lovely wife offer gourmet dinners at a fixed price.

The Nivernais Ham, Charolais Fillet in Morel Cream Sauce or with Garden Herbs, and Duck Drumsticks with Mustard are all excellent and are served with the wine of your choice. Honeymoon Gâteau should be your choice for dessert.

Honeymoon Gâteau

500 ml (1 pt) concentrated (strong) coffee, slightly sweetened
100 ml (3 oz) white rum
2 eggs
6 egg yolks
300 g (10½ oz) sugar, cooked to the thread stage*
300 g (10½ oz) dark chocolate, softened
zest* of 1 orange, grated
400 ml (1½ cups) double cream (whipping cream), softly whipped
1 box of sponge fingers
125 g (¼ lb) butter, softened
350 g (¾ lb) sweet chocolate, softened

To prepare the chocolate cream: Mix the coffee and rum together. Let cool. Whisk the eggs and egg yolks in a bain-marie* over hot water until they become thick, pale, and foamy. Pour in the sugar, cooked to the thread stage, and continue whisking over a bowl of cold water until mixture is cold. Stir in the softened dark chocolate, grated orange zest, and the softly whipped cream.

Pour the chocolate cream into a soufflé mould and finish with a layer of sponge fingers. Chill for 24 hours, then unmould.

Blend the softened sweet chocolate and butter together and frost the cake with this icing. Serve.

Serves: 10

La Bonne Etape

04160 Château-Arnoux
Tel: (92) 64-00-09
Proprietor/Chef: Pierre Gleize

This 18th century inn has had three generations of cooks and chefs. "To live in Provence," says Pierre Gleize, "with its olive trees, thyme, and rosemary which tickle your nostrils, is marvellous." Now prepared by Pierre's son, the cuisine offers a melon gâteau, rich in flavour that only a restaurant from Provence could offer.

La Bonne Etape, with its provincial Louis XIV and Louis XV furniture, offers three menus: Château, Durance, and Provence, that reflect the perpetuation of traditional gourmet cuisine. The cold Fisherman's Soup Seasoned with Vervaine, the Orange Butter Gâteau, Young Rabbit Seasoned with Hyssop, and the Duckling with Lavender Honey and Lemon are all local specialities (as are the game dishes in winter).

Melon Gâteau

125 g (¼ lb) sugar
salt, to taste
4 eggs
125 g (¼ lb) flour, sifted
50 ml (1½ oz) sugar syrup* made by boiling 200 ml (6 oz) water with
   350 g (¾ lb) sugar, then letting it cool
50 ml (1½ oz) Muscat wine
¼ litre (1 cup) pastry cream*
¼ litre (1 cup) double cream (whipping cream), whipped
400 g (14 oz) melon slices

To prepare the sponge: In a bowl, mix the sugar, salt, and eggs together. Beat the mixture in a bain-marie* over boiling water for about 10 minutes until it is pale, foamy, and thick enough to hold a shape (thread stage*). Remove from heat and continue to beat until cold. Fold the sifted flour into this mixture. Pour the mixture into a buttered and floured 23 cm (9 in) cake pan and bake in the oven at 350°F (175°C) for 25-30 minutes, then let cool.

Mix the sugar syrup with ½ the wine. Split the cooled sponge in half and soak it in the sugar syrup mixture. Mix the remaining wine, pastry cream, and whipped cream together.

Fill the bottom half of the sponge with the cream mixture, garnish with slices of melon, and replace the top half of the sponge.

Suggestion: Frost the cake with raspberry jelly and decorate it with melon slices and sweetened whipped cream.

Serves: 4

Le Train Bleu

20, boulevard Diderot, 75012 Paris
Tel: 343-3839
Proprietor: Albert Chazal • Chef: Jean-Marie Rabory

Le Train Bleu is the "buffet of the Lyon railroad station." It is right out of the Belle Epoch and the 1900 Exposition, and it is surrounded by so many historical monuments that is should also be considered one. In 1963, Albert Chazal created the menu. Today, Jean-Marie Rabory continues to cook the fine recipes. There are French regional-provincial dishes such as Snails in Chablis Wine, Hot Sausage Lyonnaise, and a Mimosa Salad (very Côte d'Azur!) and some classic Parisian recipes such as Veal Chops "Foyot" (named after a restaurant that no longer exists) and Beef with Béarnaise Sauce (the sauce is Parisian despite its name). The pastries are delicious, as is the Passion Fruit Gâteau, and the wine list is superb.

Passion Fruit Gâteau

15 egg yolks
250 g (½ lb) sugar
1 litre (2 pt) sweetened passion fruit and juice
50 g (1¾ oz) gelatine, softened in water
2 litres (½ gal) double cream (whipping cream)
1 sponge cake of 23 cm (9 in) in diameter

To prepare passion fruit cream: Whisk the egg yolks and sugar over gentle heat until thick and pale. Bring the sweetened fruit pulp to a boil in a saucepan. Add the egg yolk and sugar mixture. Add the gelatine and let cool. Whip the cream and add to the mixture when the mixture is cold but not set.

Assemble the cake inside a circular mould or soufflé dish of 23 cm (9 in). Place the sponge cake inside the mould and soak it with the passion fruit juice. Pour the passion fruit cream on top and serve.

Wine: *Sauterne, Château Guiraud, 1974*

Serves: 8

Hôtel de Paris

21, rue de Paris, 03000 Moulins
Tel: (70) 44-00-58
Proprietors: Jean and François Laustriat • Chef: Bernard Passevent

The **Hôtel de Paris** was constructed in 1934. It was built on the ruins of an ancient inn called La Belle Image. In 1935, a chef named Gilbert Laustriat acquired it, and in 1955, Jean Laustriat, Gilbert's son, took over the management of the hotel with his brother, François.

François studied at the École Hôtelière in Strasbourg and worked in the Ritz Carlton in Montreal. He maintains a traditional cuisine, especially that of Burgundy, the home of the Laustriats and of the hotel. For this reason, when the hotel was modernised recently, the Laustriat brothers were careful to keep its regional flavour.

The menu at the Hôtel de Paris offers regional specialities and traditional dishes prepared by Chef Passevent.

Pear Gâteau

50 g (1¾ oz) flour
2 eggs
200 ml (6 oz) milk
100 ml (3 oz) double cream (whipping cream)
125 g (¼ lb) sugar, and as needed
12 pears, peeled, seeded, and cut into round slices
butter, as needed

Mix the flour, eggs, milk, cream, and sugar together until they are thoroughly blended. Gently stir in the sliced pears.

Pour the mixture into a glass or pottery baking dish, sprinkle with sugar, and dot with butter. Bake in the oven at 425°F (220°C) for 50 minutes, then serve.

Serves: 6

Le Bretagne

2, place du Vainquai, 62500 Saint-Omer
Tel: (21) 38-25-78
Proprietor: Francis Beauvalot • Chef: Sylvie Beauvalot

Saint-Omer is located between Flanders and the Artois, on the holiday routes for Belgians and English. In 1972, the Beauvalots took over this almost new hotel located here. At first they hired chefs, but it brought them nothing but problems. For the last five years, Sylvie has been the cook of the house and has really come into her own. The Breton menu is most attractive due to her delicious way of presenting fish (for example, quiche with three kinds of fish), of making terrines, of finding original side dishes for meats, and of being absolutely brilliant when it comes to desserts. Sylvie wanted to become a nurse, I was told. Well, what better way is there to look after people than feeding them? And what better remedies are there than those she prepares in her kitchen?

Apple Charlotte with Brown Sugar

2 kg (4½ lb) cooking apples
10 slices white bread, crusts removed
150 g (5½ oz) butter
200 g (7 oz) brown sugar
50 - 70 ml (1½ - 2 oz) Calvados

Peel the apples, remove the pips, and cut into quarters. Brown the bread in a pan with a little butter, then drain. Place this toast on the bottom and around the edges of a large soufflé mould and set aside.

Melt the remaining butter in a large pan, add the brown sugar, then add the apples. Let cook gently for about 10 minutes, being careful to keep stirring the apples. Flame the apples with Calvados and then place them in the bread-lined mould (push them in tightly) and cook for 30 minutes at 400°F (205°C).

When cooked, put a weighted dish of about 3 - 4 kg (7 - 8 lb) over the mould and let cool. Remove the preparation from the mould.

Suggestion: Serve warm with custard.

Wine: *Champagne, Bollinger*

Serves: 8

La Ferme Saint-Simon

6, rue de Saint-Simon, 75007 Paris
Tel: 548-3574
Proprietor/Chef: Francis Vandenhende

Francis Vandenhende is a young baker-chef who can create the most expansive dinner as well as the rarest dinner in the world. He is also married to the French television star Denise Fabre, which keeps him in the spotlight as much as his fine restaurant does.

Located in a small house, **La Ferme Saint-Simon** is a warm place with an intimate ambiance and a rustic decor that is enhanced by the candlelit tables. The menu here is original and very Parisian. A tête-à-tête here makes for a delicious and romantic evening.

Chestnut Charlotte

200 g (7 oz) chestnut purée*
120 g (4 oz) pastry cream*
60 ml (1¾ oz) whisky
2 sheets gelatine
350 g (12 oz) double cream (whipping cream)
12 biscuits (cookies), crushed with a spoon
30 ml (1 oz) sygar syrup*

Thoroughly mix the chestnut purée and the pastry cream together wth a wooden spatula. Add ½ the whisky. Soak the gelatine in cold water to soften it. Squeeze the gelatine dry and dissolve it in 3 tbsp cream. Stir into the chestnut mixture. Whip the remaining cream and fold it into the chestnut mixture.

Mix the remaining whisky and the syrup together. Soak the biscuits in this mixture. Line 6 small soufflé moulds with the soaked biscuits. Pour the chestnut cream into the moulds and chill for 6 hours before serving.

Wine: *Champagne*   Serves: 6

L'Estournel

88, bis, avenue Kléber and 1, rue Léo-Delibes, 75116 Paris
Tel: 553-1079 and 553-8333
Proprietor: Claude Dray • Chef: Henri Boutier

Avenue Kléber leads to the Étoile, better known as the Arc de Triomphe. After the remodeling of the Hôtel Baltimore, M. Lo Monaco, the director, gave life to an elegant new dining room featuring 1930s decor and frescos signed by Decaris. The effect is subtle and romantic and has helped to bring success to **L'Estournel**. One could come here simply to admire the unique decor and hospitable service or to reflect on a past era, but the food is also excellent. Henri Boutier, the young chef, will prepare dishes that are a feast for your eyes as well as your stomach. His specialities include dishes such as Raw Salmon Marinated in Black Pepper and Salt, Scallops in Hazelnut Oil, Sea Bream Cooked in Fennel, Rabbit Cooked in Ginger, and Pear Charlotte.

Pear Charlotte

750 g (1½ lb) pears in syrup
250 g (½ lb) double cream (whipping cream)
20 g (¾ oz) icing (confectioners') sugar
2 egg whites
250 g (½ lb) caster (granulated) sugar
60 g (2 oz) sponge fingers
15 g (½ oz) gelatine, softened in cold water
20 ml (½ oz) pear brandy
1 kg (2¼ lb) raspberries
juice of 1 lemon

Sieve or blend 350 g (¾ lb) pears to a purée. Warm in a saucepan. Cut remaining pears into 1 cm (½ in) cubes. Whip the cream; add icing sugar. Beat egg whites until stiff; add ⅛ the caster sugar. Cover the bottom of a charlotte mould with greaseproof (wax) paper, then line with sponge fingers. Add gelatine to the pear purée in a large bowl and stir until cool. Mix in brandy and cubed pears. When cold, fold in cream and egg whites. Fill the mould with the mixture and chill for 12 hours.

To prepare rasbperry *coulis* (sauce): Purée and strain the raspberries; add lemon juice and remaining sugar. Chill.

To serve: Unmould the charlotte, surround with some sauce, and serve the remaining sauce separately.

Serves: 6

Château de Roumegouse

46500 Rignac par Gramat
Tel: (65) 33-63-81
Proprietor: Jean-Louis Laine • Chef: Raymond Lauwaert

This is an old chateau dating from the Middle Ages, or maybe the Gothic-Renaissance period. It has that period's towers, long round windows, hard beds, and huge rooms. It is located in the middle of Quercynoise country. The restaurant was originally run by a lady chef who started her career in Paris in 1955 and came to the chateau ten years later. Today, that lady's son, assisted by Chef Raymond Lauwaert, persists in improving the cuisine. The speciality here is provincial hospitality and cuisine in the best sense of the word. The Crayfish Salad, Cousses Lamb, Veal Kidney "Rocamdour," the cheeses, and the desserts (especially the Raspberry Charlotte) taste like a mother's cooking. Here, far away from the rest of the world, it feels like home.

Raspberry Charlotte

100 ml (3 oz) water
125 g (¼ lb) sugar
2 sheets gelatine, softened in cold water
300 g (10½ oz) raspberries
20 sponge fingers

Bring the water to a boil with ½ the sugar and dissolve the gelatine in it. With a fork, thoroughly crush the raspberries and the remaining sugar together. Gently fold this into the sugar and gelatine mixture.

Line the bottom of a 23 cm (9 in) mould with sponge fingers. Pour in a layer of the raspberry mixture, add a layer of sponge fingers, then another layer of raspberry mixture, and so on until the mould is filled, but finish with a layer of sponge fingers. Chill for 4 hours, then unmould and serve.

Suggestion: Serve on a plate decorated with fresh strawberries.

Le Bistrot d'Hubert

36, place du Marché-Saint-Honoré, 75001 Paris
Tel: 260-0300
Proprietor/Chef: M. Hubert

M. Hubert entered the culinary world after spending many years working as a cheese maker. He established himself in an old house in an old neighbourhood in Paris and announced the opening of **Le Bistrot d'Hubert**. One of the dining rooms is dressed in very early 1900s decor, and in the foyer there is a very *avant garde* zinc counter.

M. Hubert offers a variety of dining formulas: for lunch there is quick service and a fixed price, and the evening menu features a *grand carte*. The cuisine is very original, light, and savoury.

Don't forget to try an apéritif or some wine from Charentes, and be sure to finish your dinner with either Apple and Cider Crepes or Hot Orange Crepes. Dining in Hubert's bistro is relaxing and casual.

Hot Orange Crepes

2 oranges
sugar syrup,* as needed
6 eggs
200 g (7 oz) sugar
125 g (¼ lb) softened butter
70 ml (2 oz) Grand Marnier
2 litres (½ gal) crepe batter*

Peel the oranges. Slice the peels into very fine julienne strips. Caramelise these strips in enough sugar syrup to cover them. Squeeze the juice from the oranges and reserve.

In a bowl, mix the eggs, sugar, orange juice, and candied orange peel together. Heat the mixture, stirring constantly, over low heat until it takes on the consistency of honey. Do not boil. Add the butter and the Grand Marnier and refrigerate until cold.

Prepare 5 crepes* with the batter. Fill each crepe with the orange filling, then warm in the oven and serve.

Serves: 5

Les Roseaux

14, rue Portefoin, 75003 Paris
Tel: 887-6103
Proprietor/Chef: Jean-Pierre Lefour

Crepe Surprise

125 g (¼ lb) flour
20 g (¾ oz) sugar
1 egg
½ tbsp peanut oil
small pinch of salt
50 ml (1¾ oz) light beer
50 ml (1¾ oz) milk
3 egg yolks
170 g (6 oz) sugar
1 tsp sieved flour
1 tsp potato starch
¼ litre (1 cup) boiling milk
400 g (14 oz) strawberries (or raspberries)
water and sugar, as needed
7.5 ml (¼ oz) raspberry brandy
3 egg whites, stiffly beaten

To prepare the crepe batter: Mix the first 7 ingredients together and let rest.

To prepare *crème pâtissière* (pastry cream): Mix the egg yolks, 70 g (2½ oz) sugar, flour, and potato starch together. Pour on the boiling milk, stirring constantly. Return to stove and cook gently for 3-4 minutes. Pour into a dish and let cool.

Slice 24 strawberries and set aside. Blend the remainder with a little water and sugar, bring to a boil once, and keep hot.

Cook 8 crepes;* keep them as thin as possible. Stir the brandy, egg whites, and remaining sugar into the pastry cream and fill each crepe with 2 tbsp of this mixture. Arrange the sliced fruit on top and fold the crepe over.

Arrange 2 crepes on a plate and bake in the oven at 475°F (250°C) for 8-10 minutes or until crepes are puffed. Serve hot with the sauce on the side.

Serves: 4

Rue Portefoin is a narrow street in an old quarter of Paris. Push open the simple door of the small restaurant at number 14 and you will be surprised to find a warm ambiance with decor like an art gallery. Bouquets of lovely fresh flowers are everywhere and crystal decorates all the tables.

From his tiny kitchen, Jean-Pierre Lefour will offer you a Terrine of Artichokes, Pot-au-Feu of Sea Delights with Saffron, Turbot with Mint, Veal with Thyme, Brie Cheese from Meaux with Apples, Norwegian Omelette, and a long dessert menu with some fabulous crepe dishes.

La Petite Auberge

38, rue Laugier, 75017 Paris
Tel: 763-8551 and 763-8581
Proprietor/Chef: Léo Harbonnier

This is the very same little auberge where Léo Harbonnier set up shop some 20 years ago. He had been working with Camille Renault, a restaurateur who was a fanatic for paintings. Working alongside him, Léo, too, caught the craze, and the paintings of his own collection now decorate the walls of this intimate little restaurant on the rue Laugier where Léo is waiting to prepare veritable still lifes for you, but in his kitchen. His Eggs with Oranges, his Flemish Black Pudding, his Young Rabbit with Prunes, and his Steak Provençal are dishes where colour and perfume combine with the pleasure of taste. Equally succulent are his Fresh Foie Gras, followed by Grilled Veal Kidney, and a tart dedicated to my colleague James de Coquet. Léo Harbonnier is another word for certainty.

Eggs with Oranges

50 g (1¾ oz) butter
10 g (⅓ oz) sugar
juice of ½ orange
6 tbsp veal stock*
zest* of 2 oranges, julienne
10 ml (⅓ oz) Grand Marnier
8 eggs
2 tbsp vinegar
pinch of salt and pepper

Melt 30 g (1 oz) of the butter slowly in a saucepan. Heat the sugar to the caramel stage,* then add orange juice, veal stock, and the orange zest slices. Let reduce, then flavour with Grand Marnier.

Poach the eggs in water with vinegar for 2 minutes, then sprinkle with salt and pepper. Heat the slices of orange zest in the remaining butter. Serve the eggs with the orange slices.

Wine: *Sancerre White, Pouilly de la Loire*   Serves: 4

La Ripa Alta

32160 Plaisance
Tel: (62) 69-30-43
Proprietor/Chef: Maurice Coscuella

Maurice Coscuella belongs to the *band à Daguin;* he is one of the strongest supporters of *cuisine d'Armagnac.* A worthy student of Fernand Point (of the Troisgros and Outhier), Maurice then sailed on the *S.S. Liberty,* then on *The France.*

In 1959, he opened **La Ripa Alta**. Its cuisine is inspired by traditional and regional favourites. M. Conscuella also welcomes many young Americans who come here to serve their apprenticeship; here they learn to shell oysters, bone fish, and much more. They learn about their art.

Figs in Whisky

18 dry figs
8 sugar cubes
2 litres (½ gal) water
60 ml (2 oz) whisky
½ litre (1 pt) double cream (whipping cream)

Wash the figs in cold water. Cook them in sugared water for about 30 minutes. Leave to become cold in the juice, then drain them and reserve juice.

Heat the figs with a little of the cooking juice, add the whisky, and serve with the cream.

Serves: 6

La Belle Epoch

Châteaufort, 78530 Buc
Tel: 956-2166
Proprietor/Chef: Michel Peignaud

Raspberry Soup with Star Anise

4 containers of raspberries
juice of 1 lime
1 tbsp acacia honey
few fresh leaves of mint, shredded
4 scoops aniseed sorbet (sherbet)
4 kiwi fruits, sliced

Marinate the raspberries for 30 minutes in the lime juice, then add a spoonful of liquid acacia honey and a few finely shredded leaves of fresh mint.

Serve very cold in 4 large wine glasses. Place a ball of star anise sorbet on top of the raspberries and garnish with sliced kiwi fruit.

Serves: 4

Due to its authentic decor and long heritage (since 1781), **La Belle Epoch** could be a museum. Michel Peignaud has been here since 1974 and openly expresses his strong feelings for regionalism, hospitality, and gourmet excellence. His imaginative spirit can produce modern delights blended with the old. Michel's experience includes tenures with Maxim's, in both Tokyo and Paris, and the Véfour.

Here the Duck Foie Gras is "old school," the eggs are prepared the Berri way, the scallops are traditional, and the Langoustines in China à la Gauloise and the Squab "Façon Bécasse" are superb. The cheeses are excellent, the wine list, especially the Sancerres, is extensive, but the desserts are my favourites.

L'Escu de Runfao

5, rue du Chapître, 35000 Rennes
Tel: (99) 30-95-75
Proprietor/Chef: Jacques Granville

Spring Fruit Salad

2 oranges
100 ml (3 oz) Grenadine syrup
½ litre (1 pt) water
2 melons, 600 g (1⅓ lb) each
400 g (14 oz) strawberries, washed and stalks removed
juice of 1 orange
juice of 1 lemon
200 g (7 oz) sugar

Cut the oranges into very small, thin strips, then place strips into the Grenadine syrup and water. Heat for 10 minutes until the fruit is well blanched and impregnated with syrup. Let cool.

Cut the melons into small round pieces and put in a salad bowl with the orange strips and strawberries. Mix together well. Add the orange and lemon juice, then the sugar; mix well and serve.

Suggestion: Decorate with crystallised oranges.

Wine: *Champagne brut*

Serves: 4

Five years ago, Jacques Granville settled on this small street in the old quarter of Rennes in a house dating from Louis XIII. The dining room contains old style furniture with very old engravings on the walls, and the whole thing blends most harmoniously with a very unrevolutionary cuisine. To Jacques, anything the sea can produce is truly a treasure to be prized. His Norway Lobster Jelly with Young Vegetables and Tomato Sauce, his Warm Lobster Salad with Melon, and his Fresh Salmon with Carrots bear witness to his wonderful inspiration. Even the simple Roast Pigeon with Turnips or Breast of Duckling with Peppers will delight you, as will one of the 10 or so desserts on the menu. The Spring Fruit Salad (strawberries, melons, and crystallised oranges) is simply marvellous.

Le Métropole

15, boulevard Maréchal-Leclerc, 06310 Beaulieu-sur-Mer
Tel: (93) 01-00-08
Proprietor: Jean Badrutt • Chef: Pierre Estival

Strawberry Fritters in Raspberry Sauce

250 g (½ lb) flour, sifted
2 tbsp melted butter
1 tsp salt
150 ml (5 oz) beer
250 ml (8 oz) water
1 tbsp cognac
2 egg whites, beaten stiffly
500 g (1 lb) strawberries
100 ml (3 oz) plus 1 dash Grand Marnier
200 g (7 oz) oil, to fry
250 g (½ lb) ripe raspberries
250 g (½ lb) raspberry liqueur at 100°F (38°C)

To prepare the batter: Mix the first 6 ingredients together. Fold in the egg whites and keep in a warm place until needed.

To prepare the fritters: Put the strawberries in a bowl with 100 ml (3 oz) Grand Marnier and leave for 20 minutes. Dip the strawberries in the batter and deep-fat fry them. Set aside and keep warm.

To prepare the sauce: Purée the raspberries in a blender, then mix with the raspberry liqueur. Bring to a boil and boil for 2 minutes. Cool quickly and add a dash of Grand Marnier.

Serve the strawberry fritters on a dish or in 4 individual cups with the sauce served separately.

Suggestion: Serve topped with ice cream or custard.

Wine: *A white Bordeaux or Sauterne*

Serves: 4

The gem of Beaulieu-sur-Mer is **Le Métropole**, an oasis of aristocratic tranquillity. It is set on the sea's edge, in the tradition of Italian palaces, in the very heart of a park. The restaurant is on a terrace surrounded by exotic plants.

Jean Badrutt, the manager, who is from an old Swiss catering and hostelry family, has been in charge for 10 years. His chef, Pierre Estival, presents lunch and dinner menus that reflect an aristocratic calm and discreet luxury combined by offering classicism of all kinds and a few original dishes of "intimate" perfection such as Fillet of Angler with Avocado Sauce, Apples in Saffron with Roast Kid Goat, Mango Sorbet (Sherbet), and Strawberry Fritters.

Taillevent

75, rue Lamennais, 75008 Paris
Tel: 563-3994
Proprietor: Jean-Claude Vrinat • Chef: Claude Deligne

Blancmange

500 g (1 lb) almonds, blanched
250 g (½ lb) sugar
½ litre (1 pt) milk, boiled and cooled
5 sheets gelatine, softened
20 bitter almonds, blanched, soaked, and pounded with a mortar
½ litre (1 pt) double cream (whipping cream), whipped
1 pear, poached in syrup and diced
2 peaches, poached in syrup and diced
2 slices pineapple, poached in syrup and diced
250 g (½ lb) wild strawberries

Pound the blanched almonds and sugar together. Pour the milk over the mixture and refrigerate overnight. Strain, bring to a boil, and add gelatine and bitter almonds. Chill on ice. Fold in the whipped cream and fruit. Pour into 4 buttered moulds and chill for 4 hours.

Suggestion: Unmould onto 4 plates and serve with raspberry or strawberry sauce.

Serves: 4

It took quite a bit of courage to name a restaurant after the illustrious master of culinary art. Guillaume Tisel, a great 14th century chef and author of *Viandier,* one of the oldest books on cookery, was known as "Taillevent." In the beginning, **Taillevent** was in the 9th *arrondissement* (district) in a small space, but after much success, M. Vrinat moved to a more chic neighbourhood and larger quarters. Jean-Claude Vrinat is the son of that founder, and Claude Deligne assists him as the excellent chef. The menu is as elegant as the decor; the wine list is renowned. Taillevent expresses taste, finesse, and the highest degree of quality, from the kitchen and wine cellar to the service in the dining room. Classic dishes are never excluded, and inspiration is never absent here.

L'Aquitaine

54, rue de Dantzig, 75015 Paris
Tel: 828-6738
Proprietors: M. and Mme. Massia • Head Chef: Christiane Massia

Coffee and Dark Chocolate Mousse

6 egg yolks
200 g (7 oz) sugar
1 tsp very strong coffee
600 g (1⅓ lb) double cream (whipping cream)
200 g (7 oz) unsweetened chocolate powder

Beat the egg yolks and sugar together for about 10 minutes until the mixture stiffens. Add coffee.

Whisk the cream in a cold bowl for about 10 minutes. Gently add the first mixture to the cream. Let cool, then refrigerate for 12 hours. Before serving, scoop out each portion and roll in chocolate powder.

Suggestion: Serve the mousse on top of coffee flavoured custard.

Wine: *A sweet Jurancon wine, well chilled*   Serves: 6

In 1976, Christiane Massia opened a restaurant in this "little Italian palace" with the walls decorated with frescoes by Henri Pelletier, one of the artists from La Ruche (one of the last "villages" of famous artists to be found in Paris). She took over here with her "girls"; Christiane is a chef with a talent for teaching. She trains future chefs — young girls from France and further afield — in the sublime art of cooking, at the very highest level.

Fish dishes take the honours, along with the splendid desserts; however, the menu never overlooks the "grandmother" recipes, nor the special talents of Christiane.

Au Quai d'Orsay

49, Quai d'Orsay, 75007 Paris
Tel: 557-5858 and 705-6909
Proprietor: Etienne Bigeard • Chefs: Etienne Bigeard, Antoine Bouterin

Dark Chocolate Mousse with Strawberries

500 g (1 lb) dark chocolate
50 ml (1¾ oz) water
8 eggs, separated
6 tbsp double cream (whipping cream), whipped
200 g (7 oz) strawberries
100 ml (3 oz) sugar syrup*

Melt the chocolate in the water. Add the egg yolks, one at a time, then add the cream. Beat the egg whites until stiff, then fold them into the chocolate.

Poach the strawberries very gently in syrup. Drain and cool. Garnish the mousse with the poached strawberries and serve.

Wine: *Champagne*   Serves: 6

With a few mirrors, Etienne Bigeard has made **Au Quai d'Orsay** a most interesting Parisian restaurant. As Curnonsky said of this restaurant, it is ". . . elegant in style, yet familiar; the waitresses are alert, the noisy customers noisy, and all of Paris has stopped in at least once." Etienne (assisted by Antoine Bouterin) offers dishes that are both original and inexpensive. There is an abundance of food featuring mostly fresh vegetables (notably wild mushrooms). The Scrambled Eggs with Chanterelle Mushrooms, Artichoke Gâteau, Angler Cassoulet with Beans, Sea Bream with Ginger, Venison Steak with Whortleberries (Huckleberries), and Wild Duck with Tangerine Confit are only a few of the fine dishes served here. For dessert, try the Dark Chocolate Mousse with Strawberries.

Abbaye de Villeneuve

Route des Sables d'Olonne, 44400 Les Sorinières
Tel: (40) 54-70-25
Proprietor: Philippe Savry • Chef: Christian Heuze

Fruit Sabayon au Gratin

6 egg yolks
125 g (¼ lb) sugar
100 ml (3 oz) raspberry or strawberry brandy
250 ml (1 cup) double cream (whipping cream)
500 g (1 lb) fresh raspberries or strawberries

To prepare the sabayon: Mix the egg yolks, sugar, and fruit brandy together in a bowl, then whisk the mixture in a bain-marie* over boiling water. Turn off the heat and continue whisking until the mixture is cold.

Whip the cream until it just holds soft peaks and fold it into the sabayon.

Divide the sabayon among 6 dishes. Arrange the raspberries or strawberries decoratively on top. Place in the oven at 450°F (230°C) for a few minutes or until the sabayon is just browned lightly. Serve immediately.

Wine: *Côteaux du Layon or pink Champagne*   Serves: 6

An expression of nobility and refinement is this chateau-hotel dating from the 18th century. This is a historic location because this famous monastery was founded back in 1201 by the Duchess of Brittany. Situated in a meadow near the woods, **Abbaye de Villeneuve** is beautifully decorated and is still as peaceful as an abbey.

Christian Heuze is an extraordinary chef; salads become *feuilles du potager* (vegetable sheets) and scallops are presented as daisies. The *foie gras* comes with small turnip confit, the chicken is fricasseed with Calvados and apples, and the desserts are prepared to excellence by Christian. Do stop by the old abbey to rest a little and eat a little.

Lasserre

17, avenue Franklin-Roosevelt, 75008 Paris
Tel: 350-5343 and 359-6745
Proprietor: M. Lassere • Chef: M. Daniel

Heavenly Fruit Timbales

125 g (¼ lb) flour
125 g (¼ lb) sugar
1 egg
50 g (1¾ oz) butter, barely melted
¼ tsp vanilla extract
8 thin slices sponge cake
kirsch, as needed
8 scoops vanilla ice cream
1 kg (2¼ lb) fruits in season (strawberries, raspberries, etc.)
8 tbsp redcurrant jelly flavoured with kirsch
softly whipped cream, as needed

To prepare the pastry cups: Mix the flour, sugar, egg, barely melted butter, and vanilla together. Spread out 8 very thin circles of this batter on a buttered and floured baking sheet. Bake in the oven at 400°F (205°C) until the pastry is golden. Remove the pastry from the oven and immediately mould each circle into the shape of a dome by placing each one over the bottom of a bowl or ladle.

Fill the interior of the "dome" with a slice of sponge cake soaked in kirsch, a scoop of vanilla ice cream, and a selection of fruits in season. Glaze it with kirsch-flavoured blackcurrant jelly, decorate the inside edge of each cup with the cream, and serve.

Serves: 8

Behind the reputation of **Lasserre** is the man — René Lasserre, who began years ago as a simple cook and today owns one of the best restaurants in Paris. A restaurant of high elegance, a cuisine like the decor, and a clientele like the ambiance, all are exceptional. Lasserre is a fairy tale that has become a reality.

André Gide also agreed; Lasserre was his example of excellence when he said, "Here we have a true cuisine, total elegance, delicacy, and discretion." Lasserre is a star of restaurants recognized throughout the world.

Chez Mélanie

Place de l'Eglise, 29124 Riec-sur-Belon
Tel: (98) 06-91-05
Proprietor: Germaine Trellu • Chef: Yves Cornou

Here at **Chez Mélanie**, the cuisine preferred by Curnonsky shines. Germaine Trellu has kept up the tradition of fine classical cooking and service, and Yves Cornou, her chef, makes all the food taste exactly the way it should.

Today, Curnonsky is no longer here, however his favourite foods live on at Chez Mélanie, represented by such dishes as the Armorique Ham, Grilled or Flamed Lobster, the fine desserts (especially the famous Flan à l'Avoine, an oatmeal custard), and the fish that is as fresh as ever.

The high ceilings, marble columns, and granite walls of Chez Mélanie assure us that we are in Brittany.

Oatmeal Custard

150 g (5¼ oz) oats
1 litre (2 pt) milk
5 eggs
5 egg yolks
250 g (½ lb) sugar

To prepare the oatmeal: Boil the oats and milk together; remove from heat. Allow to steep for 20 minutes.

Mix the eggs, egg yolks, and sugar together. Stir the oatmeal into the egg and sugar mixture. Strain the mixture into custard dishes dusted with sugar. Bake in a bain-marie* in the oven at 300°F (150°C) for 20-30 minutes. Allow to cool, then turn out onto plates and serve.

Suggestion: Serve with freshly whipped cream and grilled almonds.

Le Moulin de l'Abbaye

24310 Brantôme
Tel: (53) 05-80-22
Proprietor/Chef: Régis Bulot

Régis and Catherine Bulot officially live in Courchevel where they own and manage their winter restaurant, Hôtel des Neiges de Courchevel, but they both wanted a chance to live in the sunshine for at least part of the year, so they opened **Le Moulin de l'Abbaye** in Brantôme. Here, they have transformed an old mill into a large and comfortable hotel-chateau.

In Périgord, how could one avoid the *cuisine Périgourdine?* Régis certainly doesn't — witness his Foie Gras with Confit of Duck and Cèpe Mushrooms, Veal Ribs with Garlic, Crayfish Salad, the delicious goats milk cheese, his goat cooked over an oak fire, and his Soft Fruits with Liqueur au Gratin.

Soft Fruits with Liqueur au Gratin

butter, as needed
1 apple
1 banana
200 g (7 oz) strawberries
200 g (7 oz) raspberries
400 g (14 oz) pastry cream*
4 tbsp any fruit liqueur
powdered sugar, as needed

Butter 4 individual gratin dishes. Cut the apple and banana into small dice and cover the bottom of the dishes with them. Arrange the strawberries and raspberries on top of this layer. Thin the pastry cream with the fruit liqueur. Cover the fruits carefully with the cream.

Sprinkle the dishes with powdered sugar and place under a very hot broiler for 2-3 minutes to brown them, then serve.

Serves: 4

Le Mas d'Artigny

06570 Saint-Paul-de-Vence
Tel: (93) 32-84-54
Proprietor: J.-C. Scordel • Chef: A. Dorshner

Wild Fruits au Gratin

100 ml (3 oz) fruit brandy
¼ litre (1 cup) double cream (whipping cream), whipped
¼ litre (1 cup) pastry cream*
200 g (7 oz) raspberries
200 g (7 oz) wild strawberries
125 g (¼ lb) icing (confectioners') sugar
few drops lemon juice
50 g (1¾ oz) blackberries
powdered sugar, as needed

Carefully mix the fruit brandy and the whipped cream into the pastry cream.

Purée ¾ of the raspberries, ¾ of the strawberries, and 40 g (1½ oz) blackberries and mix them together. Add the sugar, a few drops of lemon juice, and the remaining whole fruit, but reserve a few of each for decoration.

Fill 4 individual ramekins with a layer of cream, a layer of the fruit mixture, and a final layer of cream. Sprinkle with powdered sugar. Place the ramekins under a hot broiler for 1-2 minutes to brown the tops. Garnish with the reserved whole fruit and serve.

Wine: *Sauterne or Champagne*   Serves: 4

In this establishment, everything is luxurious, calm, and plush. J.-C. Scordel has created a restaurant of refinement and, with the ultimate in finesse, a cuisine worthy of **Le Mas d'Artigny**.

The Confit of Rabbit in Aspic is royal, and the Turbot with Choron Sauce is divine. The Wild Fruits au Gratin is a superb ending to a fabulous dinner.

This is *the* place in town to dine. Here you will discover one of the true stars of the culinary world.

Charvet

9, rue de la Cépède, 13100 Aix-en-Provence
Tel: (42) 38-43-82
Proprietors: Henri and Gérard Charvet • Chef: Henri Charvet

Almond Cream and Meringue Treat

2 egg whites
180 g (6⅓ oz) icing (confectioners') sugar
50 g (1¾ oz) powdered sugar
50 g (1¾ oz) softened butter
180 g (6⅓ oz) powdered almonds
1 egg
1 tbsp white rum
2 tbsp double cream (whipping cream)

To prepare the meringue: Whip egg whites until very stiff, then mix in 50 g (1¾ oz) icing sugar and all the powdered sugar. Line a baking sheet with greaseproof (wax) paper and pipe 3 circles of the mixture on it. Bake for 1 hour at 275°F (130°C). Detach the meringues from the paper and dry them for ¾ hour at 225°F (100°C).

To prepare the almond cream: Mix the softened butter, powdered almonds, and remaining icing sugar together well. Add egg, rum, and cream.

Assemble as follows: Meringue circle on the bottom, ½ the almond cream, meringue circle, remaining almond cream, meringue circle on top. Refrigerate for 1½ hours.

Suggestion: Sprinkle with icing sugar and toasted almonds before serving.

Wine: *Beaume de Provence*   Serves: 3

It is here in the Roman city of Aix-en-Provence that the Charvets, father and son, have found the ideal style that combines a refined cuisine with a bourgeois *maison*.

Henri Charvet is the chef who, with a blink of an eye, can create sumptuous regional specialities. The Saddle of Lamb with Small Cabbages and the Almond Cream and Meringue Treat are worthy of such gourmets from Provence as Mistral, Aubanel, and Daudet. The Seafood Platter in Chive Cream is also delicious, and there is also a fine wine cellar of local vintages.

Hubert Gasnier

7, boulevard Richard-Wallace, 72800 Puteaux
Tel: 506-3363
Proprietor/Chef: Hubert Gasnier

Prune Pastry

500 - 600 g (1 - 1⅓ lb) puff pastry dough*
80 g (2¾ oz) sugar
30 g (1 oz) flour
15 g (½ oz) salt
125 ml (1 cup) milk
6 eggs, beaten
20 - 25 pitted prunes, Armagnac preferred

Roll out the dough *very* thinly, then line a 23 cm (9 in) cake mould with the dough. Chill for 2 hours in the refrigerator.

In an earthenware bowl, mix 70 g (2½ oz) sugar, the flour, and the salt together. Gradually add the milk and mix to a smooth, creamy consistency. Stir in the beaten eggs.

Take the mould from the refrigerator and prick the pastry all over with a fork. Arrange the prunes on the bottom and pour the egg mixture on top. Bake at 425°F (220°C) for 40 - 45 minutes. A few minutes before the end of the cooking time, sprinkle with the remaining sugar to produce a caramelised finish. Serve warm.

Wine: *Champagne*   Serves: 8

It is difficult to talk about Hubert Gasnier or his cuisine. Both are so extraordinary that you think you're dreaming. The easiest thing to do is simply visit his restaurant in Puteaux and try the delectable Duck Confit with Cèpes Mushrooms Sautéed "Bordelais" Style, the fabulous Cassoulet à la Castlenaudray, or the tasty Prune Pastry.

The warm and cozy ambiance here will help you to relax and enjoy this man's fine talent for creating excellent dishes.

L'Espérance

89450 Saint-Pierre-sous-Vézelay
Tel: (86) 33-20-45
Proprietor/Chef: Marc Meneau

Viennese Pastry

175 g (6 oz) flour
275 g (9½ oz) sugar
125 g (4 oz) butter, melted
4 egg whites
500 ml (1 pt) double cream (whipping cream)
500 g (1 lb) raspberries

Mix the flour, 125 g (4 oz) sugar, melted butter, and egg whites together. Use this batter to form 16 very thin circles, 8 cm (3¼ in) in diameter, on a baking sheet. Bake the circles for approximately 10 minutes at 425°F (220°C). Remove them from the oven when they are golden brown. Place the circles on a cold, flat tray.

Whip the cream. Thoroughly crush the raspberries and sweeten them with the remaining sugar. Mix the cream and almost all of the raspberries together and place on each of the baked circles.

To assemble: Sandwich 4 circles together to make small layer cakes. Decorate each one by surrounding it with a little of the reserved sweetened raspberries, and serve.

Wine: *A sweet Sauterne or Vouvray Moelleux*   Serves: 4

Vézelay is situated on the edge of a hill in the shade of the celebrated Madeleine Cathedral. This is a famous tourist attraction and a perfect location for **L'Espérance**. In this bourgeois house, you will discover a winter garden and a summer night's delight.

The regional dishes served here are beautifully and originally prepared. The *foie gras* is accompanied by a fig compote, the spinach comes in a pie, and dishes such as Terrine of Calf's Head en Tortue and Pigeon Hotchpotch are enduring symbols of this traditional, regional cuisine at its best. There are also very fine desserts and Chablis wines.

Le Gambetta

41, rue Gambetta, 78800 Houilles
Tel: 968-5212
Proprietor/Chef: Francis Poirier

What was once a suburban bistro has been transformed into a first-class suburban restaurant through the hard work of Annie and Francis Poirier. The ambiance of **Le Gambetta** is warm and romantic. The cuisine is excellent, as prepared by Francis, who once worked for Les Troisgros and Michel Oliver.

Le Gambetta has the greatest respect for everything from the sea; Lobster Ragout with Girolle Mushrooms, Salmon with Mustard Seeds, and Langoustine Mousseline with Avocado Cream Sauce are only a few examples. The Duck in Cider with Corn is also a fine dish. For dessert, try the Dark Chocolate Mousse with Orange Preserves, Hot Apple Tart with Almond Cream, or the Chestnut Soufflé with Cocoa Sauce. Everything here is delightful and tasty.

Chestnut Soufflé with Cocoa Sauce

75 g (2½ oz) blanched chestnuts
1.1 kg (2½ lb) sugar
75 g (2½ oz) apple or apricot jelly
½ litre (1 pt) water
140 g (5 oz) glucose
8 eggs, separated
250 ml (½ pt) double cream (whipping cream), whipped
2 tbsp rum
300 g (10½ oz) glazed chestnuts (sold as *marrons glacés*)
125 g (¼ lb) powdered cocoa
½ litre (1 pt) milk
200 g (7 oz) grated cocoa

To prepare *pâté de marrons* (chestnut candy): Pound the blanched chestnuts in a mortar. Mix with 75 g (2½ oz) sugar, cooked to the ball stage.* Mix with jelly and roll out thinly on a baking sheet. Place in the oven at 275°F (135°C) until dry.

To prepare the syrup: Mix 300 g (10½ oz) sugar, ½ the water, and 40 g (1½ oz) glucose together and then heat it. Beat 4 egg whites until stiff. Pour the syrup over the egg whites in the bowl of a mixer and keep mixing until cool.

Boil the remaining water, 600 g (1⅓ lb) sugar, and remaining glucose together. Beat remaining 4 egg whites until stiff. Pour this syrup over the egg whites in the mixing bowl and let turn until cool.

Slowly mix the *pâté de marrons*, the 2 egg white mixtures, the rum, and the whipped cream together. Line 8 ramekins with greaseproof (wax) paper, fill them with this mixture, and sprinkle all with cocoa powder. Freeze for 2 hours. Unmould, remove paper, and place equal amounts of glazed chestnuts on each.

To prepare cocoa sauce: In a saucepan, bring the milk and grated cocoa to a boil. Remove from heat and let soak for 10 minutes. Whisk the egg yolks and remaining sugar together for 5 minutes. Return saucepan to heat and bring to a boil. While whisking, pour some of the hot mixture over the egg yolk mixture, then pour all back into the saucepan and, over low heat, fold together with a spatula. *This mixture must not boil.* Let cool.

Cover each unmoulded mixture with the sauce and serve.

Serves: 8

Le Royal Monceau

35 – 39, avenue Hoche, 75008 Paris
Tel: 561-9800
Proprietor: Philippe Serre • Chef: Hervé Plisson

Orange Soufflé

1 litre (2 pt) milk
6 - 8 oranges
1 vanilla pod, grated
250 g (½ lb) powdered sugar
50 g (1¾ oz) flour
30 g (1 oz) cornstarch
30 g (1 oz) whole wheat flour
10 eggs, separated
100 ml (3 oz) curaçao

To prepare the pastry cream: Bring the milk and the grated vanilla to a boil. Mix the sugar, flour, cornstarch, whole wheat flour, and 8 egg yolks together with a spatula. Pour in the boiling milk. Stir well, then pour back into the saucepan the milk was boiled in and return to the stove. Bring mixture just to the boiling point, but do not allow to boil.

Remove the pulp from the oranges without spoiling the skin. (Reserve 6 - 8 shells.) Squeeze the juice from the pulp into the pastry cream. Add the curaçao and 2 remaining egg yolks to the pastry cream. Beat the egg whites until stiff and fold into the pastry cream.

Fill the reserved orange shells with the cream mixture and bake in the oven at 325°F (160°C) for 15 minutes.

Wine: *Château d'Yquem, 1961*   Serves: 6 - 8

During a gay and frolicsome bygone era, Lucien Serre opened his beautiful restaurant, which he decorated with authentic Eastern accessories. He, then, went on to manage it for 40 years with much success.

His son, Philippe, has since taken over his father's restaurant and appears to have had just as much success. Hervé Plisson is the chef, and he excels in the preparation of elaborate cuisine such as Roast Angler with Pink Peppercorns, Veal Knuckle with Lemon, and Orange Soufflé Tart (along with an assortment of other delicate desserts).

Prunier Traktir

16, avenue Victor-Hugo, 75116 Paris
Tel: 500-8912
Proprietor: Claude Barnagaud Prunier • Chef: Robert Thaissen

Orange Soufflé "Côte d'Azur"

4 large oranges
200 g (7 oz) sugar
sugar syrup,* as needed
100 ml (3 oz) curaçao
4 tbsp pastry cream*
3 egg whites
butter, as needed
2 tbsp icing (confectioners') sugar

Gently remove the orange segments from their skins. Separate the segments and remove seeds and pith. Dice. Place the diced segments on a plate and coat generously with sugar. Put in a warm oven and leave until oranges soak up all the sugar.

Cut the peels into thin julienne slices. Blanch them in boiling water. Rinse thoroughly, then cook until no more liquid is left in them. Add enough syrup to cover the peel. Cook until all liquid evaporates. Add the curaçao.

Mix the cooked orange peel and the orange dice with the pastry cream. Beat the egg whites until stiff, then add to the orange and cream mixture. Fill 4 buttered soufflé moulds with the new mixture. Cook for 20 - 30 minutes in the oven at 275°F (135°C). Sprinkle with icing sugar just before serving.

Wine: *Sauterne*   Serves: 4

"Everything that comes from the sea is in the kingdom of Prunier Traktir," says the owner, Claude Barnagaud Prunier, of this very exclusive and very famous restaurant, which specialises in delicacies from the sea.

Prunier Traktier, also a beautiful restaurant, is located in the sophisticated 16th *arrondissement* (district) of Paris. The building is an excellent example of mid - 1920s architecture, the era when it was built.

M. Barnagaud Prunier and his chef, Robert Thaissen, have nicely blended their talents to offer traditional service of classic cuisine that aptly matches the milieu. You must try the Scallops in Champagne, the "Sunstroke" Tart, and the Orange Soufflé "Côte d'Azur."

La Coquille

6, rue du Débarcadère, 75017 Paris
Tel: 380-2595
Proprietor: Paul Blache • Chef: Jean-Claude Renault

La Coquille is as quaint and enchanting as ever. Since 1898, La Coquille, a perennial establishment and a favourite of Curnonsky, has been pleasing the discriminating gourmets of Paris.

Since 1970, Paul Blache has been managing La Coquille. He has altered the atmosphere a bit, but everything else has remained unchanged. Jean-Claude Renault definitely proves his talent for creating fabulous dishes, especially the Scallops au Naturel, Frogs Legs in a Pan, Lobster Américaine, Black Pudding with Two Purées, Braised Duck with Burgundy Wine, Chicken Fricassee with Morel Mushrooms and Cream, and to finish any meal, the Praline Soufflé. These are all a gourmet's delight.

Praline Soufflé

200 g (7 oz) pralines
¼ litre (1 cup) warm pastry cream* made with flour and 4 egg yolks
2 egg yolks
6 egg whites, stiffly beaten
butter and sugar, as needed
100 ml (3 oz) kirsch

Crush or grind the pralines to a powder. Mix 4 tbsp of the pralines into the warm pastry cream. Stir in the 2 egg yolks. Fold in the 6 stiffly beaten egg whites.

Pour the mixture into a buttered and sugared soufflé dish. Sprinkle the top with the remaining powdered pralines (this will form the crust when the soufflé is cooked). Cook in the oven for 10 - 15 minutes at 325°F (160°C). Sprinkle with kirsch and serve.

Serves: 4

La Réserve de Beaulieu

06310 Beaulieu-sur-Mer
Tel: (93) 01-00-01
Proprietor: Henri Maria • Chef: Gilbert Picard

Beaulieu has just celebrated the centennial anniversary of this illustrious restaurant, "a place," wrote an admirer, "where one should arrive only by the Blue Train." This means the elegance and sophisticated patronage of this establishment is incomparable. The restaurant faces the sea and has the most panoramic view of the Mediterranean possible.

The great hôtelière, M. Potfler has made La Réserve de Beaulieu one of the finest establishments on the Côte d'Azur. Assisted by Gilbert Picard, the chef, Henri Maria offers a stunning bilingual menu, epitomizing classicism. Dinner is served on a patrician terrace. Here you will enjoy superb Foie Gras in Brioche, Fillet of Beef in Chervil, Scallops in Whisky Velouté, and Hot Raspberry Soufflé, among other delicacies.

Hot Raspbery Soufflé

8 egg yolks
1 dash kirsch
300 g (10½ oz) sugar
8 egg whites
butter, as needed
500 g (1 lb) raspberries
125 g (¼ lb) génoise,* soaked in kirsch

Whisk the egg yolks, kirsch, and sugar together until mixture is very pale and thick. Beat the egg whites until stiff, then fold into the yolk mixture.

Butter a soufflé mould well. Fill the mould as follows: A layer of egg mixture, a layer of génoise, a layer of whole raspberries. Repeat as necessary until all ingredients are used, but finish with a layer of egg mixture. Bake in the oven at 400°F (205°C) for 15 - 20 minutes.

Suggestion: Serve with icing (confectioners') sugar and raspberry purée on the side.

Wine: *Pink Champagne or Sauterne*

Serves: 4

L'Escale

Promenade du Pont, 13 Carry-Le-Rouet
Tel: (47) 45-00-47
Proprietor: S.A. Charles Bérot • Chef: Gérard Clor

Iced Raspberry Soufflé

400 g (14 oz) fresh raspberries
400 g (7 oz) sugar, and as needed
½ litre (1 pt) double cream (whipping cream), softly whipped
2 egg whites

Sort and clean the raspberries. Keep the finest on one side to decorate the soufflé. Crush and sieve the remainder, then mix with 400 g (7 oz) sugar. Fold in the whipped cream.

Beat the egg whites until very stiff, adding a little sugar towards the end of the process. Fold them carefully into the raspberry mixture.

Line the edge of a soufflé dish with greaseproof (wax) paper so the paper raises the height of the sides by 5-7 cm (2-2¾ in). Fill the mould with the raspberry and cream mixture. Freeze for at least 6 hours.

When the soufflé is set, remove the paper and decorate with the reserved whole raspberries.

Suggestion: Serve with puréed fresh raspberries.

Serves: 6

Carry-Le-Rouet is Charles Bérot's native town. For the past 25 years, he has been reigning over this charming little restaurant. **L'Escale** is a beautiful little house facing the port of Provence, which guarantees that the freshest fish are available here. A flowered terrace and a gracious welcome from Mme. Bérot greet you as you enter.

To assist him in his business, Charles found Gérard Clor, a successful associate with a lot of class. Gérard's cuisine would be the envy of the people of Marseilles if it weren't for the fact that Carry-Le-Rouet is close enough for them to travel to easily and taste the delicious Fish Soup, Clam Cassoulette, Gâteau of Lamb, and Iced Raspberry Soufflé. At L'Escale, the gentle blue decor of the tables is as appeasing as the blue Mediterranean sky.

Grill de l'Hôtel de Paris

Place du Casino, Monte Carlo, Monaco
Tel: (93) 50-80-80
Proprietor: Société des Bains de Mer • Chef: Sébastien Bonsignore

Tangerine Soufflé

100 ml (3 oz) milk
40 g (1½ oz) sugar
30 g (1 oz) flour
4 egg yolks
3 egg whites, stiffly beaten
zest* of 3 tangerines, grated
juice of 3 tangerines
powdered sugar, as needed

Bring the milk to a boil. Mix the sugar, flour, and egg yolks together. Gradually stir the boiling milk into the mixture. Put into a saucepan on the stove and cook gently for 2 minutes, then let cool.

While the cream is cooling, softly beat the egg whites. Stir the grated tangerine zest and the tangerine juice into the cooled cream. Gradually fold in the egg whites with a wooden spatula.

Butter the sides of a soufflé mould and sprinkle with powdered sugar. Fill the mould up to the top with the soufflé mixture and bake for 15-18 minutes at 475°F (250°C). Sprinkle the cooked soufflé with powdered sugar and serve.

Serves: 4

What could be more breathtaking than dining at the top of **L'Hôtel de Paris**, with its panoramic view of Monaco, the palace, the casino, and, on the horizon, the gorgeous blue Mediterannean?

Sébastien Bonsignore began to coordinate the cuisine here in 1946 and has reigned at L'Hôtel de Paris ever since.

L'Hôtel de Paris is truly a monument to luxury and beauty, and Sébastien continues to maintain these traditions.

The Langoustines in String, the Bouillabaisse in Aspic, the Loin of Lamb, and the numerous desserts are but a few of the many sumptuous foods Sébastien offers.

Hostellerie de Pont-Sainte-Marie

10150 Pont-Sainte-Marie
Tel: (25) 81-13-09
Proprietor/Chef: Jean-Paul Duquesnay

Beyond the meadows, at the edge of Troyes, and in the shade of the Pont-Sainte-Marie Church, you will discover the **Hostellerie de Pont-Sainte-Marie**. On the other side of the white shutters, seated at a very refined table, Jean-Paul Duquesnay demonstrates his arts; the art of greeting you and serving dishes that he has prepared with love and inspiration are Jean-Paul's most admirable talents.

If you agree, you will stay and try the fresh vegetables, shrimp, baby rabbit, tart, and everything else Jean-Paul will tempt you with.

Apple Tart

320 g (¾ lb) puff pastry dough*
4 apples, peeled and finely sliced
125 g (¼ lb) icing (confectioners') sugar
4 tsp honey

Roll out 4 pieces of puff pastry dough, each to the size and shape of a dessert plate (about 20 cm or 8 in). Prick the circles with a fork. Arrange the sliced apples on each circle and sprinkle with sugar.

Bake the tart in the oven at 425-450°F (220-230°C) for 18-20 minutes. Spread a spoonful of honey over each tart 5 minutes before the end of the cooking time. Serve hot.

Wine: *Champagne*   Serves: 4

Château de Teildras

Cheffes, 49330 Châteauneuf-sur-Sarthe
Tel: (41) 42-61-08
Proprietor/Chef: Mme. De Bernard du Breil

There is a feeling of looking back into time here. This chateau, built in 1542, has been in the same family since the 17th century. Madame the Countess du Breil resides in this castle and is also the chef. What an aroma her guinea chick has, and what flavour there is in the Pike Perch Scallops with Sorrel!

Steeped in discreet charm and elegance, this lordly manor could almost be overwhelming, but don't be intimidated. Rent a room and stay for a while so that you may enjoy the many marvels the chateau has to offer while discovering the fabulous cuisine.

Brown Sugar Tart

500 g (1 lb) short pastry*
200 g (7 oz) soft brown sugar
50 g (1¾ oz) powdered almonds
50 g (1¾ oz) butter
2 tbsp double cream (whipping cream)
2 egg yolks

Line a 23 cm (9 in) pie dish with short pastry and bake it at 400°F (205°C) for 8-9 minutes.

Mix the sugar, powdered almonds, butter, and cream in a saucepan. Melt these ingredients very gently. Stir in the egg yolks at the last minute.

Fill the pie crust with the cream and bake it for 20 minutes at 350°F (175°C). Serve warm.

Serves: 6

Benoît

20, rue Saint-Martin, 75004 Paris
Tel: 272-2576
Proprietor/Chef: Michel Petit

In 1912, Benoît Matray, a native of Saint-Jean-d'Ardières, in Beaujolais, opened his bistro near the famous Halles de Paris (the old marketplace). A person of vitality and dynamic spirit, he quickly brought **Benoît** to success. Before the war, we could see Galtier-Boissière, accompanied by Henry Béraud, dining on his favourite dish — a dozen Portuguese oysters, accompanied by Bouzy champenois wine.

In 1959, Michel Petit, Benoît's grandson, acquired Benoît. He enlarged it, but kept the decor and the cuisine the same. The Hot Sausage Salad with Lard, Black Pudding with Apples, Calf's Tongue "Verdurette," Pickled Lentils, and Pig's Ear and Tail Fried in Bread Crumbs have remained a Benoît tradition, and I think the Pear Tart is Michel's best dessert.

Pear Tart

4 eggs
225 g (7¾ oz) sugar
pinch of salt
280 g (9¾ oz) flour
250 g (½ lb) butter
150 g (5¼ oz) ground almonds
1 tbsp rum
vanilla-flavoured sugar,* to taste
4 pears, peeled and sliced
2 tbsp apricot jam

To prepare the pastry: Beat 2 eggs, 100 g (3½ oz) sugar, and a pinch of salt together in a bowl. Add 250 g (½ lb) flour, then add ½ the butter, piece by piece. Line a pie dish with the dough. Bake it in the oven for 25 minutes at 375°F (190°C).

To prepare the almond cream: Mix all the remaining ingredients except the pears and jam with a spatula in a bowl until they are blended.

When the pastry shell is cooked, garnish it with pear slices, glaze it with jam, and cover all with almond cream. Bake until golden (10 - 15 minutes) in the oven at 425°F (220°C). Serve cold.

Serves: 6 - 8

Le Relais

12, avenue George V, 75008 Paris
Tel: 723-3958
Proprietor: Gérard Lucien • Chef: Maurice Lorang

At **Le Relais** in the evening, at the bar, you might well meet up with the most attractive young ladies from Alain Bernadin's Crazy Horse Saloon bar next door. At noon, businessmen hurry to get a table here. And in the squeeze of the midday rush or the more relaxed atmosphere of the evening, the decor and menu here are most pleasing — all thanks to Christiane (and with good reason, since she is the niece of Marinette who runs La Petite Tour) and Maurice Lorang, the chef from Alsace.

May I say that each time I come here I simply cannot resist the Scallop of Veal "Holstein" Style? It's a dish of somewhat vague origins, which is rarely to be found on menus. Accompanied by fried potatoes, it really is delicious! The pastries are also excellent . . . especially the Prune Tart.

Prune Tart

500 g (1 lb) large prunes, stones removed
1 litre (2 pt) tea
100 ml (3 oz) rum or liqueur
500 g (1 lb) flour, and as needed
8 egg yolks
50 - 70 ml (1½ - 2 oz) water
50 g (1¾ oz) sugar, and as needed
pinch of salt
500 g (1 lb) butter, and as needed
6 tbsp double cream (whipping cream)

Soak the prunes in the tea and rum overnight.

To prepare the dough: Shape the flour on a pastry board into the shape of a flattened cone, then knead in 2 egg yolks, a little water, sugar, and the butter. Knead thoroughly, adding a little flour to prevent the dough from sticking to the board if necessary. Roll out the dough with a rolling pin and set ⅓ of it aside.

Butter a tart pan and place ⅔ of the pastry dough in it. Flatten by doubling the edges around the tin. Place the prunes tightly together in the tin. Roll out the remaining ⅓ dough and cut out 1 cm (½ in) thick strips.

Beat the remaining 6 egg yolks with the cream and sugar, to taste, in a separate bowl (keep the mixture runny), then pour onto the prunes.

Place the strips of pastry dough on top of the prunes in a crisscross pattern, then bake in the oven at 375°F (190°C) for about 30 minutes.

Serves: 6 - 8

Appendix

Glossary

al dente

Slightly undercooked, firm to the touch, but not soft. Usually applies to cooking pasta, rice, and vegetables.

Américaine sauce

A sauce for fish, shellfish, and eggs. To prepare enough for 4 people: Reduce the pan drippings from 1 kg (2¼ lb) lobster until thick. Pound lobster coral and liver together, add to the reduced drippings, and whisk until smooth over high heat. Remove pan from heat, whisk in 125 g (4 oz) butter (a piece at a time), then add pepper to taste and a dash of lemon juice. *Variations* — Add cognac, shallots, garlic, tarragon, chervil, etc. to taste.

Anglaise sauce

A mixture used to prepare fish or meat that is to be coated with bread crumbs before cooking. Made by mixing 2 eggs, 1 tbsp oil, 125 ml (½ cup) water, and salt and pepper (to taste) together, then reducing it gently to the desired consistency.

auberge

An inn, public-house, or tavern.

bain-marie

A large vessel filled with hot water in which other pans can be placed. Water should come no more than halfway up the sides of the other pans. Used over low heat on the stove or in the oven. Transfer of heat from hot water to other pans heats delicate foods gently.

Béarnaise sauce

A famous sauce served with broiled and grilled meats. To prepare about 400 ml (1½ cups): Blend 125 ml (½ cup) white wine, 2 tbsp tarragon vinegar, 2 finely chopped shallots, ½ clove finely chopped garlic, and a sprig each of tarragon, chervil, and parsley together in a saucepan and reduce by half. Place saucepan in a bain-marie* and beat in 3 egg yolks. Gradually whisk in 150 g (5¼ oz) softened butter and continue to whisk until mixture reaches sauce consistency. Do not boil.

Béchamel sauce

A basic cream sauce used for vegetables and fish and as a base for other sauces. To prepare about ½ litre (2 cups): Melt 30 g (1 oz) butter in a saucepan. Add 40 g (1½ oz) flour. Mix well and cook gently for 2 minutes, whisking constantly. Gradually add ½ litre (2 cups) milk, reduce heat, and simmer gently for 15 minutes, stirring occasionally. Strain through a fine sieve, then season with salt and pepper to taste and add a pinch of nutmeg. Sauce will keep refrigerated for 10 days or frozen for about 3 months.

bistro / bistrot

A pub.

Glossary

blanch

To boil quickly in water, then rinse in cold water to tenderize, fix colour, and remove strong flavours.

blind bake

To bake a pie crust or other crust shell without its final filling.

bouquet garni

Aromatic herbs, usually parsley, thyme, and a bay leaf in proportions to taste, that are tied together in a porous cloth (muslin or cheesecloth). If fresh herbs are used, the stems may be tied together with a string and then used.

Brillat-Savarin, Jean Anthelme

A French politician and gastronome born in 1755 who wrote *La Physiologie du Goût,* published just before his death in 1826.

brut

Unsweetened, very dry.

caramelise

To dissolve sugar slowly in water and then boil steadily without stirring until a dark brown colour is reached. (Also, see **stages of sugar**.)

chantilly cream

Double cream (whipping cream) beaten to the consistency of mousse (soft peaks), then sweetened and flavoured with vanilla, orange liqueur, sugar, etc. to taste.

chestnut purée

A mixture made by peeling chestnuts, steaming them, then puréeing them in a blender.

chicken stock

A broth made from chicken parts and used for soups, sauces, etc. To prepare 800 ml (about 3 cups): Combine 1 stalk chopped celery, 1 chopped carrot, 1 chopped onion, 450 g (1 lb) chicken parts (backs, necks, wings, feet, gizzards), 6 peppercorns, and 125 ml (½ cup) chopped mushrooms in a heavy pan. Add 1.5 litres (6 cups) cold water and bring slowly to a boil. Reduce the heat and simmer for 2½ - 3 hours or until reduced by half, stirring occasionally. Let cool. Strain when cold, then season with salt to taste when ready to use. For **duck stock** or **guinea fowl stock**, use same recipe, but use duck or guinea fowl parts.

choux paste / choux pastry

Cream puff pastry. To prepare ½ litre (2 cups): Blend 250 ml (1 cup) water, 6 tbsp butter in small pieces, 1 tsp salt, ⅛ tsp pepper, and a pinch of nutmeg together in a saucepan. Bring to a boil, then remove from heat. Beat in 250 ml (1 cup) sifted flour, then beat in 4 eggs, one at a time. *Variation —* For dessert dough, use 1 tsp sugar and a pinch of salt instead of 1 tsp salt.

concasse

Coarsely chopped or shredded. Usually refers to tomatoes; tomatoes should be peeled, then squeezed gently to remove the seeds before being chopped.

court bouillon

A flavoured broth in which meat, fish, or vegetables are cooked. To prepare **vinegar court bouillon**: Combine 1 litre (2 pt) water, 125 ml (½ cup) vinegar, 1 sliced carrot, 2 small onions stuck with cloves, 1 bouquet garni,* and salt and pepper to taste in a large pan. Boil for 15 - 20 minutes, then simmer until ready for use. *Variations* — To prepare **white wine court bouillon**: as above, but replace vinegar with 250 ml (1 cup) dry white wine. To prepare **red wine court bouillon**: as above, but replace vinegar with 500 ml (2 cups) red wine.

cream

Recipes in this book call for double cream or whipping cream. For an extra rich liquid comparable to the French *crème fraîche,* heat 250 ml (1 cup) double cream (whipping cream) through, then mix in 1 tbsp buttermilk, pour into a glass and allow to stand at room temperature for 12 hours. Will keep for several days covered in the refrigerator.

crepe batter

To prepare enough batter for 12 crepes: Blend 250 g (½ lb) flour, 3 eggs, 1 tbsp oil, and a pinch of salt together in a bowl. Add ½ litre (1 pt) milk. Mix well. Let rest for 1 hour before using.

crepes

Heat a 10 - 12 cm (4 - 5 in) skillet, then grease it with a few drops of oil or butter. Add about 2 tbsp crepe batter.* Tip the skillet so the batter spreads over the bottom. (Crepe should be paper thin; pour off any excess batter.) Cook over moderate heat for about 1 minute or until brown on 1 side. Turn over and cook another minute or until brown. Slide the finished crepe onto a plate. Continue until all batter is used.

Curnonsky

A French gastronomer, born Maurice-Edmond Sailland in 1872. Awarded the name "Prince of Gastronomers" in a French newspaper contest. After his death in 1956, it was decided that no one else would ever be given that title.

deglaze

To dissolve the caramelised juices remaining at the bottom of a pan. Remove all excess fat from the pan, add stock, vinegar, or wine, and heat with the sediment remaining.

duck stock

See **chicken stock**.

fine herbs

See **herbs**.

Glossary

fish fumet/stock
>A strong, flavoured broth used for cooking and as a base for sauces. To prepare about 675 ml (2½ cups): Melt 3 tbsp butter in a saucepan. Add 500 - 600 g (1 - 1⅓ lb) fish bones and trimmings (skin, heads, tails, etc.), 1 chopped carrot, 1 chopped onion, 4 tbsp parsley, and 2 stalks chopped celery. Cover and cook gently for 7 - 10 minutes. Add 500 ml (2 cups) water, 1 bouquet garni,* 250 ml (1 cup) white wine or 2 tbsp vinegar, 3 - 6 crushed peppercorns, and salt to taste. Cook gently, still covered, for 30 minutes, then strain and use as needed.

foie gras
>The liver of a goose or duck; chicken liver may be substituted.

fumet
>See **fish fumet**.

génoise
>A sponge cake mixture. Whisk 4 eggs and 125 g (¼ lb) sugar together in a saucepan over low heat. When mixture becomes thick and pale, remove from heat. Fold in 100 g (3½ oz) flour and 75 g (2¾ oz) softened butter. Pour mixture into a buttered 23 cm (9 in) mould and bake at 350°F (175°C) for 30 - 35 minutes.

gratin
>To brown the top of a dish under a hot broiler. Often, bread crumbs or grated cheese are sprinkled on the top of the dish first.

guinea fowl stock
>See **chicken stock**.

herbs
>Aromatic plants used for flavouring and as garniture. Usually, 2 tbsp fresh herbs equals 1 tbsp crushed, dried herbs or 2 tsp pulverized herbs, but adjustments according to taste are best. **Fine herbs** traditionally means a mixture of any herbs, but usually is a combination of chopped chives, parsley, chervil, and tarragon to taste.

Hollandaise sauce
>A butter sauce for fish, eggs, and vegetables. To prepare 250 ml (1 cup): Melt 125 ml (½ cup) butter over low heat in a saucepan. In a blender or food processor, blend 3 egg yolks, 2 tbsp lemon juice, 1 tbsp sherry (optional), ¼ tsp salt, and a pinch of white pepper. While machine is still on, slowly add melted butter and continue to blend until mixture thickens. Pour into a sauceboat and let set a few minutes to finish thickening. Serve warm.

hostellerie
>An inn.

hôtellerie

An inn, hotel, or hostelry.

John Dory

A European marine fish, also called "golden haddock," that has a firm, white flesh and a delicate flavour that rivals turbot and sole. Porgy or scup can be used for John Dory recipes.

julienne

To cut vegetables lengthwise into matchstick shapes, about 3 mm (⅛ in) thick.

mirepoix

Vegetables cut into 1 cm (½ in) dice and used in sauces and when braising. Usually, onions, carrots, celery, leeks, and turnips.

nap

To coat thinly with a gravy or sauce.

pare / trim

To cut into a regular shape or to remove unwanted parts such as fat or gristle.

pastry cream

A custard filling, also called *crème pâtissière*. To prepare about 675 ml (2½ cups): Scald ½ litre (2 cups) milk with 1 vanilla bean or 2 drops vanilla essence or extract. Let steep. Combine 60 g (⅔ cup) flour, 80 g (1 cup) sugar, 2 well-beaten whole eggs and 2 egg yolks, and a pinch of salt in a thick-bottomed pan. Remove the vanilla bean from the scalded milk and slowly stir the scalded milk into the egg mixture. On moderately high heat, bring the mixture to a boil, whisking constantly to beat out the lumps. Put heat on low and continue to beat and cook for 2 - 3 minutes. Take pan from heat and let cool, stirring occasionally. Pastry cream will keep for 1 week in the refrigerator or it can be frozen.

pâte

Paste, dough, or batter; pastry. Also refers to pasta.

pâté / terrine

A mixture of ground meats, liver, game, etc. that has been seasoned and baked. If the mixture is baked in a pastry crust, it is called a pâté. If it is baked in a dish lined with pork or bacon fat, it is called a terrine. (Also, *see* **terrine**.)

Glossary

Périgourdine / Périgueux sauce

A classic Madeira sauce made with truffles and served with meats. To prepare about 125 ml (½ cup): Lightly sauté 2 tbsp diced truffles in butter, then season with salt and pepper to taste. Remove from pan. Add 2 tbsp Madeira wine to the pan juices, then stir in 250 ml (1 cup) concentrated brown stock or beef bouillon. Simmer for 5 minutes then strain. Return truffles to the pan. Keep hot but do not boil. If sauce becomes too thick, add more wine. *Variation* — If truffles are sliced into thick round pieces, this is called Périgourdine sauce.

poach

To cook gently by submerging in water or seasoned liquid that is simmering, but not boiling. Used for cooking fish, fruit, vegetables, and eggs.

Poivrade sauce

A spicy pepper sauce served with meats. To prepare about 250 ml (1 cup): Combine 2 tbsp wine vinegar with 125 ml (½ cup) red wine. Add 2 diced shallots, 1 bay leaf, and 15 peppercorns. Simmer until reduced by half. Strain and mix the liquid into 250 ml (1 cup) hot brown sauce or concentrated beef bouillon. Season to taste with cayenne pepper, white pepper, and freshly ground black pepper; sauce should be spicy.

pot-au-feu

A broth made from meat and vegetables that is served in the pot in which it was made. The meat and vegetables are served separately with a choice of sauces such as cream sauce with mustard or mayonnaise flavoured with herbs on the side. The broth is served as a clear soup.

provincial

An adjective used to describe the cuisine, architecture, customs, etc. of the different regions or provinces of France. It does *not* mean oafish, limited, or countrified.

puff pastry dough

A flaky pastry, also called *feuilletage,* in which the layers of butter are kept separate from the layers of dough. Dough can be purchased or it can be prepared as follows. To prepare about 750 g (2½ lb) dough: Mound 500 g (1 lb) sifted flour on a board and make a well in the centre. Put 1½ tsp salt and about ⅓ litre (1¼ cups) water in the well. Mix and knead the mixture until a smooth and elastic dough is formed. Form into a ball and let stand 25 minutes in a cool place. Roll out the dough to 20 cm (8 in) square. Knead 500 g (1 lb) butter on a lightly floured board, then flatten and shape to slightly smaller than half the dough. Place the butter "pad" on ½ the dough, fold the remaining dough over, and seal the edges of the dough together to make a pouch. On a floured surface, roll the pouch with a rolling pin to about 60 cm (24 in) long by 20 cm (8 in) wide by 15 mm (½ in) thick. Fold the rectangle into thirds, wrap in foil, and chill for 30 minutes. Repeat this process 5 times (with 30 minute rests in between), but be sure to turn the dough with each rolling so the length is in front of you (½ turn to the right). Refrigerate until needed.

purée

To mash solid foods (meat, fish, vegetables, fruit) in a mortar, food processor, or blender or to press it through a sieve. The resulting substance is called a purée.

reduce

To thicken by evaporation, usually in a saucepan over low heat. This concentrates the flavour.

relais

A relay station or way station; often an inn on a thoroughfare between towns.

saddle

For mutton, lamb, or venison: the part of the hindquarters extending from the last ribs to the leg on each side. For rabbit and hare: the fleshy part extending from the base of the shoulder to the tail; the part remaining after removing the head, legs, ribs, and tail.

sauce

A liquid seasoning for food used to enhance flavour and to act as a binder. For recipes, see individual sauce entries (**Américaine**, **Béchamel**, **Poivrade**, etc.).

Saupiquet sauce

A wine sauce, often thickened with croutons, that is served with hare and game fowl. See recipes on pages 66, 67, and 68 for variations.

sauté

To cook and brown a small quantity of food in very hot fat, oil, butter, or a combination of these, in a frying pan or skillet. The food must be absolutely dry before being put into the pan, and it must not be crowded in the pan.

scallops, whole

If scallops are purchased in the shell, they must be washed and scrubbed thoroughly. To open: Place in the oven at 300°F (150°C) on a baking tray, deep shell side down, until they open. The hinge muscle is the kernel referred to in the recipes. The bean-like material is the coral.

short pastry

A short crust pastry, also called *pâte brisée,* used for pies, tarts, and turnovers. To prepare enough for one 23 cm (9 in) pie shell: Rapidly mix together 200 g (7 oz) sifted flour, a pinch of salt, 1 tbsp oil, 125 g (4 oz) butter in small pieces, and 3 - 4 tbsp water. Knead rapidly with the palm of the hand, then refrigerate overnight. Bake at 400°F (205°C) for 8 - 9 minutes to set the pastry or for 15 - 20 minutes to cook completely.

stock

The liquid obtained by slowly simmering the juices derived from various foods as they cook; used as the base for soups and sauces. For recipes, see **fish fumet / stock**, **chicken stock**, and **veal stock**.

Glossary

sugar, stages of

There are a number of desired degrees of consistency that can be accurately obtained by boiling sugar. Begin by preparing **sugar syrup**: Combine 2 parts sugar with 1 part water and dissolve in a saucepan over medium heat. Bring solution to a boil and skim the impurities as they rise to the surface, but do not stir. When small bubbles, close together, appear, the water has evaporated and the sugar has begun to cook.

When the temperature on a candy thermometer reads 214 - 217°F (101 - 103°C), the sugar has reached the **thread stage**. To test, put a small amount of sugar (1 tsp) in cold water, then put the cooled sugar between the thumb and forefinger and pull apart. Short or long threads will appear.

To reach the **ball stage**, boil the syrup until the temperature is 241 - 250°F (116 - 121°C). To test, put ½ tsp sugar into cold water, then roll cooled sugar between thumb and forefinger and it should form a ball.

If the syrup continues to boil, it will reach the **caramel stage** at 356°F (180°C).

sugar syrup

See **stages of sugar**.

sugar, vanilla-flavoured

Break a vanilla pod into thirds, place these into a jar of sugar, close tightly, and leave for several weeks before using.

sweat

To cook gently until the food, usually vegetables, exudes juice.

terrine

A deep, earthenware dish with a cover. Also, the food cooked in such a dish; see **pâté**.

tournedos

Small, but fairly thick, slices cut from the fillet or tenderloin.

veal stock

A broth made from veal knuckles or cut up pieces of veal and used for soups, sauces, etc. To prepare 2 litres (about 2 qt): Blanch 2 kg (4½ lb) veal knuckles and cut off meat (or use 1 kg / 2¼ lb browned veal cut in pieces and its drippings). Add meat and bones to 4 litres (1 gal) cold water. Add 1 diced carrot, 3 stalks diced celery, 1 bouquet garni,* 8 peppercorns, 1 diced onion, 6 cloves, and 1 tbsp salt or to taste. Bring to a boil, reduce heat immediately, and let simmer 2½ - 3 hours or until reduced by half. Strain, cool, and refrigerate until ready for use.

vanilla sugar

See **sugar, vanilla-flavoured**.

velouté

A white sauce made with chicken stock,* fish stock,* or veal stock* and used as a base for other sauces; also, used to describe thick soups. To prepare 375 ml (1½ cups): Melt 2 tbsp butter in a saucepan, mix in 2 tbsp flour, then gradually add 500 ml (2 cups) chicken, fish, or veal stock and stir over low heat until thickened. Simmer in a bain-marie* or in a double-boiler for 1 hour, stirring occasionally, then strain and season to taste with salt, pepper, and nutmeg.

vinaigrette

A mixture of 1 part vinegar to 3 parts olive oil and seasoned to taste with salt, pepper, and herbs. Classic vinaigrette dressing includes 1 part mustard.

walnut liqueur

Split 20 green walnuts in half, then put in a jar with 1.5 litres (3 pt) brandy and seal tightly. Leave for 6 weeks in a cool place, shaking the jar occasionally. Strain. Mix 500 g (1 lb) sugar with 250 ml (1 cup) water; bring to a boil, cover, and cook gently for 3 minutes. Add a pinch of cinnamon and a pinch of coriander. Add the seasoned sugar mixture to the walnut and brandy mixture and leave for another month. Strain and bottle.

zest

The peel or outside rind of any citrus fruit used for flavouring. This is the coloured part only. It can be scraped off with a fine grater or cut off with a paring knife.

Index of Recipes

Recipes . . .

Recipes . . .

Recipes . . .

VEGETABLES & SIDE DISHES

SWEETS / DESSERTS

Index of Restaurants

Restaurants . . .

Restaurants . . .

A Note from the Director of the Master Chefs Institute

The Master Chefs Institute is an international affiliation of great chefs and restaurateurs whose primary function is to provide a bridge between the professional working chef and the public. Through its worldwide membership, the Institute is now the repository of the most important contemporary recipes, cooking techniques, menu developments — everything that relates to the art of cuisine. We do have a limited number of public memberships available in each country where the Institute functions. These members receive special discounts on most Institute publications, are invited to receptions held at various sites within each country where Master Chefs demonstrate their speciality recipes, receive the chef-to-chef newsletter, are entitled to reduced tuition rates at our cooking school in France, etc. If you would like more specific information about public membership to the Institute, write to me directly and I promise you a prompt reply. My address is:

Sandy Lesberg, Director
The Master Chefs Institute
World Headquarters
1865 Broadway
New York, New York 10023 U.S.A.